Afternoons in
ITHAKA

Afternoons in ITHAKA

SPIRI TSINTZIRAS

ABC
Books

The ABC 'Wave' device is a trademark of the Australian Broadcasting Corporation and is used under licence by HarperCollins*Publishers* Australia.

First published in Australia in 2014
by HarperCollins*Publishers* Australia Pty Limited
ABN 36 009 913 517
harpercollins.com.au

HarperCollins*Publishers*
Level 13, 201 Elizabeth Street, Sydney, NSW 2000, Australia
Unit D1, 63 Apollo Drive, Rosedale, Auckland 0632, New Zealand
A 53, Sector 57, Noida, UP, India
77–85 Fulham Palace Road, London W6 8JB, United Kingdom
2 Bloor Street East, 20th floor, Toronto, Ontario M4W 1A8, Canada
10 East 53rd Street, New York NY 10022, USA

National Library of Australia Cataloguing-in-Publication entry:

Tsintziras, Spiridoula, author.
  Afternoons in Ithaka / Spiridoula Tsintziras.
  ISBN 978 0 7333 3208 1 (paperback)
  ISBN 978 1 7430 9914 8 (e-book)
  Subjects: Tsintziras, Spiridoula.
  Women – Australia – Biography.
  Gastronomy – Greece – Ithaka Island – Anecdotes.
920.72

Cover design and illustration by Hazel Lam, HarperCollins Design Studio
Cover images: background texture by shutterstock.com; other images and author photo by George Mifsud
Typeset in 11/16pt Bembo Std by Kirby Jones
Printed and bound in Australia by Griffin Press
The papers used by HarperCollins in the manufacture of this book are a natural, recyclable product made from wood grown in sustainable plantation forests. The fibre source and manufacturing processes meet recognised international environmental standards, and carry certification.

6 5 4 3   14 15 16 17

For Chrysoula, Panayioti and Katerina

Contents

PART I
The seed

ITHAKA

As you set out for Ithaka
hope the voyage is a long one,
full of adventure, full of discovery.

Laistrygonians and Cyclops,
angry Poseidon – don't be afraid of them:
you'll never find things like that on your way
as long as you keep your thoughts raised high,
as long as a rare excitement
stirs your spirit and your body.

Laistrygonians and Cyclops,
wild Poseidon – you won't encounter them
unless you bring them along inside your soul,
unless your soul sets them up in front of you.

Constantine Cavafy

Tomato sandwiches

He who is hungry dreams of bread loaves

Greek proverb

Yiayia's knotty brown hands pummel the dough, punching it in, bringing it together and pushing it out, over and over. What was flour and water and a scrap of old dough a few moments ago is now like a living, breathing being beneath her hands. My grandmother's floral apron, the one Mum sent her from Australia, strains against her belly. A wisp of wavy hair escapes from beneath her brown headscarf. Her forehead is wet with sweat and I catch a whiff on her skin of the goat that's tethered in the back yard.

'Yiayia, can I try?'

She pulls off a small piece of dough and passes it to me.

I stand up beside her and try to copy her. I like the elastic, floury feel of the dough in my hands, but my movements are clumsy. Maybe if I had a bigger piece …? But I know not to ask. We mustn't waste any.

'You make it look so easy,' I say, envious.

'I've baked bread every week since I was little.'

'In Australia, we mostly buy ours at the supermarket. It's sliced.' I don't know how to say 'sliced' in Greek, so I make cutting movements with my hands.

Yiayia shrugs. Australia is so far away, so strange. She says, 'Your mum used to be in charge of the baking when she lived here.' She stops, a sad look in her eyes. 'We need to let the dough rise. We'll come back later.'

She puts her big lump into a huge bowl and places my little one beside it. She covers them with a sheet and a goat-hair blanket to keep the dough warm and make it rise more quickly. While we've been in the village, I've been sleeping under similar blankets. I hate the prickly feel of them against my chin at night but they are warm. I think the bread will be happy.

I run outside to find Pappou, my grandfather. I know he will be in the *baxe*, the orchard where he dries grapes and figs. Mum tells me to be careful, as there are things that can trip me up: stones embedded in the soil and unexpected holes near the creek that runs along the end of the yard. When she was little, she fell on a large rock and split her forehead. She points to the scar near her hairline in warning.

I hold my nose as I walk past the toilet. Its walls are made of the very stones that are strewn around the yard. Inside, there is a hole in the ground like a black, toothless mouth. The smell is horrendous, but it's the shadowy presence of weeks and months and years of poo that makes my stomach turn. Every time I need to go, I worry that I will fall in. I grip the walls with my hands. This leaves me nothing with which to block my nose. Yiayia and Pappou use newspaper to wipe their bottoms, but Mum bought toilet paper on the first day we were here after my brother and I complained about the scratchy newspaper. Dad said he used to use rocks to wipe his bottom in his village, and we should count ourselves lucky. I don't know if he was joking. Mum bought the toilet paper anyway, even though it cost a lot. She likes to make everyone happy.

I pass the prickly pear tree with its fleshy leaves covered in spikes and look hopefully to the egg-shaped fruit, but it hasn't yet turned orange to show that it's ready to eat. In Melbourne, Mum and I pick prickly pears from plants that grow beside the rail lines. Mum usually carries a paper bag and tongs to wedge the fruit off so that the prickles don't pierce her skin. Back in our yard in Collingwood, we place the pears on a newspaper and Mum slits the tight skin with the tip of a knife while she holds the fruit with the tongs. Inside, the flesh glistens like a jewel – sometimes ruby red, sometimes orange, depending on the variety. Each time, I am surprised anew that such a fierce-looking plant can make such beautiful fruit. By the time the fruit on the tree here is ready, we will have gone home to Melbourne.

I walk past Yiayia's vegetable patch, with its tomato plants towering over me and long cucumbers that curl in on themselves. Alongside the black, round eggplants and dark-green zucchinis, string beans climb up sticks of cane. Mum is picking beans and zucchini for our dinner tonight. I lean down beside her and smell the damp earth, cradling the eggplant in my hands. It's like a baby. I want to wrap it in a blanket and hold it to my chest, but I'm too old to do things like that. I'm seven and I know that the eggplant is for eating, not playing with.

Pappou is at the end of the garden, bent over piles of small green sultana grapes. He is laying these out on a plastic sheet to dry. The morning sun is already hot. I never knew that the little brown shrivelled sultanas, which we buy in packets from the supermarket back home, came from grapes. Pappou stops what he is doing to smile at me. He reaches into his worn pants and pulls out an ouzo sweet.

'What are you doing, Pappou?' I ask through a mouth full of lolly.

'I'm drying the grapes. Then we'll take them off the stems and sort them. Your mum and aunts used to do that when they lived here.'

'There's a lot. Will you eat them all?'

'No, we'll send them off to town to be cleaned and then sell most of them.'

He turns to go back to work. I try to help but I soon get bored. There's nothing to do here – no television and no other kids in the house, except my brother, Dennis. He doesn't really count. I make my way to the front yard down the side of the house, past Yiayia, who is putting wood in the outdoor oven, and out onto the road. I can just see the sea winking at me down below. I look at it longingly before walking back into the kitchen.

'Maaa, when can we go to the beach?'

'Later, Spirithoula. Later. Now, just sit still.'

I look in the fridge. There's a plate of feta cheese, some eggs and the bowl of string beans that Mum has just picked.

'There's nothing to eat here. Why does Yiayia even have a fridge if there's nothing in it?'

Mum rolls her eyes towards the ceiling. 'It's new. I think she bought it with the money I sent her. Because we were coming.'

She points to a small chest.

'When I was little, in the summer we would buy ice and put it in here. Not that we had much to keep cold then. If we had meat from the pig, we usually cured it.'

'There's nothing to eat, nothing to do. I miss home.'

'We'll be home in a few months. Now come and look at this.'

She lifts the covers. The dough has risen; it looks like a plump, sleeping baby. I poke it and my finger sinks in, leaving an indent on the smooth surface.

'Yiayia would have had my head if I'd done that when I was a girl. God, to think how many curses she threw at me and my sisters when we did even the smallest thing wrong.'

'What sort of curses?'

'May you go where the sun is hot enough to bake bread and dry salt.'

'What does that mean?'

'May you be thrust far away from here – into the desert.'

Mum looks doubtful, like she regrets telling me. She doesn't want to say anything that will make Yiayia look bad. 'Yiayia's life was hard. I can't blame her.'

I can never imagine my own mother cursing me like that, willing me to be far from her.

'Now, the bread is ready to knock back.'

Mum takes the dough and cuts it into seven pieces, one loaf for each day. She kneads each of these and returns them to their sleeping place.

I go into the bedroom next to the kitchen, which I'm sharing with my brother. He is playing with his Matchbox cars on the floor and doesn't look up when I come in. I flop onto the bed and look at the pictures in the one book I have – my Greek school reader. The familiar characters, Anna and Mimi, play with their *topi*, their ball. They go to church with their family, visit their relatives. The things that Anna and Mimi's family do are familiar to me because our family does them too. Now that we have been in Greece for a few weeks, I recognise that the book is about life here. The words get harder as the book goes on and in the end, I just look at the pictures.

Outside, the wood that Yiayia fed into the oven has turned to ash. She sweeps it to the back of the oven and wipes down the floor with a damp sheet tied to a wooden pole. Mum and I carry the bread out to Yiayia, who feeds the loaves into the mouth of the oven. Finally, she pushes a heavy piece of metal across the entrance and wedges this shut with a broomstick to keep the heat in.

Mum takes us for a walk to the *vrissi*, the freshwater tap down at the beach that runs from a deep well in the ground. She tells us that her uncle funded the building of the wall that holds the tap. He went to the United States, made some money, then came back to set up a café on the beach and educate his daughters. Building the wall was his way of giving back to the village. We drink the cold, clear water and fill an earthenware jug to take back to the house. When we pass the square, Mum gives in to our whining and buys us a small packet of *yaridakia*, puffy savouries. I crunch them, relishing the salty crispness on my tongue.

When we get back to the house, Yiayia is taking the seven golden orbs out of the oven. I move the things on the table to one side – the bottle of red wine, the bottle of olive oil, the salt and pepper shakers – and lay down a rough cotton sheet. Yiayia turns the bread onto the covered table. I feel giddy with hunger and want to sink my face into it, but I have to wait a little longer for it to cool. Finally, Mum takes the serrated knife and cuts me a wedge. She tears a tomato apart with her hands and mashes it along the bread, then drizzles the bread with olive oil, crumbles a wedge of feta over it, and sprinkles some of Yiayia's dried oregano on top. She hands it to me on a plate.

I bite into the warm bread. It's chewy and dense, wet with the juice of Yiayia's tomato and the green olive oil. The briny, creamy taste of the feta and the bitter aftertaste of the oregano are better than anything I have ever eaten back home. Flies buzz around me, wanting to share my sandwich. I shoo them away. I've waited a long time for this. It's mine.

Chrysoula's tomato, feta, olive oil and oregano sandwich

Serves 1

Ingredients
1 thick wedge of dense, good quality bread (to make your own, see page 75)
1 ripe tomato (to grow your own, see page 275), halved
1 small piece of feta (or, if you are feeling brave, fig-sap ricotta – to make your own, see page 165)
A drizzle of olive oil
A pinch of dried oregano (to dry your own, see page 282)

Method
Place the bread onto a large plate. Rub the seeded side of the tomato against the bread so that the juice seeps out. Break up the remaining tomato and place it on the bread. Crumble the feta over the top, drizzle with oil and sprinkle with dried oregano.

Horiatiko kotopoulo

It's the old chicken that makes good broth

Greek proverb

Yiayia Spirithoula and Pappou Dionysios are waiting at the gate when our taxi pulls up. They squint into the sunshine, looking a little bewildered. When we pile out, I kiss their leathery brown cheeks and taste the dust from the road, mixed with their tears and laughter and high-pitched voices. Theio Spiro, Dad's brother, helps the taxi driver pull our heavy suitcases from the boot of the car. We make our way up the stone steps to the inside of the house where it's cool and quiet.

Now that we are here in Vanada, the village where Dad grew up, I don't know what to do with myself. Yiayia takes charge – first, we need to choose where to sleep. Our cousins will be arriving next week to stay too, and while there are lots of blankets piled up against one wall, there is not much room. Some of the kids will have to sleep on the floor. I don't mind; I like it when Mum lays out blankets that span the whole room when my cousins sleep over back in Melbourne.

'*Ela*, come, our new daughter-in-law, you must be hungry. How was the trip from Petalidi? How are your parents? We met them at a feast day a few years back.'

Yiayia looks Mum straight in the eye, appraises her. Mum looks down. Although they have spoken many times on the phone, this is the first time Mum has met Dad's parents.

'Yes, my parents are well. It was hard to leave them. It was like leaving for Australia all over again.'

'Yes, I know how it feels to say goodbye,' Yiayia clucks and looks away.

'We slaughtered a chicken yesterday. I bet you haven't had a *horiatiko kotopoulo*, a village chicken, for a while,' Pappou says to Dad with a laugh. I think he's trying to make things lighter again.

We wash our hands in the kitchen basin with its blue and white tiles, and sit down to the meal. The chicken tastes strong. The cheese on the pasta smells like goat, but I'm getting used to strange smells, and I'm hungry. I eat everything on my plate and wipe the sauce with the bread.

'After we rest, we can go down to the *cafeneion* and you can see everyone.'

Dad nods. For the second time today, he blinks away tears. Until today, I'd never seen Dad cry.

Mum helps Yiayia clear up and make the beds, and we all lie down for a rest. The blankets are scratchy and I can't sleep.

We've been in Greece a month now, but I can't get used to the afternoon sleeps. My limbs are too jittery; I'm too excited to sit still.

Later, we open the suitcase with the presents. Mum pulls out the things she has brought for everybody – thermal underwear and sheepskin slippers, nighties and warm socks. I can tell my grandparents like this new daughter-in-law of theirs.

Mum makes us put on our best clothes and we walk down to the *cafeneion*. Pappou's brother, Fotis, and his wife, Fotena, 'she who belongs to Fotis', come out from their house and embrace Dad. They pick my brother and me up and kiss Mum on both cheeks, touching her arms as if she is a chicken they are testing for plumpness. She laughs, embarrassed.

'Oohh, Nephew, we never thought we would see the day. *Perimene mas. Eimeis kername.*' Wait up for us. It's our shout.

Our little group walks along the dirt road. Pappou points out the church, and the rooms at the back of it that serve as school and mayor's office. Pappou is the mayor of the town, and I feel myself puff up with pride to be walking with him. He has an important-looking moustache that tickles when he holds me close.

It takes us half an hour to get to the *cafenieon*, even though it's only 200 metres from Pappou's house. Nearly every door of every house along the way opens. The same cry is repeated. *Tsintziras's son has returned.*

The *cafenieon* is a large room, piled high with boxes of soft-drink bottles, coffee and tinned milk. At the end of the room, a man is making coffee in an oversized *briki*, an Ottoman-style coffee pot. Everyone stops talking as soon as we come in. Suddenly, they are up, hugging my father, tousling our hair, appraising my mother. I have no idea who all these people are, but Dad knows everyone. He's crying again. A priest in a tall hat is smoking. I gather he is the father of my brother's godfather, who lives back in Melbourne. Everyone is talking at once, wanting to know how their families are in the *xenitia*, the foreign land. We are treated to Fanta and small packets of *yaridakia*. There's talking and drinking and more tears and we don't go home until late.

When we get back to the house, Yiayia brings out pork pieces pickled in fat, and olives, cheese, tomatoes, bread. More is brought out as people drop in, and the men drink wine and beer and little shots of ouzo. I am sleepy, but I daren't go to bed; I might miss something. Pappou brings out a rifle from under his bed and we all go outside to watch him shoot it into the night air. His eldest son has come back from abroad, and it calls for celebration. It's been such a big day; when Mum leads me to the scratchy goat's hair blankets laid out on the floor, my eyes finally close.

The next day, I wake to find Mum making *mitzithra*, a hard goat's cheese for grating on spaghetti. She is laughing with Yiayia, wondering if she might be able to sneak a few of the bowling-ball-sized cheeses through customs when the time comes to leave.

Yiayia turns to Dad. 'What did you do to deserve this good woman?' Dad looks a bit taken aback, but then he smiles.

To Mum she says, 'That son of mine used to run around with Vlahos's son, making slingshots and terrorising the town. And don't even ask what he got up to when we sent him to Kyparissia for high school. You've made a *noikokiri* out of him' – a good master of the home.

Next week, our first cousins are coming from Amaliada. Yiayia is still worried about where everyone will sleep. Dad decides that he and Mum will sleep outside, on top of the mulberry tree in the garden.

'What will people say? That I don't have enough room in my house for my own son?' Yiayia balks.

But Pappou tells her to shush. 'Let the man do what he wants.'

Dad orders wood, which some villagers help to carry to Pappou's house. He and Theio Spiro rig up a platform on top of the tree. A few days later, Mum and Dad are sleeping under the stars. I am very jealous, but they won't let my brother and me up there – we might fall off.

Pappou has been busy too. He has set up a tank on top of the outhouse with a hose running down so that we can have showers. He and Yiayia still wash in the basin below the house with Yiayia's handmade soaps. The shower is for us. To get to the outhouse, we have to walk past the chook house and the goat tethered up to a tree. I remind myself to go to the toilet before it gets dark.

In the afternoons when everyone is sleeping, Dad lets me visit his aunt in the neighbouring village over the hill. It's a long walk and I'm surprised he lets me go by myself. At home, I'm not allowed to walk around our neighbourhood like this, but I think Dad feels safe here. Yiayia Dimitra makes me warm milk, gives me lollies, and talks with me while her husband sleeps in the next room. I know I'm keeping her up, but I love the warmth of her house, her kind eyes.

Most days, I take my dolls and play with Georgia, an older cousin who lives down the road. She hasn't got nice dollies like me. I have one that even has a bottle, with milk that disappears when you feed her. One day the milk bottle goes missing and, soon after, I see it attached to Georgia's doll's mouth.

'That's mine!'

'No it's not. The milkman brought it for me.'

I know it's a lie, but I don't know what to say. She speaks so fast, seems so much more confident than I am.

The days turn into weeks and we pass the time: we press grapes in the big cement trough in the back garden, swing on the rope Pappou has rigged up for us, play with our cousins. The three boys, Stathis, Dionysios and Nikos, are like wild animals, climbing trees, throwing stones, wreaking havoc. We go to a saint's day festival in a neighbouring village, all of us piling into Theio Spiro's little Fiat and the few other cars in the village. Theio is the last-born of Yiayia's children, much younger than Dad; he was barely a teenager when Dad left for Australia, and he seems to look up to Dad. I wear my sparkly blue dress that Mum made especially for this trip. Theio tousles my hair and we take a photo together. I feel so proud.

At the end of the summer, the village school starts. I tell Dad I want to go too. The school room is airy, full of light. The small kids sit up the front and the big kids at the back. The teacher lets me help myself to books from the big bookcase at one end of the room. What the students are learning is too hard for me to understand, but I look at the pictures in the books and try to make sense of the letters. I would like to be able to read all the words, understand the stories. The kids look at me with a mixture of awe and pity – I am the *Australeza*, the Australian. I keep looking at the words on the page; maybe one day I will know what they say. I know my grandfather would be proud. Perhaps by the time we go back to Australia, the letters will make sense. I keep staring at the pages, wishing and pretending.

Yiayia Spirithoula's horiatiko kotopoulo me makaronatha (village chicken stew with spaghetti)

Serves 6 to 8

Ingredients

4 tablespoons olive oil
1 whole chicken (preferably free range and organic, in the absence of one from a Greek village), cut into chunks and washed
1 large onion, diced
3 cloves garlic, peeled and sliced
4 tablespoons tomato paste
3 ripe tomatoes, quartered and grated (discard the skins)
1 teaspoon dried oregano
1 pinch each of ground cinnamon, clove and nutmeg
500 grams spaghetti
Grated *mitzithra* (a hard cheese available at Greek delicatessens), if desired

Method

Heat the oil in a heavy-based pot and brown the chicken pieces until golden.

Add the onion, garlic and tomato paste and stir until the onions are soft and the chicken is coated with the mixture.

Add the grated tomato to the pot along with the cinnamon, clove, oregano and nutmeg. Boil some water and pour it over the chicken mixture until it is just covered. Simmer on low heat until the chicken is tender and the sauce is thick, around 45 minutes, stirring occasionally and adding water if it looks to be drying out. Season to taste.

Bring a pot of salted water to the boil and cook the spaghetti until *al dente.* Drain the spaghetti, then place it in a large serving dish and top with the chicken and sauce. Sprinkle with *mitzithra* if desired.

Coffee cup connections

Curses are like chickens: they come home to roost

Greek proverb

The grind of the overlocker is relentless; it churns through flannelette nighties, the sharp needles binding the fabric together, the knife cutting through the excess material. A thick dust fills the air. It's hard to breathe in the little tin shed in our back yard in Collingwood.

Mum wakes early in the morning and works well into the night until her fingers hurt. I often sit and watch, mesmerised. She takes a piece from one pile of cut fabric and expertly joins it with another to form the body of the garment. Every evening, Dad counts and ties the bundles of completed nighties into lots of one hundred, making a pile that reaches the ceiling by the end of the week.

When the factory boss comes to pick them up, my mother has to haggle over the price.

'But you paid thirty-five cents apiece last time.'

'It's gone down to thirty cents. The companies are squeezing us. What can I do, Chrysoula?'

'I can't keep doing them at that price, Niko. You know I can't. I'll have to work for someone else.'

But everywhere is the same – the pay pitiful, the conditions hard, the expectations high. Mum avoids the factories. She wants to be home with her children, even if it means less money and more work.

I learn to make coffee early for the constant trail of visitors. Mum tells me that by the age of two, I could stand on a chair and stir the sugar and coffee in the *briki*, pouring it into small coffee cups without spilling it. I take great pride in making sure that each cup has a *kaimaki*, a crema on the top.

'What a good *noikokira* she is,' visitors remark. A good mistress of the home. They smile encouragingly at Mum – I will make a good wife one day.

My mother's sisters and Dad's many family friends usually come by on weekends, and neighbours drop in during the week. There is the gypsy-eyed Despina from the housing commission flats, with her band of eight grubby children. There is Maria from next door, who teaches me to play solitaire and pontoon before I have started school. Even I know, small as I am, that her cheeky smile masks her troubles with her hard-drinking husband, who heads off to the factory each morning in a grey overcoat. And there is Yiayia Yiannoula, the undisputed matriarch of the street, clad from head to foot in black, still mourning her husband who died decades ago. Despite her diminutive size, I am scared of her penetrating black eyes, which are framed by her *tsebera*, her headscarf. Mum listens to each visitor's woes, gives sage advice, and always manages to see something promising in their coffee grounds – they will come into some money unexpectedly, their husband is going to stop drinking, or their daughter will finally start showing some respect.

One day Mum goes out to use the payphone at the milk bar. She needs to order more work from the factory.

'I want to come with you,' I whine.

'No, I'll just be a few minutes.' She turns on the television, and Tom and Jerry flash by.

My brother and I are still sitting there half an hour later when Yiayia Yiannoula knocks on the door. Dennis lets her in.

'Mum's not here,' he says.

'She's been in an accident. A car accident. I'll look after you for a while.' She sounds shaken.

Dad comes home later that night. He has a wild look in his eyes. He bundles us into the Valiant, straps our mattresses to the roof and we make our way to my aunt's house in Northcote, where we will be staying for the next few weeks. That means it's serious. It's exciting being with my cousins, but I want my mum. A few days later, we visit her in hospital. Her hand is in plaster, and her knee too. Her room is all white and it smells like disinfectant. I hold Dad's hand, scared.

She finds it hard to talk; tears roll down her cheeks. She tells us she's lucky to be alive – a fire engine hit a car, which climbed onto the footpath and ran her over. At the time, all she could say was, '*Ta paidia mou, ta paidia mou*' – my children, my children – before she passed out.

A month later, she comes home. Mum's sister walks us home from Northcote with her own two children, my cousins Kathy and Georgia, in tow. Georgia is in the pram, and my aunty pushes her uncomfortably – her pregnant belly is in the way. Even though Kathy is three months younger than me, I have to force my little legs to keep up with her. I collect flowers along the way and have a posy ready to welcome Mum home. I don't want her to leave ever again.

It takes more than a year, but Mum recovers. She has a bent finger that won't straighten. She has a bung knee, which aches when she presses on the sewing machine pedal. And her pelvis hurts. But still, the piles of nighties keep reaching the ceiling.

Often I have to vie for Mum's attention, offering to help if I want to speak to her. Even then, someone or other interrupts us: 'Chrysoula, are you home?' they shout from the front gate. Sometimes I wish she was less kind, less generous, and that people would leave her alone; I want more of her to myself. Still, I have no choice and so I sit in on the whispered stories about their lives, about their troubles. I learn to listen carefully, as she does.

I love it best of all when Mum tells me stories of her own childhood in Greece. Of her stern mother and her gentle father, both of whom worked hard to eke out a living for their family of five children. How Mum hated school and how the

letters on the page just didn't seem to penetrate her 'hollow skull'. How the sea was a few hundred metres from their door, but she and her sisters were not allowed to swim because the boys might see their bodies. How she worked in her father's fields, singing with her cousins, and how free they felt. Now that we have been to Greece, I can imagine her in these places, roaming as a youngster with her siblings.

She speaks joyously of studying to be a seamstress. Her father couldn't afford to educate her and her siblings, but he did send her to learn the sewing trade in the nearby town of Kalamata as an apprentice. She remembers how hard it was to save for a sewing machine. How the village girls and women would come to her for their once-a-year new dress, usually around Easter. She speaks reverently of the exotic fabrics they would buy when they could afford to. How no matter how poor you were, it was important to dress well; anyone could flatter her body shape with just the right dress; there was no excuse for going about in torn clothes. She is horrified by how some people dress in Australia. Men in singlets and thongs. Women in tank tops, their backsides hanging out of their jeans. *What sort of dress is that? Do they not have any self-respect?*

She describes sponsoring her sisters to come out to Australia for a better life. And how hard it was for them – all had difficult relationships, had married men who gambled or were violent.

'Why did you have to leave Greece?' I would ask.

'We were too many girls. In those days, if a girl didn't have a dowry, you couldn't get married. My father gave the dowry to the oldest girl, and there was none left. So I had to come out. And I brought your *theies*, your aunts. It was different for your Theio Niko. He was a boy.'

She missed her parents, her older sister and younger brother. Everyone cried for weeks before she left. But what choice did she have?

Now, in Australia, women still come to her for clothes. They bring a jar of coffee in exchange for her to take up a skirt. A length of fabric for a new dress. A bag of oranges to let out a top. Money is rarely exchanged.

'Why don't you take money, Mama?'

'They don't have much money, like us. Anyway, it's no trouble for me to do it.'

34

'You could charge. Maybe one day have your own business. You wouldn't need to work for the factories.'

'Spirithoula *mou*, I can't speak English. How would I run a business with no English?'

And there the conversation ends. Mum turns her head back to the machine, expertly reaching for the pieces of the nighty.

Spiri's Turkish-style coffee

Telling one's fortune using coffee grounds is an ancient practice, widespread in Africa, the Middle East and the Mediterranean. It goes by the name tasseography. In the Greek tradition, the brew is drunk, the sediment rotated counter-clockwise, and the cup overturned on a napkin. The reader then 'tells' the cup, using her knowledge of the shape and placement of the grounds, as well as a hefty dose of intuition.

Before you can go there, you'll need a well-brewed cup of coffee. This is how I've been making it since I was old enough to stand on a chair to reach the stove.

You need a *briki* (a coffee pot sold in Greek and Middle Eastern delicatessens), some small espresso cups, and finely ground Turkish- or Arabic-style coffee.

Fill one espresso cup with cold water and pour it into the *briki*. One cup serves one person, so multiply this by the number of guests. It is important to use a *briki* whose size corresponds to the number of guests – if your *briki* is too big, the all-important *kaimaki* (crema) won't form.

For a medium-sweet (*metrio*) coffee, add 1 teaspoon of sugar per person to the cold water and stir briefly. Then add 1 heaped teaspoon of coffee per person and stir again. Heat the *briki* over a low heat until the coffee starts to rise and bubble, but do not let it boil. Take the *briki* off the stove and slowly pour it into the espresso cups, being careful to include a little *kaimaki* with each serve.

Mine is bigger than yours

Don't sprout where you haven't been planted

Greek proverb

'*Faye, faye.*' Eat, eat.

My Theio Nick Tasiopoulos thrusts a cucumber at me as I walk past. I take it. I know he'll be offended if I refuse. Theio Nick has just picked half a dozen cucumbers from his garden – they are displayed on a garden table, the faux-marble top of which is peeling away to reveal bloated chipboard. The cucumbers look like stunned snakes in the summer sun, turgid and still. Theio takes them inside and his wife, Tasia, peels and cuts them into quarters, sprinkling them with salt. They feel crisp and cool in my mouth.

Theio Vlahos and Dad are standing in front of Nick's tomato plants.

'My tomatoes are good this year, no?' says Nick. It's more a statement than a question. 'And my cucumbers, they're huge. I brought the seeds back from Greece.'

Dad and Theio Vlahos nod. There's no doubt about the size of Nick's cucumbers.

Vlahos counters, 'I tried sheep manure this year for the first time and the cucumbers like it.' I'm willing to bet that Theio Vlahos has bigger cucumbers, but he's too modest to admit it.

My uncles' back yards in Preston and Reservoir are so much bigger than our tiny patch in Collingwood. Their cucumbers are always bigger; they have more string beans; their tomatoes are plump with seeds. Still, our few metres of soil are packed with spring onions, beans, tomatoes, peppers and eggplants. A grape vine winds its way up recycled iron plumbing pipes. A prolific fig tree drops fruit all over the tin shed that houses the barrel of wine and Dad's tools. My brother and I clamber up to get the fruit before the birds do. On hot summer days, I like to watch the heat coming up in waves off the concrete. When my cousins come over, we eat watermelon or grapes, spitting the big pips as far as we can – into the garden, over the fence, into the drain under the garden tap. We have fun, but our yard is so small compared to Theio's.

The back flyscreen door bangs and Theia Tasia comes out.

'Ah, Nick, are you bragging about your cucumbers again?' She looks to the men. '*Café*?'

The men nod and turn back to the garden.

Theia goes back inside and I follow her. She takes out the big *briki* and puts the coffee on to brew. She produces a jar filled with glistening pieces of preserved grapefruit skin, and places these onto little crystal plates, which she arranges on a tray along with tiny forks. I carry the tray of sweets and Theia brings the coffees. The men finally tear themselves away from the cucumbers. I join Theia inside with the women.

'Tasia, these grapefruit are lovely,' Mum says.

'Yes, we had a good crop last year. I made lots. I nearly killed myself peeling them. Here, have a jar to take home when you go.'

Mum makes as if to refuse, but I can tell she doesn't mean it. She places the jar near her bag. They talk about the recipe and Mum says she will try it next time. Her grapefruit always turn out a bit watery.

I wander back outside. The men have moved on to talking about pest repellents.

'Beer is good for snails. You put it in little pots. They drink it and they drown.'

'What a way to go.' The men laugh. The coffee is finished and Theio has brought out a slab of beer and wheeled out the oversized barbecue. He has a tray piled with chops marinated in olive oil, lemon and oregano, and sausages for the kids. Soon the coals are hot and he places the meat onto the hot plate. We only came for coffee, but now we're staying for dinner.

I join my 'cousins' John and Peter, Tina and Arthur; we are distantly related through marriages that happened in Dad's village a few generations ago. John and Peter are older than my brother and me and have exciting things in their rooms:

an electric guitar, a tape recorder, a football. But soon even these things bore us and we move outside to play hide and seek in the back yard. In the twilight, I can hear snatches of conversation ...

'That bastard boss; he doesn't even let you go for a piss unless you're on a break,' says Dad.

'The union should do something.'

'What can they do? Pfft. Nothing!'

They talk about the royalists and leftists in Greece, about how you can't get a job there unless your political party is in power. Even though they work hard here, in dirty workplaces, they agree there are more opportunities in Australia – especially for their kids.

The women are putting the final touches on dinner: chopped cucumbers and tomatoes, plates of olives and feta, a mound of bread. The platter of meat arrives and we each grab a plate. The men take their food first, then the kids, and, finally, the women.

It's late when we leave. Mum takes the jar of grapefruit.

'Drop in next Saturday if you like,' she says to Theia Tasia, kissing her on both cheeks.

Dad has some cucumber seeds wrapped up in a napkin, the ones Nick brought back from Greece in the bottom of his suitcase.

As we make our way home to Collingwood, Dad says, 'I'll plant these seeds next year. Maybe my cucumbers will grow as big as Tasiopoulos's ...'

'I hope so, my husband, I hope so ...'

VLASIOS ON DRYING SEEDS

For many years, eighty-year-old Vlasios Tzikas, the father of my close friend Katerina, worked in takeaway food shops, selling steak sandwiches and hamburgers to make a living. He raised four kids.

One look at Mr Tzikas's garden and you realise that in another life, he could have been an engineer. His garden houses a massive covered water-storage area that he has dug into the ground, into which storm water drains from the down pipes. A homemade electric pump pushes water up an incline into the lush garden. He has built a wood-fired oven to a design of his own devising, using clay and twigs from his back yard.

Mr Tzikas saves seeds from most plants. The process below works best with 'wet' seeds that are embedded in the damp flesh of fruits and vegetables, such as tomatoes, cucumbers, marrows and cherries.

Leave the largest, healthiest-looking fruit on the plant. When the fruit ceases to grow, or the rest of the plant has died off, harvest it. With clean hands, break the fruit open and scoop out the seeds. With smaller fruits or berries, you can crush the fruit into a pulp.

Wash the seeds in a bowl of water, agitating in order to remove the 'wet' membrane around each seed. Discard any seeds that float to the top, then throw away the water and repeat. This helps to stop the seeds fermenting in their own wet skins.

Place the seeds onto kitchen paper, leaving 1 or 2 centimetres between each. If it is not easy to separate the seeds, spread them as smoothly as you can onto the paper. Put the sheets of paper in a warm, well-ventilated spot such as a window ledge.

In a few weeks, when the seeds are completely dry, cut up the kitchen paper so that each seed is on a little bit of paper. Store these in an airtight glass container in a dry, dark place until you are ready to plant them (paper and all) in the appropriate season.

The good grape

He who drinks on credit gets twice as drunk

Greek proverb

The sticky, ruby-red juice oozes through the gaps between my toes, rises up around my feet, and sinks back into the wooden vat. The smell that wafts up is sweet, almost sickly.

'Okay, that's enough, Spirithoula.'

Dad let me get up first, humouring me, but now the men mean business. Reluctantly, I take Dad's hand. He helps me down onto a crate and back onto the ground. He hoses my feet and then washes his own with soap. He steps up to take my place.

The glistening juice squishes through his toes at a great rate. He presses down with one foot, then the other, working up a rhythm. I watch, mesmerised. The sack beneath his feet is plump with muscatel grapes, filled to the brim and then sewn tightly shut at one end. It has been placed in a vat that has a hole in one corner. The juice from the grapes drains out through the hole into a clean bucket. When the bucket is full, its contents are poured into the covered oak barrel in the small corrugated-iron shed. And so goes the annual wine-making ritual.

My uncles take it in turns to press the grapes. When the juice is spent and the sack is flat, they open it up. They remove the grape must and give this to my mother. She will boil it down, adding cornflour and semolina to make *moustalevria*, a jelly-like sweet. Nothing is wasted.

The men fill the sack from a few of the twelve boxes of grapes that are stacked up in one corner of our yard. As always, there has been careful deliberation about where to buy the grapes. Sometimes they come from the Preston or Queen Victoria markets, or from roadside vans piled high with crates of sweet-smelling muscatels or sultana grapes. Our Italian neighbours always know where to find these. Word spreads like wildfire about which supplier has the best and cheapest fruit. Dad wishes he had enough grapes from his own yard to make wine. While the bunches on the vine above us are full and lush, there are not enough to make a whole barrel. This year Dad bought the grapes from a farmer who drove his truck around our neighbourhood, spruiking his wares through a loudspeaker just as I heard gypsies do in Greece.

Although it's only eight o'clock in the morning, it is already hot. The men work quickly in a bid to avoid the heat.

I run off to play with my cousins Kathy, Georgia, Dimitra and George. Our mothers are busy, and Kathy and I need to keep an eye on George, who climbs our high fence and runs out onto the road on a whim. My cousins are here on holidays, down from a small NSW town called Narrandera, where they now own a fish and chip shop. It's exciting when they come to visit.

'Mama, can I take these?' I hold up a bag of large black bin liners.

She nods without looking at me, preoccupied. She's filling tomatoes, zucchinis, eggplants and zucchini flowers with rice to make *yemista*. I furtively take the dishwashing liquid, and a pair of scissors. My cousins and I cut the bags down the side and spread them out along our concrete drive. It's just like the Slip 'n Slide we've seen on television. We squirt the bags with dishwashing liquid and spray them with the hose. One by one, we slide along the drive. We have to push one another, as there's no slope. As the morning progresses, we get braver, tumbling and sliding, slipping and slopping our way even more energetically. Tomorrow we will have bruises, but today our laughter can be heard all the way down the street. We are sopping wet in our shorts and T-shirts when we finally go inside to ask for food. Mum produces a tub of Neapolitan ice-cream and we fight over the last of the chocolate.

By early afternoon, the boxes of grapes are empty. The men's sticky feet leave marks on the concrete. Mum hoses the yard and we sit down under the grape vine to a tray full of *yemista* and salad. I mop my plate with bread to make sure I get all the oil. Everything tastes delicious after the activities of the morning.

'It's going to be a good one this year, Panayioti. The grapes are sweet, very juicy …' my uncle says.

'*Makari*,' Dad says superstitiously. May God grant it.

Finally, Dad and my uncle tie the empty, washed vat onto the top of my uncle's car with thick ropes. Tomorrow, we will be at his place, doing the same again.

A few weeks later, when I open the door of the shed, the smell of fermenting grapes is sweet, yeasty. Dad has plastered the plug at the top of the barrel down so that it doesn't burst out. I can hear the juices bubbling wildly as if desperate to escape. Dad has lovingly placed a small heater in the shed to help the fermentation process along during the colder autumn mornings.

When my uncles come over, they turn the tap on the barrel to try the wine, knowing full well it's too early. It won't be ready for months.

'You shouldn't leave it too long, Panayioti.'

There's no risk of Dad leaving it too long – he is like a child with a toy, pulling it apart to see what makes it tick. He decants his wine well before my uncles do.

I am allowed to have a sip. It smells and tastes awful. But clearly I lack a suitably refined palette. Dad and my uncles are so proud of their creations, exchanging bottles, comparing colour and flavour. Invariably, each claims his is the best. The women look on, amused.

Chrysoula's yemista (vegetables stuffed with rice and herbs)

Serves 6 to 8

This recipe is superb when there is a glut of summer vegetables –
tomatoes, zucchini, eggplants, zucchini flowers. If you prefer,
you can make it using only one type of vegetable. It's a great one
for larger groups and it's worth making a lot.

Ingredients
5 large tomatoes
5 medium capsicums
5 medium zucchinis
5 small eggplants
4 cups long-grain rice
2 or 3 onions, finely chopped
5 or 6 cloves garlic, finely chopped
5 or 6 sprigs mint, finely chopped
1 bunch parsley, finely chopped
1 cup olive oil
250 ml passata (or 1 cup freshly grated ripe tomatoes, skins
discarded)
1 cup water
Salt and pepper to taste
2 cups boiling water

Method
Preheat the oven to 200°C.

Slice the tops off the tomatoes and scoop out the seeds with a teaspoon, leaving a hollowed-out shell approximately 1 centimetre thick. Put the tops back on and place the tomatoes into a deep baking dish. Do the same with the capsicums and zucchinis. Roll the eggplants on a hard surface to soften them, then remove the seeds from the middle as with the other vegetables.

In a large bowl, combine the rice, onions, garlic, herbs, oil, passata, 1 cup of cold water and salt and pepper.

Fill each vegetable with the rice mixture and replace the vegetable 'lids'. Pour any remaining liquid into the pan, but discard any leftover rice. Place the pan in the preheated oven and raise the heat to 250°C.

After about 30 minutes, when the vegetables start to brown, add 2 cups of boiling water to the pan (this will help to cook the rice). Rotate the eggplants and zucchinis. Continue to bake until the vegetables are soft and have crispy skins (around 1 hour). If the rice starts to look dry, add some more boiling water to the sides of the dish.

Serve with a fresh green salad and homemade bread.

Pubs and pedals

Wine and children speak the truth

Greek proverb

'Don't tell Mum,' he says as I sit beside him, struggling to get my feet off the sticky carpet and my bottom onto the tall stool.

'What'll it be, Peter?'

'The usual, John. A pot of VB. And lemonade for my daughter.'

I look shyly at the bartender with the handlebar moustache, but he doesn't take any notice of me. Nor do the men sitting alongside us – bum cracks and potbellies showing over Hard Yakka shorts as they down a few quick ones before going back to nearby worksites. The beer is set on a soggy placemat and Dad downs it fast. He orders another 'for the road', drinks it and we are off.

The pub is a few streets away from our house. We walk past tiny weatherboards, a factory that makes cookware, and a few newer, brick-veneer homes. When we get to our house, Mum is waiting at the door.

'You took your time at the milk bar.'

'Dad let me buy chips, Mama,' I say quickly.

Dad scurries into the garden. I can tell Mum wants him to get a job again, fast. The unemployment benefits don't stretch far, what with the middle-of-the-day visits to the pub. But he keeps changing jobs; he gets bored, or has disagreements with the bosses. Luckily, factory work is plentiful and it shouldn't be too long now. It's nice having him home when I get back after school. When I'm sick, he brings me potato chips and lemonade in bed. I like the feel of his cool palm on my forehead, even the worried look on his face. It means he loves me.

Maria from next door and her family have moved away to a big house in Bulleen. Mum says we will visit her sometime, but that sometime doesn't come around. I miss jumping the corrugated-iron fence to visit, and playing cards on her laminated table. Now a new family has moved in. They have a daughter my age, Bella. Her parents are often out, and she asks to sleep at our house one night when they won't be home. As we squish into my single bed, she tells me she sleeps without undies on. I am intrigued. In our family, everyone sleeps with their undies under their nightwear.

It's not long before we hear arguments next door. Our wall is two metres from theirs.

'Fuck you! Get out of my house ...'

'Piss off, bitch! It's not your house. If anyone's going to get out, it's you ...'

Dad looks at Mum and turns the TV up.

One night, Bella's eight-year-old brother comes to our door. He has red freckles, a downy splash of golden hair and a scared look in his eyes.

'Can I use the phone? Mum won't wake up. Dad's not home.'

I watch as he rings the ambulance. I can tell the operator doesn't believe him, thinks it's a prank call.

I grab the phone. 'Please can you come? This is not a prank call. His mother is sick,' I say in my most mature voice.

Later, we hear that they pumped his mum's stomach; she had downed fifty aspirin. Within days, she is back home. The arguments continue.

My godfather, who works at a bike factory in Clifton Hill, brings me a bike for my birthday. He has kept me in wheels over the years, from my first small red trike to the bike with the white vinyl seat and colourful tassels that he steers down the drive now. I can barely contain my excitement. I love the feel of the wind in my hair, the power of the muscles in my legs pumping the pedals. I love how strong I feel. I strain at the inclines, whizz at dizzying speed down hills, splash through puddles after a big rain and ride up and down the bluestone gutters.

On my bike, I wind my way around Collingwood. Past the community youth centre, where kids are sniffing glue out the back. Past Theia Georgia and Theio Vassili's house, friends of ours who have no children of their own and who spoil my brother and me with lollies and excursions into the city. Every adult who is a good friend of my parents is a *theia*, aunty or a *theio*, uncle. Every time Theia Georgia sees me, she holds me tight against her generous bosom and I turn my head to avoid the moles on her face.

More often than not, I cycle past the house of my friends, two sisters who live in the street around the corner.

'*Pop*-py! *An*-gela!' I call in a sing-song voice.

Angela's head appears in the doorway.

'Come out and play.'

'Wait there. We're coming.'

I'm not encouraged to go into the girls' house. Their mother has white carpets. She lays clear plastic sheeting over them so they don't get dirty. We have vinyl on our floors and Mum doesn't care who steps on it.

Poppy brings out a few dented tennis rackets. We hit the ball back and forth over the hot bitumen of the road. The buzz of traffic on Hoddle Street is buffered by the row of houses on our street. We move onto the footpath when the odd car comes by. More kids join us. Our game of tennis morphs into a game of cricket and we don't stop playing until our mothers call us in for dinner.

One day, I'm riding back from the milk bar and I see a bundle of clothes on the footpath. I approach slowly and realise it's Bella's father. I think that maybe he's drunk, sleeping it off on the street. But then I notice blood on his T-shirt. I run in to tell Mum. Soon an ambulance arrives. And a police car. When the paramedics have carried Bella's dad away, the police knock on the door of his home.

'Mum's getting dressed. You can't come in,' says Bella.

But they make their way in anyway, and find a knife buried in the back yard. Later, my parents whisper when they think my brother and I can't hear: *Will she go to jail? What about the kids?* But Bella's dad decides not to press charges, and within weeks her parents are back together again. I know without asking that my parents prefer I don't play with Bella anymore. They are not a 'good' family.

But there are times when we make our own noise through the walls, when Dad can't control his drinking and Mum is fed up. At times like these, my brother Dennis and I retire to our bedroom; we stare at each other across the small space between our beds. Dennis nervously makes a hole in the plaster with his finger and we both watch the dust fall onto his nylon bedspread.

One day, Dad's anger is out of control. Mum gets us out of the house before I can even get my shoes on. I can feel the burn of gravel on the soles of my feet as we hurry along in the dark towards Theia Georgia's house. There's no freeing wind in my hair, no pedals underfoot, just the rush of adrenalin as we hurry along in case Dad decides to follow us out onto the street.

My mother pushes me forward. I feel her distress in the pressure of her hand as it steers me by the elbow. We are heading towards the safety of Theia's lit porch and her understanding ear.

I imagine Dad, back at home, still throwing chairs across the kitchen, drunk. Or perhaps he will be sitting on our vinyl green couch, his rage spent. With a cigarette in his hand, listening to the empty sounds of the house. The clock ticking, the lino creaking as it contracts in the cold night.

The following day, he is repentant. Says he can't remember what he said. He promises it will never happen again. But the next time we walk to the milk bar together, I pull at his hand. I don't want to stop at the pub for lemonade.

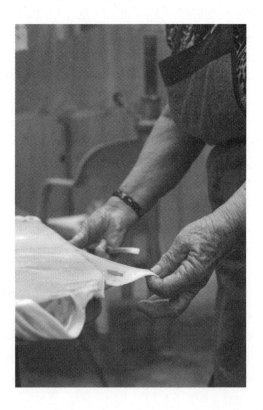

Georgia's spanakopita (spinach pie)

Makes 2 family-sized pies

Septuagenarian Theia Georgia and her husband still live in Collingwood. Walking down the narrow path alongside her single-fronted weatherboard, I am transported back to my own childhood home just streets away. In Theia's garden, there is a chaotic array of pumpkins, silverbeet, herbs, spring onions and beetroot, just as there was in ours all those years ago. And her hugs are just as heartfelt, her lollies just as sweet.

When I asked her to show me how to make her famous *spanakopita* – all buttery, flaky, spinachy goodness – she quickly obliged. The beauty of this recipe is that you can replace the spinach with almost anything else that is in season: leek, silverbeet, wild greens or pumpkin, for example.

The recipe comes with a warning: the pastry needs to be elastic, and rolled and pulled until it is papery thin. Suffice to say, this takes practice. Do not be dejected if this does not happen the first or second time you try; I had to ring Theia Georgia for advice the first time I attempted it on my own. If it all sounds too much, there is no shame in purchasing some of the traditional filo pastry now available in supermarkets and Greek delicatessens.

Ingredients

For the dough
1 kilogram plain flour
1 teaspoon salt
1 cup vegetable oil
2 cups lukewarm water
200 grams unsalted butter, melted

For the filling
1 bunch spinach, finely chopped
4 or 5 stalks silverbeet, finely chopped
1 leek, pale part only, finely chopped
½ bunch spring onions, finely chopped
1 handful of fresh herbs (eg dill, mint, thyme and/or oregano),
finely chopped
2 eggs
150 grams feta cheese
300 grams ricotta cheese
Salt and pepper to taste

Method
Preheat the oven to 200°C.

Put the flour and salt into a large mixing bowl. Make a hole in
the middle and pour in the oil and water.

Using your hands, gradually combine the flour with the wet
ingredients. When they have come together, lay the mound on a
clean, floured surface and knead gently until you have a smooth,
silky dough. Cut this into 4 portions and cover them with a
damp tea towel.

Place the chopped vegetables and herbs into a large bowl.
Scatter half a teaspoon of salt over the top and mix well. After
10 minutes, squeeze out any excess liquid.

In a separate bowl, whisk the eggs. Crumble in the feta, then add the ricotta, salt and pepper. Add this mixture to the greens and mix well.

Use a rolling pin to roll out 1 portion of the pastry. When it is the size of a large pizza, drizzle a few tablespoons of melted butter onto it.

Slide both hands under the pastry and gently stretch it evenly, until it is at least 60 or 70 centimetres square and translucent. Cut the pastry into 15-centimetre squares. Place the most irregular of these squares, buttered side down, onto your work surface. Add another square, buttered side down, and continue until you have used up all the 15-centimetre squares. Round the edges by patting them with your hands, then put the stack aside under a damp tea towel while you repeat the process with the other 3 portions of pastry.

Have ready 2 round baking trays, about 30 centimetres in diameter. Roll 1 stack of pastry out to the size of the base of the baking tray, and then lift it into the tray. Edge the pastry 2 centimetres up the side of the tray.

Spread half of the filling onto the pastry. Roll out another stack of pastry and place it over the top of the filling. Pinch the sides shut, using a little water if the pastry is too dry. Brush a generous amount of melted butter over the top and gently score the pastry in a criss-cross fashion. Repeat the steps with the remaining pastry to make the second pie. Bake for 45 minutes or until golden and flaky.

Heidelberg hiatus

Show me the teacher and I will show you the student

Greek proverb

I stick my finger into the solidified fat. It intrigues me. How can such a dark, bubbling mass of oil cool into a solid block of yellow overnight? My finger leaves a dent. I wipe my hand on the tall stacks of butcher's paper on the counter. I quietly open the till and take out a small handful of twenty-cent coins. Dad won't notice. He's been so busy since we moved from Collingwood to West Heidelberg in Melbourne's east, where my parents now run a fish and chip shop. Dad's out the back, loading a sack of potatoes into a machine that looks like a cement mixer. I hear him press the switch and it starts whirring, grinding the skin off the potatoes. When it's done, he transfers the great vats of peeled potatoes into another machine, which spits them out as chips. The familiar starchy smell rises up. I carefully step across the wet floor to get to our living area out the back of the shop.

I walk through Mum and Dad's bedroom. Mum's sewing machine is crammed into one corner of the room. If I'm lucky, she'll let me use it again tonight. I have learnt to sew small dresses for my dolls, spinning the wheel by hand without turning the electricity on. I walk past the lounge room, where the TV is blaring already and Dennis is sitting bleary-eyed on the couch, eating Corn Flakes. I go to the kitchen, where Mum is cooking *spanakorizo*, spinach and rice casserole, for tonight's dinner.

'I'm just going to the newsagent's next door to look around.'

'Again?'

'I'll be back soon.'

The newsagency has a big poster in the window with multiple images of a topless woman. In each frame, she wears stickers on her breasts, with tassels hanging from her nipples. I lean my head in for a closer look at the glitzy diamantes. I wonder how they stay on. I can't imagine my own mother wearing such things. I know not to ask her what they are for.

But I have no time to waste – there are more exciting things to be found, and it will be time to go to school soon. I make my way past the rows of notebooks, coloured paper, ballpoint pens and textas. Past little jars of glitter and gold and silver stars. Past the towering boxes of dolls that crawl and cry, which are far beyond my means. I find what I am looking for: the new book of paper dolls with fancy dresses and matching handbags and shoes. The dolls have big eyes and sweet mouths, rouged cheeks and tiny feet. I check my stack of change. I think I have enough. The man at the counter raises an eyebrow when I pay with two fistfuls of coins, but doesn't say anything. Outside, I put the book under my jumper and round the corner to the back of our shop. I open the gate, clamber around the boxes of drinks and over the rubbish bins to my room, where I carefully start to take the dolls out of the book. I dress them in different outfits, take them to dances and to the park, make them have conversations and kiss each other goodbye as they go back to their homes.

'Come and have breakfast, Spirithoula. It's nearly time to go.'

I hide my booty under the bed and start getting ready for school.

The school ground here in West Heidelberg is so much bigger than our intimate little patch of bitumen at Victoria Park Primary School. Tall gums dot the playground. There's bark on the ground and oversized tyres to play on. I look for Eva. When I find her, her nose is wet with snot as usual. Anna joins us, chewing at the wet tail-end of her dark hair. We Greek girls stick together, like scared rabbits.

I'm still worried that the petite, blonde-haired Sarah will get me back for what I did last week. She tried to push in when we were waiting to go on the gym equipment; when I protested, she punched me in the stomach and I told the teacher. Since then, every time she passes me, she taunts me: *Lagger, you wait and see, I'll get you.* But today she is nowhere to be seen. Her friends tell me she has had to leave the school and it's all my fault.

In class, our teacher asks us to write about a part of our body that we can't do without. She says that she can't do without her hand. With it she writes on the blackboard, teaching us important things. I think she's very clever. So clever in fact that I copy her: my hand is the most important part of my body, too. I'm not confident enough to come up with my own body part.

In the afternoon, a kind teacher comes around and takes Eva and me out of class. I am proud to be made a fuss of, love the special attention, but ashamed, too. I can't read as well as the others. I have to go to special classes to catch up. The only books we have at home are my Greek school readers and a copy of *Dot and the Kangaroo*, in which cartoon characters have adventures in the bush. This was given to my brother by his godparents. I look at the pictures over and over, fascinated, but the words are a little too hard for me to understand. We don't speak English at home like most of the other kids. I envy the others, the way English slips from their mouths so naturally.

Back at home, I am bored.

'Mum, why can't I work in the shop?'

'You're too young. It's no place for a child.'

'But I'm bored.'

'Then go and do your homework, so you don't end up like them.' She points her chin to the young people on the other side of the counter, who are more often than not swearing and drunk. She is careful not to look them in the eye, for fear that they will turn on her. I am fascinated by these youths who play for hours on the pinball machine in the shop. They can't afford the minimum chips – *Come on, Peter, can't we buy a half serve? We've only got ten cents!* – but they constantly feed the machine with coins. They don't seem to go to school. And they threaten to get violent when Dad tries to close the shop at night. *Oorrrhhh, come on, just a few more minutes.*

Dad always gives in. He calls then 'bodgies', but I know he's got a soft spot for them. Mum keeps telling him, *They'll eat you alive. How are we ever going to get ahead?*

When I was little, we lived for a few years in Narrandera; my parents worked in a fish and chip shop with my mother's sister and her husband. Bikies took over the town for days on end, fights broke out in the shop – I was only four, but I knew even then that Dad wasn't cut out for it. Mum says his hands were made for working at a desk, not frying chips. I wonder what we are doing back in a fish and chip shop again.

I go to visit Nicki, whose family runs the milk bar a few doors down. Her house is more interesting than ours; it has two levels. Upstairs, she and her three sisters share a large bedroom. We play jacks on her bed and dress her dolls. She has real Barbies with elbows and knees that bend, not like the hollow stiffs I've got. She gets the blondes; I get the brunettes. When we sing in front of the mirror, she is always ABBA's beautiful Agnetha while I am the plainer Frida. But it's her house, and I'm grateful she lets me play with her.

A bit later, Mum sings out from downstairs, 'Come home, Spirithoula, your *nouno* and his family are here.' My godparents. I run home – I can't wait to see my godsister, who is a few years older than me, and her brothers. Our parents eat *spankorizo* and we kids have fish and chips, eaten straight out of the paper parcel. Mum and Dad take it in turns to serve in the shop when the bell tinkles, while we talk and laugh and play Murder in the Dark well into the night as the adult conversation drones in the background …

'The cost of potatoes has gone up from two dollars a sack a few years ago to ten dollars now. How are we supposed to make a living?'

They talk about the long hours they work, the drunken youths my father is struggling to control. Should they stay or go?

We check on the house in Collingwood every now and then. My parents have rented it out to a Vietnamese family, who do most of their living in the front room. The windows are covered with sheets. We are taken aback at how they have made our home theirs. Dennis and I miss Collingwood, miss the neighbours and the familiar streets. I think my parents do too.

Two years after we moved to Heidelberg, it's time to load the removal truck up again and return to Collingwood. I breathe a sigh of relief. It's nice to be home.

Chrysoula's tyganites patates (potato chips)

Serves 3 to 4

According to my mother, the secret to making the best chips ever is to cut the potatoes thick, salt them well and make sure the oil is plentiful and very hot. Vegetable oil is fine, but if you want to splash out, use olive oil.

Ingredients
6 large potatoes
1 teaspoon salt
4 cups vegetable or olive oil

Method
Peel the potatoes and cut them longways into thick wedges. Place them in a colander and rinse them to wash off the starch. Allow them to drain, then mix through the salt with your fingers.

Heat the oil in a heavy pot or deep pan over very high heat. To test it, drop one chip into the oil. If it sizzles instantly, the oil is ready. Cook the chips in batches, a handful at a time; they should be just covered by the oil.

Agitate the pot occasionally so that the chips don't stick to the bottom. When they are golden, remove them with a slotted spoon and place them onto a napkin-lined plate. Serve immediately to waiting guests or hungry children.

Sweetbreads and other tidbits

We don't have bread, yet we ask for cheese

Greek proverb

He always smiles widely, even though he holds a bloodied cleaver in his hand.

'What will it be today, Chrysoula?'

Mum looks at the gleaming pig's head with its hairy snout, the oversized calf livers, the ox tongues and lamb's brains.

She points. 'One kilo these please.' Lamb sweetbreads. The round, identical pieces of the thymus gland are like a tray of tiny, perfectly formed clouds.

'And half kilo these too.' Chicken hearts.

She turns to the main counter, where the more conventional cuts of meat are displayed.

'The chops, they are very expensive today.'

Our butcher shrugs and smiles again.

'For you, Chrysoula, I will take fifty cents off.' Winks. I look down to the sawdust on the floor, sensing Mum's embarrassment. But she's got her bargain, and that's the main thing.

He wraps it all up for us. We leave the shop and walk home down Hoddle Street. There's a steady stream of people heading to the Victoria Park football stadium. It's going to be packed today. Collingwood versus Carlton. In the road outside our house, Dad has set two chairs and balanced a plank between them, staking his claim to our parking spot. Our street is fast filling up with cars.

Mum opens each of the packages. Some of the meat will go in the freezer. We'll have the sweetbreads for lunch today. I'm excited. I love their soft texture in my mouth, their delicate flavour. Dad loves them, too; they are usually eaten as a *meze*, a snack with ouzo. It's very much a man's food. It's my job to remove the little hairs. Mum boils them briefly to firm them up and to get rid of any impurities. Before long they are sizzling in the pan with wine and oil. I start to get a salad ready.

Dad gets back from the market and plants three boxes of fruit and vegetables onto the kitchen floor.

'The potatoes were cheap. I got a box.'

'Good. I'll give half to Sophia this afternoon.' Mum's sister is always cooking fried potatoes and sausages, going through at least a box of potatoes a week.

'Mum, are we going to visit Theia?' First we had sweetbreads, and now we're visiting my aunty and cousins' house. It's turning out to be a good day.

'Yes, we will get there quicker if you wash the dishes.'

After lunch, we pack the boot of the Valiant with half of everything Dad brought home.

'Be careful. Don't scratch the car,' Dad cautions.

Dad's proud of the new car, even though it's second-hand. He bought it off our family friend Theodore, or *Psomas*, 'The Bread Man'. In a former life, the Valiant carted bread. Now it carts potatoes.

We drive to Northcote. My cousins surround us like excited puppy dogs, and everyone helps bring things into the house. Our mothers stay in the kitchen, packing the food away. My uncle and father go out into the back yard and crack open beers. There's not much room to play in the house.

'We're going to the park. Can we have some money to get an icy pole from the milk bar?'

'Be careful how you cross the road. And don't speak to any strangers.' They hand over the requisite coins. It's turning out to be a *very* good day.

The bell on the door of the shop tinkles when we go in. The sweet milk-bar aroma rolls over us: milkbottles, musks and liquorice allsorts; Four'N Twenty pies; tobacco. We take forever to decide what we want. Will it be a raspberry icy pole or a packet of candy cigarettes? Smith's crisps or a Paddlepop? Mixed lollies or a Freddo Frog? Once we've made the all-important decisions, we head to the park. We don't leave until our mothers round the corner and tell us it's time to go home.

That night, Dad and I sit on the green vinyl couch to watch TV. Bill Collins is introducing *True Grit* with John Wayne. Mums says it's late, that I should go to bed, but Dad winks and says I can stay up. He smokes during the commercials. I think he's a bit like John Wayne, except he doesn't own an eye patch and his nose is bigger.

The next day is boring. I wander around the house, turn the TV on, turn it back off. There's a stack of Greek records in the stereo cabinet, but only one record in English: I put it on and start dancing to 'Skinny Girls'. It's not as much fun as dancing with my cousins; together, we hitch our dresses up, writhe around the lounge room and have dance competitions like on *Young Talent Time*. After a while, I turn my attention to my homework, trying to wrap my head around long division. Dad shows me how he did it in his day and gets frustrated that I need to write my workings down – *Can't you just do it in your head?* Then it's time to do my Greek homework. When I make yet another simple grammatical error, Dad scowls and calls me 'Skippy the bush kangaroo'. Even though I do very well at Greek school, I can't do well enough for Dad. Dennis falls even further short of his expectations. Dad finally gives up on us and goes outside for a smoke.

I'm glad when Monday comes around and I can see my friends. But first, there is the torturous run around the Victoria Park football oval. The grass is muddy from Saturday's game. The circumference of the ground seems an impossible distance. I envy my classmates their long running strides, their easy relationships with their bodies. My body is chunky, the back of my thighs dimpled. I already have my mother's generous bottom. Sure enough, I am among the last to struggle across the finish line. For our troubles, we stragglers are made to do twenty push-ups. The looming bleachers seem to mock my incompetence as I stare at the feet of those more athletic than me. *One … two …*

Over the road, we cross the black bitumen of the schoolyard and enter our classroom. The room echoes with thirty pairs of shoes as we clamber to get to our desks. The scrape of metal on wood makes the teacher grimace. He glares at us. We lift our chairs and sit down.

I pull out my books and look up expectantly. I want to put my hand up and say I have finally mastered long division. I look around at my classmates. Apart from Megan, who wears thick black-rimmed glasses, I know no one else will appreciate the information. I put my head down and start my work.

Chrysoula's pan-fried glykathakia (sweetbreads)

Serves 8 as an appetiser

Ingredients
1 kilogram lamb sweetbreads (pre-order these from your butcher)
1 glass dry white wine
½ cup olive oil
½ teaspoon oregano
Salt and pepper to taste

Method
Wash the sweetbreads carefully, removing the fine hairs. Place in a saucepan of cold water and bring to the boil. As soon as the water bubbles, transfer the sweetbreads to a colander and rinse them with cold water.

Place the sweetbreads and the wine in a frying pan over low heat. Cover and simmer until the wine has reduced. Add the oil, oregano, salt and pepper and cook until tender. Serve with crusty bread and salad.

Inky squid sandwiches

A priest blesses his own bread first

Greek proverb

'That's disgusting!'

'Urrrgghh, what *is* that?'

'It's squid.'

I look down at my sandwich. Black inky squid on white sandwich bread. It seemed a good idea this morning, but now it has turned into a dark, soggy mess.

My friends shuffle along the wooden bench, staying well clear of my smelly sandwich and me. I eat quickly, then make my way to the monkey bars, where I might redeem myself with my flips. But before lunch is over, everyone knows. Spiridoula ate squid sandwiches for lunch.

It's Easter week and we're fasting at home. This means we don't eat milk, eggs or meat. Mum fasts for forty days, but she's satisfied if the rest of us fast for the week.

'Mama, tomorrow I'll take tomato-sauce sandwiches for lunch,' I announce when I get home.

'*Oti thelis*,' she says absently. Whatever you want. She's standing on a chair, taking down curtains. There are piles of them on the floor. She plans to wash them in the bath. It's important to have everything clean for Easter. This is what they did in the village, and this is what she does here. 'Please can you get a rag and start dusting?'

I do as I am told. The house must be spotless before we can get on to the cooking. Once the curtains are soaking, Mum starts on some bread. I watch as she expertly rolls out the dough, putting her whole body into it. She lets me have a go, but my strokes are nowhere near as good. She puts the dough into a huge basin and covers it with a few blankets, just as my grandmother did when we were in Greece. When the dough has doubled in size, she places it into large round tins and puts these in the oven. The house fills with its heady aroma. Before we go to sleep, she lets me have a wedge with oil and oregano on top.

The next day we make *koulourakia*, coiled Easter cookies. I place my clumsy shapes next to Mum's. 'Bravo, Spirithoula, bravo,' she says. Then we dye a few dozen eggs. Mum drops them gently into the pot and I watch in wonder as they come out, blood red. The egg is a symbol of the renewal of life, representing victory over death. It's my job to polish them with olive oil and place them in the blue bowl with the ornate silver handle.

Good Friday arrives and in the evening we pile into the Valiant and head down to Ayia Triada, the Holy Trinity church in Richmond.

The smell of honey, incense and perfume assaults me as we enter the church. Rhythmic chants cut through the stifling haze. High above, mournful Byzantine saints look down at us. The immense gold chandeliers look dangerously heavy and I wonder whether we would survive if they were to fall on our heads. I look up, expecting God to say something, but He doesn't.

My father lifts me to kiss the myriad icons; I am careful to avoid the lipstick marks. A middle-aged man guides us to the front, away from the aisle.

'*Yriyora, min stekese stin mesi,*' he says impatiently. Quickly, don't stand in the middle. There are many hundreds of people in the church, and it's his job to make sure they move in an orderly fashion.

We are ushered to the *Epitaphio,* the symbolic bier of Christ. I look in awe at this ornate casket, its canopy of chrysanthemums intricately woven like a rich tapestry. I have to stand on my toes to kiss the image of Him. Then we are pushed onward and outside by the mass of bodies behind us. The cool night air is a welcome relief. I clutch my father's hand tightly so that I don't lose him among the thousands of people lining the streets.

The priest finally emerges from inside the church. In the doorway, he seems immense in his vestments, a dark figure backlit by the light from inside. The jingling of his incense holder announces that the bier is approaching behind him. Men

73

strain under its weight. We part to give it room. The bier is carried slowly down the stairs like a coffin, step by careful step.

We follow behind, each carrying a candle. As far as the eye can see, lights flicker in the night air. We slowly follow the bier and the sound of chanting. I play with the warm wax of my candle, seeing how close I can get my fingers to the flame before they burn. My father takes a firmer hold of my hand, concerned for the skirt of the woman in front of me.

Locals come to their front gates to watch the passing parade. The dark bodies and little lights buffer me. I feel protected, part of something so much bigger than myself. I think back to the week of squid and tomato sauce sandwiches, the cleaning, the cooking; it all leads to the service commemorating the resurrection of Christ tomorrow night. There will be fireworks and laughter at midnight, and we will go home to eat soup and crack our eggs and say *Christos anesti*, Christ has risen. I clasp Dad's hand a little tighter. I'm glad to be here.

Chrysoula's bread

Makes 3 or 4 loaves

Mum regularly bakes both for the family and as a *prosforo*, an offering for church. In Greece, she baked from a sourdough starter, but in Australia she usually uses the live yeast available from most Greek delicatessens. There is a hefty dose of intuition involved – she will know instinctively if a little more flour or water is required, and if the dough has risen enough. Below is her recipe translated into cups and grams.

Ingredients
30 grams fresh yeast or 2 tablespoons dry yeast
3 cups lukewarm water
8½ cups flour (whole wheat, barley, white and/or cornflour)
1 tablespoon salt
2 tablespoons olive oil
1 tablespoon sugar

Method
In a small bowl, dissolve the yeast in half a cup of lukewarm water. Cover with cling wrap and place a blanket over the top, then set it aside for an hour.

In a large bowl, sift the flour with the salt and make a well in the centre. Add the oil, sugar, yeast mixture and 2 cups of lukewarm water. Using your hands, slowly mix everything together, pulling in the flour until it all comes together. If more water is needed, add a little at a time. Turn out the dough onto a floured surface and continue kneading until it is smooth and no longer sticks to the hands.

Lightly oil another mixing bowl. Place the dough inside and roll it around until it is coated in oil. Cover the bowl with a clean, damp dishcloth and a light blanket. Allow to rise for around 1 hour.

After an hour, punch the dough down and knead for 5 or 6 minutes on a floured surface. Divide the dough into 3 or 4 portions and form them into round, oblong or baguette-shaped loaves. Place the loaves several centimetres apart on floured trays and cover with a damp tea towel and a blanket. Allow the loaves to rise for 1 hour or until they have doubled in size.

Preheat the oven to 220°C, then bake the loaves for 1 hour. When the bread is golden and makes a 'hollow' sound when tapped on the bottom, it is ready.

The sacrificial lamb

The good housewife cooks before she gets hungry

Greek proverb

I try not to look at the lamb's eyes, or at the mouth clamped shut with wire, the sharp teeth still visible as it turns around, slowly, slowly. The lamb's body has been secured to the spit so that it doesn't move, metal skewers pushed through the flesh and clamped on. I feel sorry for the animal, but I know I will not be able to resist eating it – it smells delicious.

The spit has a small motor attached, perhaps from an old lawn mower or washing machine, which is connected to a rubber belt. The spit itself is made from a 44-gallon drum cut in half. When I was very little, we used to turn the lamb by hand. Sometimes I was allowed to have a turn, but my face quickly burnt with the heat and the job would be handed back to the men.

There's a regular *ssszzz* sound as fat drips from the lamb into the coals. The heat is unbearable, but I reach out to pluck a piece of skin. I've been waiting so long. I pull away a large strip, much bigger than I expected. I stuff it into my mouth before anyone sees. It's crisp and salty and leaves a pleasant oily taste on my tongue.

Soon after, the motor stops. All the men are off their vinyl seats and talking loudly, arguing about the best way to stop the whole lamb catching fire as the fat pools on the coals below. My uncle pulls out an old piece of corrugated iron; he puts it between the lamb and the coals while he fixes the motor. I scurry off, my cheeks burning.

Inside, my cousins are playing cards, my Theio Niko dealing. They move over for me and hand me a stack of one- and two-cent coins. The card game is one in which luck plays some part, but the willingness of players to pit themselves against the dealer is what makes or breaks them.

Theio Niko flips the cards over, counting like he's working at the casino.

'*Se efaga!*' he says when we bust, with a dramatic flourish of his trump card and a smug chuckle. I've eaten you.

John, his son, itches to deal so that he can 'eat' his dad in return.

My stack of coins dwindles quickly. I take too many risks and am too distracted by the lamb smells emanating from the back yard.

It's New Year's Eve and Cousin Tom's house is full of people. The women are putting the final touches to the food on the kitchen table; the men are outside drinking and talking, keeping an eye on the spit; the teenagers have holed up in the front room. I am restless and move from room to room.

Tomorrow, New Year's Day, is Saint Basil's Day, when we will visit all the people we know by that name. Theio Vassili in Collingwood will have enough chops, sausages and rissoles on his barbecue to feed the whole street. Then we might go to my godfather Vassili's house – perhaps he'll have another lamb on the spit going. I might not want to eat it again tomorrow, but I doubt it.

'Why don't women have parties on their name days?' I ask Mum. It seems men get all the honours – parties on their saint days, pride of place at the head of the table.

'I don't know,' she says. 'That's how it's always been in Greece.'

Her answer doesn't make sense to me. I see that most women we know work in factories and shops just like their husbands. It's not like Greece here at all.

When the sun goes down, the lamb is ready, and the table in the kitchen is brimming. There are three types of everything: roasted potatoes, potato salad and *scordalia* (potato and garlic dip); Greek salad, coleslaw, and lettuce and cucumber pieces; *taramosalata* (caviar dip), *tzatziki* and *melitzanosalata* (eggplant dip). There's a basket of bread piled high and the platter of juicy chunks of lamb, as well as sausages and other meats. I fill my plate with meat, bread, salads. We sit wherever there is a free space, eating and talking.

At the end of the night, Theio Niko lines us kids up and gives us the money he has won, saying '*Fai yiati pinases*' – Eat, because you are hungry – as he hands over the coins. His son John pipes up '*Akoma pinao*' after he gets his share: I'm still hungry. His father tells him not to be a smart-arse. His mother overhears and gives her husband a serve for swearing at the child on New Year's Eve; it is bad luck. She asks John if he really is hungry. 'Not for food,' he replies with a grin.

Finally, the clock strikes midnight and we kiss and hug one another. '*Hronia polla.*' Many years to you. '*Panta me uyeia.*' May you always have good health.

We cut the *vasilopita*, the New Year's cake. The first piece is dedicated to God, the second to the home, the third to the man of the house, and so on until everyone has been covered. There's a coin baked into the bottom; whoever gets it will have luck for the rest of the year. I miss out this year, but I am hopeful that next time it will be my turn.

I'm tired, but it's time for sweets, so I perk up. The kitchen table has been cleared of savouries and is now filled from corner to corner with *baklava*, *melamakarona* (honeyed sweets that look like oversized macaroni), *kourabiethes* (shortbread dusted with icing sugar), *galahktobouriko* (filo pastry filled with custard) and *karithopita* (walnut cake). This year someone has brought pavlova. My aunts and Mum gather around; they wonder at how the egg base can be made so crisp on the outside and so soft in the middle. I love the crunchy shell and the soft eggy mixture that melts in your mouth. Then there's the freshness of the fruit and the delicious fattiness of the cream. It's so different from the syrupy cakes I am used to.

I go outside with my cousins and we pick up coals and throw them against the concrete, watching them burst into sparks until the adults tell us off.

The lamb looks nude now, its bones showing, the fat coagulating. I secretly whisper a 'thank you' under my breath for being so tasty and then I join the others inside.

The women are washing the dishes and soon we pile into the Valiant to head home. Dad drives especially carefully, going through the back streets of Richmond and Collingwood to avoid police. Mum is alert; she hates it when Dad drinks and drives. But I rest sleepily in the back, knowing that with his hands on the wheel, and with a belly full of roast lamb, we will get home to greet New Year's Day safe and sound.

Lamb on the spit

Serves 20 to 25 people

Whenever someone in our family wants to roast a lamb on the spit, my Uncle John is called in to help. He kindly shared his secrets to the perfect fire-cooked lamb.

The lamb is usually skewered and marinated the night before and put onto the fire early in the morning. An early start is called for if the lamb is to be eaten for lunch: the fire will take some time to get going, and a 10- or 12-kilogram lamb requires around 3 hours to cook. Care needs to be taken: that the lamb doesn't catch fire, that it cooks evenly, and that your fire chiefs don't get so drunk they can't lift it from the stand. It's an acquired art, but one worth perfecting; a slow-cooked, beautifully marinated lamb is an unforgettable eating experience. I still make a habit of thanking the lamb for giving its life for my pleasure.

Equipment
1 spit roast, about 120 centimetres long
20 kilograms briquettes or charcoal
A large sewing needle and very fine wire or cooking twine
A few bags of ice if the weather is warm

Ingredients
1 whole lamb, between 10 and 12 kilograms
1 cup olive oil

1 cup dried oregano
12 to 16 whole cloves garlic, peeled
A few sprigs rosemary or oregano
1 cup salt
Freshly ground pepper to taste
3 lemons to serve

The spit

Gas spits are available for hire, but traditionally the lamb is cooked over a fire, giving it its distinctive smoky flavour. The best spits have a movable stake, so that you can easily lower it once your lamb is cooked.

The lamb

Order your lamb a week or two in advance. Most butchers remove the head, but you can ask them to keep it on if you prefer. Pick up the lamb the day before you need it. The butcher generally removes the innards, so no cleaning of the cavity is required. Have a clean surface ready on which to marinate and store it – a table covered in a clean sheet is ideal. If the weather is warm, cover the lamb with a sheet and pack a few bags of ice around it. Keep it away from pets and other animals.

Before putting the lamb onto the spit, wash and dry all the components of the skewer. Push the skewer through the cavity of the lamb, starting at the neck (or the mouth, if the head is still attached) and coming out under the tail.

Use the U-bolts to brace the lamb's legs, then secure these with the nuts. Repeat the process to secure the back of the lamb to the middle of the spit. Use wire to tie the lamb's legs to either end of the spit; there should be very little movement as the lamb rotates. There is nothing worse than dropping your lamb into the fire. Takeaway, anyone?

Combine ¼ cup of salt with ¼ cup dried oregano and pepper to taste. With clean hands, rub this mixture into the cavity and massage it generously into the flesh of the lamb. Make a few small incisions with a small, sharp knife in the fleshy parts of the lamb, such as the shoulders and thighs, and, with your fingers, push peeled garlic cloves into these as far as they will go.

Using the needle and cooking twine or wire, stitch the abdominal cavity up securely from one end of the lamb to the other.

The fire

If you are using charcoal briquettes, place about 20 kilograms of briquettes in the tray of the spit, lining them up along one side. They should be well lit before you load the lamb on. Ensure that the thicker parts of the meat (such as the shoulders and buttocks) have more coals under them than the thinner parts. Aim to start with a very hot fire for the first half hour of cooking, and slow it down as the meat cooks.

Rig the lamb up at the highest setting on your spit. After an hour, lower the lamb and add more fuel if the fire is burning too low. Cook for another hour or so, or until you see that the meat is cooked as described below.

In the last 30 minutes of cooking, baste the lamb with a mixture of oil, the remaining oregano, salt and pepper, using a sprig of rosemary or oregano as a basting brush.

The meat is ready when the skin is golden brown and has peeled well away from the flesh, and the flesh is starting to come off the bone. Check the thighs and shoulders to see if the meat is tender. When the lamb is done, use heatproof gloves or a thick towel to lift it off the stand, then place it onto a clean surface such as a bench or table covered in foil or plastic. This is a job for two people.

Slice off pieces of meat and serve hot to the waiting masses with wedges of lemon.

The hungry caterpillar

He who becomes a sheep is eaten by the wolf

Greek proverb

'I'm going to flush your head down the toilet,' she spits down at me. 'You're going to be sorry you ever came to this school.'

I look up at the girl, who towers over me by more than a head. Her body reminds me of the character Bea from the television show *Prisoner*, solid and unmoving. Her friends stand behind her and together they push me up against the lockers. Scores of feet echo up and down the linoleum corridor, but I might as well be alone – no one can help me here.

Debbie, a girl from my primary school class, walks past. I quickly slide away from my tormentors and fall into stride with her, looking back all the while to check that I am not being followed.

'What have you got on next?' she says. 'I've got art. Isn't this fun?'

'Um, I've got art too. It's very big, isn't it?'

We are at an orientation day at our local high school, designed to prepare us for year seven next year. The school, Collingwood Education Centre, appears massive. Dozens of rooms and offices sprawl across three floors; there is a full-sized theatre, a gymnasium and an oval. There's a smoking area for the older kids and most of the classrooms are open plan, separated from each other by low partitions. I find it overwhelming compared to the contained rooms of Victoria Park Primary. How am I going to cope?

Debbie and I join a few others in drawing class. Debbie effortlessly makes a beautiful Aboriginal motif using dots. I look at my own clumsy efforts to draw a face and push the paper deep down into my bag. We then make our way to the cafeteria. I am astounded by the choices: hot chips and pies and sausage rolls; salad rolls and sandwiches; chocolates and crisps. If I do get my head flushed down the toilet, at least I can turn to the cafeteria for comfort.

The following year, when we start real classes, Bea is nowhere to be seen, but I stick with Debbie even so. We negotiate the corridors together, somehow finding our way to classrooms. There are some pleasant surprises, like the specialised art rooms where we can study textiles, woodwork and ceramics. Perhaps I can prove myself with my sewing skills, which I have honed on my mother's machine. But I quickly realise that if I want to move up in the pecking order, sewing isn't going to cut it. Debbie, who lives in the high-rise housing-commission flats near the school, keeps me in the loop with gossip: who stole what; who is in trouble with the police; what everyone is doing. I listen, open-mouthed. There's a sports store down the road, and there are whispers about who has stolen the latest gear – oversized baseball shirts and high-topped runners, mimicking the rap videos I watch on Saturday mornings. No one can afford these things, but there's so much kudos in wearing them that it's worth risking arrest to get them.

Debbie introduces me to the 'club' at the base of the flats. Here there are pool tables and a trampoline and young people everywhere, smoking, talking and laughing. They know how to do somersaults on the trampoline, play pool like pros, and break into Michael Jackson moves when the mood strikes. They carry ghetto blasters and seem not to bother with school much.

I, on the other hand, take the pool cue clumsily, aware that there is a row of Maori boys behind me on a velour couch, sniggering when I bend over. I bounce up and down on the trampoline, my repertoire limited. All the while, I'm conscious of the time.

'Debbie, I've got to go. My parents don't know I'm here. I have to get home.'

She shrugs. She's getting used to my limited freedom. She can roam the grounds of the housing-commission estate as she pleases.

My parents do let me go to the library on my own. It seems like everything you could ever want to know is on offer at Collingwood's Carringbush Library. Books tantalise me from rotating displays, seduce me from metal shelves. It's like a smorgasbord of words, and I am greedy. I chomp my way through the children's section, catching up on all the books I've never read – *The Very Hungry Caterpillar, The Cat in the Hat, The Magic Faraway Tree* – then move on to teen fiction. I read everything I can get my hands on. The librarian raises an eyebrow when I hand over a tome with a woman on all fours baring her breasts. She looks even more worried when I lie, 'It's for my father.'

I spend every spare minute lying on my bed, reading. I hear my mother washing dishes and know I should get up and help, but it's too late. I have entered a parallel universe of adventure, romance, sex and danger. I live vicariously through the characters and am sad to let them go at the end of a book. I play around The Rocks like the orphans in *Playing Beatie Bow*. I am swept up in forbidden passions with the heroines of *The Thorn Birds*. I become wicked like the fiendish characters in *The Wonderful Story of Henry Sugar*.

At lunchtime, Debbie often goes home to eat with her family, and sometimes I join her. After we eat, her blue-eyed, softly spoken father does the dishes. I've rarely seen my father wash up. Debbie's mother has a cheeky smile and freckles on her dark skin. She smokes at the table, just like my dad, and tells me Archie Roach is her baby brother. I like the casualness of Debbie's family, the way they chat with one another and seem to trust Debbie to do the right thing. I recognise the strong ties of my own family, without the fear.

When Debbie comes to my house after school, my mother plies her with food.

'*Faye, faye,* you are too skinny,' Mum says.

'Argh, Mama, don't,' I say.

'It's alright,' Debbie says, obliging by eating everything put in front of her, from lemony baked potatoes to sweet little plates of syrupy preserves.

At other times, we run across the eight lanes of Hoddle Street, zigzagging between the traffic to get fish and chips for lunch. We eat them at the park, where packs of kids are smoking furtively. I try a cigarette but gag at the taste.

At school, although Bea is gone, there are still groups of girls out to get me. One afternoon I find myself cornered.

'You're in for it, Spiri.'

I am head to head with Jenny. Her friends Anna and Effie stand behind her. I make a snap decision.

'I don't care. I'll fight you. After school, in the park.'

Jenny looks at her friends, then backs off. A new respect comes into their eyes; they are three, I am one, and yet I stood up to them. The fight doesn't happen, but I'm prepared to follow through if it does.

These girls aren't the biggest threat, however. As the year goes on, the boys become our common enemy. They steal our pencil cases and push them through the down pipes from second-floor windows, tear pages from our books and tease us mercilessly. Jenny becomes the target of Jim, a diminutive boy who puts her down at every opportunity. He makes her life hell for months on end.

One day, when the teacher has left the room, he starts mocking Jenny, then pulls her hair. She stands up, rage in her face. She turns around, and the crack of her slap against his cheek silences us all. He is so shocked, he moves slowly back to his chair, speechless. Jenny sits down, her back straight, her anger surrounding her like a force field. I doubt he will tease her again.

The teachers do their best to control the rowdy bunch of students, who come from so many backgrounds and have so many needs. There are the Cambodian and Vietnamese refugees, who sit in groups and bother no one. There are the Turks, the boys prancing around, *Siktir lan* this and *Siktir lan* that: *Fuck this, dude*, and *Fuck that, dude*. Some of the Turkish girls are quiet and studious; others apply lipstick in the toilets and hitch up their skirts. I sense that their families are even stricter than mine – that they need to take what freedoms they can at school.

We are allowed to call our teachers by their first names, and to go into the staff room at lunchtime. I love this new freedom to speak with my teachers as equals. I take pride in lining up with them in the 'health food' section of the canteen to order my salad roll, after the hot food has lost its lustre. I know it's not cool to be chummy with the teachers, but they make me feel that I have something to say, that my views are important.

I especially like my English teacher, Joy. She has red hair and wears flowing skirts and brown leather sandals. She is gentle but speaks passionately about the English language.

'Today, we are going to learn about poetry. We're going to read some poems, and then I want you to have a try at writing your own. They don't have to rhyme. Just write what comes to you.'

I enjoy this; the words reel off my pen and onto the page. The following week, she takes me aside. Have I done something wrong?

She hands me back my poem. 'This is really lovely, Spiri. You should keep writing. I've bought you something to help you along.'

She gives me a journal. I open it up and find it is filled with clean, lined sheets.

She smiles. 'I hope you find lots of things to write in these pages.'

I feel sure that I will. Perhaps this high-school caper won't be so bad after all.

Christina's mtomatoula glyko (preserved tomato sweet)

Preserving fruits and vegetables was once widespread in Greece, particularly in villages. It ensured that in times of plenty, enough was put aside for the leaner months. It also meant there was always something to serve people who came calling.

This tomato sweet is traditionally made on the island of Kos. My friend Sevi was shown how to make it by her mother, Christina. Like many Greek recipes that take some time to prepare (this one needs to be left overnight and requires 2 to 3 hours' cooking time), it tends to be made in bulk. It is also best done in company. This jewel-like dessert makes for a novel and delicious gift.

Equipment
2 large glass jars with lids, sterilised (or several smaller jars, if you prefer).

Ingredients
50 medium-sized Roma tomatoes that are not too ripe
4 tablespoons lime powder (available from Asian groceries)
50 whole blanched almonds
50 whole cloves
2 kilograms white sugar
8 tablespoons lemon juice (the juice of approximately 2 lemons)
2 cups water
15 grams vanilla powder (available from Greek delicatessens)
1 tablespoon honey

Method

Peel the tomatoes, taking care not to remove too thick a layer; the exterior of the flesh still needs to be firm. Place the peeled tomatoes in the basin of a clean kitchen sink, with the plug in.

Put the lime powder into a strainer and hold this above the tomatoes. Turn on the tap so that the water runs through the powder and onto the tomatoes. When no powder remains in the strainer, let the water fill the sink until the tomatoes are completely submerged. Leave the tomatoes in the lime for 30 minutes, stirring with a spoon every 3 or 4 minutes. The lime firms the tomatoes up.

Using a dessert spoon or fork, pierce the base of each tomato and scrape out the seeds. Wash the tomatoes thoroughly and give them one last vigorous shake to remove any seeds that might still be lodged inside.

Insert an almond into the cavity of each tomato. Poke a clove into the stalk end of each. Put the tomatoes into a large, heavy-based pot. Add the sugar, lemon juice and two cups of water, then cover the pot and leave it overnight. The tomatoes will expel a fair bit of liquid.

The next day, put the pot onto the stove and bring to the boil. Simmer over a low heat for 2 to 3 hours, stirring every 30 minutes, until the liquid has turned into a syrup. After 2 hours, place a little of the liquid into a small bowl and wait until it has cooled slightly. The cooled syrup should be the consistency of honey. If it is not yet ready, let it simmer for a bit longer.

When the syrup is the right consistency, take the pot off the stove. Add the vanilla powder and the honey and stir. When the syrup has cooled, pour it into the sterilised jars, ensuring that it covers the tomatoes.

This sweet keeps for a year if refrigerated.

Cavafy connections

Wonder is the beginning of wisdom

Greek proverb

Constantine Cavafy. Someone in the class has heard that Cavafy was gay. There's also a rumour he was a necrophiliac. We're paying attention now.

We are studying Cavafy's poem 'Ithaka' in our year twelve Modern Greek class. We explore the sordid details of the poet's life (what does a necrophiliac *do*, exactly?). Stella, our teacher, smiles, and then deftly diverts the discussion to more literary questions. Cavafy was known for his hedonistic poems. Does anyone know what 'hedonistic' means? We do not. The word comes from the Ancient Greek word *hédoné*, which means 'pleasure'. We perk up again.

The poem itself feels like hard work. Stella makes us read it in Greek. She refuses to give us the translation just yet. The words are difficult; some are in Katharevousa, an educated, purist form of Greek; others are in Dimotiki – the modern, everyday language – and still others in dialect. We read that

94

Cavafy was born in Alexandria, that Greek was not his first language. At any rate, the poem was written in 1911. What relevance can it have to my life now?

I go back to daydreaming about the charms of George, one of the boys in the class. I stare vacantly out the window, across the park where a group of Maori boys are rap dancing, towards the flats looming up into a grey sky. I can just make out a figure sleeping on a bench, covered in an old blanket. I fantasise about George's full lips on mine, my thighs intertwined with his. But there the fantasy stops. My father's face looms. *Ti tha pei o kosmos?* What will people say?

I've watched George grow from an awkward child who played cricket on our street to a bad-boy Adonis. If the rumours are true, George is juggling two girlfriends at once. I shake myself from my reverie. George is not the man for me.

It's confirmed beyond doubt when he leans across the table and says provocatively, 'Why are men superior to women?'

'Mmm. Why?'

'Because they can piss on a wall.'

The boys in the class snigger, the girls groan. George watches me get angry and smirks even more.

I try to concentrate on what Stella is saying. She challenges us to get inside the poem, get under its skin. What does it mean? What do you think the author wants us to learn? What might 'Ithaka' stand for in this context?

Although I don't understand all the words, I like the shape of them, the way they roll off my tongue. There are no superfluities, no pretentions. I put my hand up.

'I think the poem is about going on a journey, on life's journey. Maybe it's about finding out where you belong, where home is?'

Stella nods. 'Bravo, Spirithoula.'

We pull the poem apart, line by line. I scribble notes beside it.

Laistrygonians and Cyclops,
angry Poseidon – don't be afraid of them:
you'll never find things like that on your way

'Don't let obstacles get in your way. Don't let fear stop you from exploring things.'

And if you find her poor, Ithaka won't have fooled you.
Wise as you will have become, so full of experience,
you will have understood by then what these Ithakas mean.

'You can't just pick and choose from good and bad experiences. The biggest riches are the ones we have gained from the journey.'

I think about my own journey, about where I'm going. I want so many things. Mostly, I want more freedom to go out, to explore. I want to escape my chunky thighs and large bottom – where are the bottoms like mine in *Dolly* magazine?

And I want to know where I belong. Am I Australian? Am I Greek? I feel that I exist in no-man's-land – somewhere in the middle, with one foot in each camp. I want *out*, but I have no idea what I want *into*. Or how the heck I'm going to get there.

Mum has her own ideas about what I should want. At parent–teacher night she makes straight for Stella, the only teacher who speaks Greek. 'Is my daughter good enough to go to university?'

I roll my eyes, embarrassed.

Stella glances at me and says diplomatically, 'She has great potential. If she continues to apply herself as she has, she will do well.'

Mum is pleased; she doesn't bother to speak to any other teachers. On the way home she tells me, 'If you don't go to university, you'll turn out like me – sewing nighties for a living. We came to Australia for our children, for a better life. Make me proud, Spirithoula, make us all proud.'

I know by 'us' she means not just our family, but also all the *theies* and *theios* and the neighbours too. I feel as if the whole tribe is sitting on my shoulders, and the weight of it gives me a headache.

Luckily I too want to go to university, although for a different reason – escape. I try to apply myself to my studies. But in my regular bouts of procrastination, I take solace in my trusty companions: books. Cavafy echoes in my head … *May you visit many Egyptian cities to learn and go on learning from their scholars.* The school library becomes my little Egyptian city, allowing me to step out of my life and into another, more exciting one. I let the words in books overrun me; I soak in them, get lost in their sensual charms.

I start with the year twelve English reading list, on which is George Orwell's *Nineteen Eighty-Four*. I work diligently through his *Animal Farm*, and then through the books that led him to these seminal ones, tracing his journey backwards. His writing leads me to Aldous Huxley's *Brave New World*. From there I peek into Virginia Woolf's *A Room of One's Own* and Simone de Beauvoir's *The Second Sex*. I want very much to understand de Beauvoir and her fellow existentialist Camus, but their language is beyond me as I sit on the carpet, reading passages during my lunch hour. George Johnston's *My Brother Jack*, another prescribed text, leads me to its sequels, *Clean Straw for Nothing* and *A Cartload of Clay*. Our English teacher, Michael, tells us that the character Cressida Morley is based on Johnston's real-life partner Charmian Clift. I seek out her exquisite stories, in which she describes eking out a living on the Greek island of Kalymnos with Johnston and their young children. Clift writes of trying to balance her writing career with her family, and of their longing to escape their 'civilisation-sick' existence in Australia and England. In *Mermaid Singing*, published in 1958, the irony is not lost on Clift when she describes an islander addressing her husband:

> *Well you see Mister George, it seems funny to these fellers*
> *here, all these fellers who don't want nothin' but to get away*

*from Kalymnos. They all want to go to Australia. They
don't want to have to go on diving for sponges. Ain't nothin'
here but sponges, Mister George.*

Clift whets my appetite for other expatriate writers who have
lived in Greece: Gillian Bouras, Gerald Durrell. These writers
have made the inverse of my parents' journey, leaving affluent
city lives for poor, rural ones.

My very favourite author, however, is supremely civilised.
I read Oscar Wilde's plays, his stories, his biography. *The Picture
of Dorian Gray* becomes a kind of manifesto: the duality of
Dorian's character seems like a strange metaphor for my own
life. 'Live! Live the wonderful life that is in you! Let nothing
be lost upon you. Be always searching for new sensations. Be
afraid of nothing.' I am torn – am I a dutiful Greek daughter,
or a … what? What is the alternative? Will my true self always
be hidden away like Dorian's portrait?

Perhaps the answer to my dilemma lies in laughter. Our
Modern Greek class goes to see *Wogs Out of Work*, a show
about 'New Australians' sending themselves up. Suddenly
being a Greek-Australian doesn't seem so bad. The strict
fathers, the factory-working mothers: I've never seen them as
funny before. There's a skit about a Greek girl who has a sharp
tongue and big hair – 'I'll have to tell Dad I'm going out with
people from the office,' she says as she dons red high heels to go
out with her boyfriend. She is a stereotype, I know, but she is
larger than life, endearing, *out there*.

After the show, we stop for coffee in Brunswick Street's Black Cat Café. I have my first real cappuccino; I watch the coffee ooze from the machine, the barista flamboyantly frothing the milk. There are Formica tables with retro chairs like the ones my parents threw out only a few years ago. The waiters have long hair and ripped jeans. Mum would never let me wear ripped jeans. *We're not that poor that you have to wear torn pants*, I can hear her saying.

There's a camaraderie in the group, a sense of being grown up. Our teachers talk a little more than usual about their lives, about their young kids. About their divorces. I realise for the first time that they are in their early thirties, not really that much older than us. And that they too have problems.

When I get home, Dad is waiting anxiously at the door. As soon as Stella drives off, he closes the door and starts yelling: 'What time is this? I was so worried. I don't trust that Stella. What sort of teacher is she anyway to bring you home so late? I thought you would be home hours ago. You'll never go out at night again!'

Mum stands behind him, imploring him to calm down. He walks off in a huff, ranting, and she ushers me to my room.

'Why were you so late? You know how much he worries. Something could have happened to you out there on the streets.'

'But Mama, we just went out for coffee …'

'Go to bed now. I'll calm him down …'

I cry myself to sleep.

The next morning, I talk to Stella and burst into tears.

'Why must it be like this? What have I done wrong? I had such a good time.'

She's concerned, perhaps feels a bit guilty. She organises for me to see a psychologist, a woman with a Greek background who will come and see me at school. Finally, someone is going to solve my problems.

When I meet with the psychologist, I talk non-stop. About my over-protective father. About feeling so damned *responsible* for my parents. About worrying about their feelings all the time, about feeling trapped. I lay my problems out on the little brown school desk in front of us. I want desperately for her to make sense of them, to give me some answers. She listens patiently. She nods. She sympathises. I get the feeling she has been through it too.

After three sessions, she says, 'Spiri, you sound like a 25-year-old. You feel you have to shoulder everything. You are a very responsible, sensible young woman.'

Yes, this I already know.

'I can't keep seeing you. It's too far to come. But I feel you'll be okay. You'll work through it.'

I am gutted. So much for solving my problems. And yet I can't blame her. Deep down, I always knew I would have to work them out for myself.

MARY COUSTAS, AKA 'EFFIE', ON MULLETS AND MOUSSAKA

The stage production Wogs Out of Work *opened at Melbourne's Athenaeum Theatre in 1987, with a planned running season of two weeks. In the end, the show ran for over three years, reaching an audience of more than 750,000 people across Australia.*

Wogs Out of Work *launched the acting career of Mary Coustas, aka Effie Stephanides. Mary went on to play Effie in* Acropolis Now *(1989–92),* Effie: Just Quietly *(2001), and* Greeks on the Roof *(2003). She talks here about why* Wogs Out of Work *was a hit, what was good about growing up in Collingwood, and why hair was so big in the '80s.*

Everything was large in the '80s – the economy, the fashion, the possibilities. It was an era of flamboyancy, a loud and proud era. The big shoulder pads, the loud colours, the mullets, the root perms. In *Wogs Out of Work*, we ran with those feelings. By chance, we gave birth to a phenomenon.

The character of Effie was essentially a love letter to my childhood. I grew up in Collingwood. Back then, you weren't made to feel like an outsider there, as the suburb was so diverse. I continue to do Effie because I feel she has found a place in the Australian psyche, and in mine, which I cannot overlook.

In one of my favourite scenes from *Wogs Out of Work*, Nick Giannopoulos plays a wannabe surfie called Spiro – complete with wetsuit, fluorescent zinc cream and blond wig. It's his way of picking up blonde chicks at the beach. Spiro is not the brightest of bulbs.

One day he comes home to discover half the street gathered in his lounge room, with their heads bowed like somebody has died. What he doesn't know is that this gathering is over his bad Higher School Certificate results. A Greek female neighbour says to him, '*Tst tst tst*. No good, Spiro. No good for you mother, no good for you father. No good for the whole street.' I loved that line because it perfectly captured the big role community plays for the Greeks. It's absurd and true at the same time.

In another scene, Nick and Simon Palomares play their mothers, working on an assembly line. Petroula, Nick's mother, says, 'I was cleaning in my daughter's bedroom, and between her T-shirts I find drungs!'

Simon's character replies, 'Oh no, signora!'

Petroula continues, 'Drungs, signora, drungs! And she takes them every day, because on the packeto it says Monday, Tuesday, Wednesday ... every day, every day!'

The snooping, the misinterpretation and the melodrama of that moment got the biggest response from the audience every single night.

My personal philosophy is that no matter what it is we want to do, there comes a point when we have to step outside our comfort zone, take a risk and prove something major to ourselves. The impetus has to come from within. I've grown to realise that difficulty can push us forward to a place that buys us more individuality and strength.

Mary's moussaka

Serves 6 to 8

I am mad about a great moussaka, especially one with a Middle Eastern twist – I love it when the cinnamon, nutmeg and chilli tastes rise above all the other ingredients.

Ingredients
3 or 4 eggplants, sliced lengthwise into ½-inch pieces
6 potatoes, peeled
1½ kilogram ground beef
2 large onions, finely diced
1 teaspoon ground cinnamon
¼ teaspoon chilli flakes
1 teaspoon nutmeg
2 tablespoons tomato paste
1 cup crushed tomatoes or tomato puree
1 teaspoon sugar
Salt and pepper to taste
1 cup grated *kefalotyri* cheese (available at most Greek delicatessens) or parmesan

Béchamel sauce
1 cup salted butter
1 cup plain flour
4 cups milk, warmed
8 egg yolks, lightly beaten
A pinch of ground nutmeg

Method

Place the slices of eggplant in a colander and salt them liberally. Cover them with an inverted plate, weigh this down with a heavy can or jar, and place the colander in the sink so that excess moisture can run off. They will need to sit for at least 15 minutes, preferably for an hour.

Boil the potatoes until they are just tender. Drain, cool and slice them into ¼-inch pieces. Set aside.

Preheat the oven to 200°C. Rinse the eggplant and potato slices and dry them with paper towels. Place them on a greased baking tray and grill until golden brown. Take them out and put them aside to cool. Reduce the heat to 180°C.

In a large, heavy-based pan, brown the ground beef. Add the onion and sauté until it is translucent, about 5 minutes. Add the cinnamon, chilli, nutmeg, tomato paste, crushed tomatoes and sugar. Simmer uncovered for approximately 30 minutes so that excess liquid can evaporate. Season to taste with salt and pepper.

To make the béchamel sauce, melt the butter over a low heat. Add the flour to the melted butter, whisking continuously to make a smooth paste. Allow the flour to cook for a minute but do not let it brown. Add the warm milk in a steady stream, whisking continuously. Simmer over low heat until it thickens but does not boil. Remove from the heat and stir in the egg yolks and a pinch of nutmeg. Return to the heat and stir until the sauce thickens.

Lightly grease a large, deep baking pan. Place a layer of potatoes on the bottom. Top with a layer of eggplant slices. Add the meat sauce and sprinkle it with ¼ of the grated cheese. Top with another layer of potato, then another layer of eggplant, and sprinkle it with another ¼ of the cheese. Pour the béchamel sauce over the top, making sure that the sauce fills the sides and corners of the pan. Smooth the top with a spatula and sprinkle with the remaining grated cheese.

Bake for 45 minutes or until the béchamel sauce is a nice golden-brown colour. Allow to cool for 15 to 20 minutes, then slice and serve with a fresh green salad.

The rebellious vegetarian

Nothing in excess

Greek proverb

'You'll die,' my mother states matter-of-factly when I tell her I am giving up meat. She crosses her arms against her chest, daring me to challenge the evident truth of her statement.

I scoff. With all my sixteen-year-old self-righteousness, I point out that in her village, and in those of other Greeks of her generation, meat was a luxury, and *she* didn't die.

'Yes, but that was in Greece, and we were always hungry. Here it's different,' my mother counters. 'We can afford to eat well.' She is now waving her arms about.

Mum and Dad regularly buy half a lamb and have our butcher cut it into pieces to store in our jumbo-sized freezer. Endless roast dinners and stews follow. Every weekend, barbecues sizzle away in the back yards of our relatives, the smells competing with those emanating from the yards of the neighbours. 'Eat meat, it's good for you,' my Uncle John says whenever we eat at his house. He won't rest until my cousins and I have eaten at least three chops apiece.

A couple of times a year, the extended family treks out to parks in Sorrento or Rye, where we play loud Greek music and fry up Esky-loads of cutlets, sausages and meat patties. Sometimes there is a lamb on the spit, but now I turn even that down. I am more evolved than my meat-eating elders. I am different.

When the weeks of my meatless folly turn into months, Mum realises this is not a passing phase. And *of course* it is personal. I am slighting her efforts to feed me, to sustain me. It is a slap in the face. For me, it is a way of saying, 'I'm not a child any more. I can decide what to feed myself.' Despite (or perhaps because of) her daily protests, I stubbornly persevere. I cook my own sauces to put over her pasta. I self-importantly add wedges of tofu to one untainted corner of the barbecue. I offend my uncles by turning down their cutlets.

Finally, when Mum can stand it no longer, she resorts to guerrilla tactics. She adds ladlefuls of strained liquid from her beef stew to my vegetarian sauce when I'm not looking. She pours juices from a lamb roast over my baked vegetables. When I discover small bits of flesh in my food, we fight.

'You've put meat in here, Mum! How could you?'

'I didn't,' she counters, eyes twinkling.

When she is caught, she restrains herself for a few days. Then she starts scheming again.

Still, even she acknowledges that there are perks. I start cooking a lot more, branching out from packet-mix cakes and toffee apples. Mum has always encouraged me to cook, letting me handle knives and ovens from a very early age. She lets me make my own mistakes and overlooks the messes. How else am I going to learn?

I begin making more extravagant meals. From my first cookbook, the *Women's Weekly Italian Cooking Class*, I make vegetarian risotto, spaghetti puttanesca and minestrone. When I have mastered ricotta cannoli and profiteroles, I start experimenting with Chinese food – spring rolls and vegetarian wontons, chow mein and stir-fried mushrooms.

My family tries these new foods, quietly pleased that I am becoming so adept in the kitchen. My father, a notoriously fussy eater, approves my flavoursome sauces with a small smile. But he always makes comical gestures, as if he is chewing rocks, when he tastes my *al dente* pasta; Greeks are notorious for cooking their pasta until it is soft and bloated. My mother starts to appreciate the joys of tofu and Asian flavours. She never comments on the undercooked vegetables.

It is during my Chinese period that I invite a group of friends over for a meal. I go shopping at the exotic grocers in Richmond for spring-roll wrappers, Chinese broccoli, fresh ginger, oyster sauce and tofu. I spend the better part of a day preparing what is for me an ambitious menu: vegetarian spring rolls, a tofu and vegetable hotpot, stir-fried Chinese broccoli and fragrant rice. When my friends arrive, I spend most of my time in the kitchen, frying and stirring so that each dish arrives at the table hot. Just as I finally sit down to enjoy my guests, my mother appears with a bowl of meatballs, hot from the pan and smelling tantalisingly of garlic and parsley. Before I have time to protest ('This is a *vegetarian* meal'; 'The theme is *Chinese*'; 'These are *my* friends'), my friend Chris has tucked into the meatballs as if he hasn't eaten for a month. He realises his folly when he looks up at me. I am nearly in tears.

'You need meat,' my mother insists as he swallows the offending meatball.

I realise then that I can't possibly compete with my mother. Her meatballs will always trump my tofu. She will always win in the kitchen.

Chrysoula's keftedes (fried meatballs)

1 kilogram mince meat
3 eggs
½ cup breadcrumbs
1 tablespoon self-raising flour
2 medium onions, grated
6 cloves garlic, finely sliced
3 sprigs mint, finely chopped
1 teaspoon dried oregano
1 cup red or white wine
½ cup lukewarm water
Salt and pepper to taste
1 cup vegetable oil, for frying

Method

Mix all of the ingredients (except the oil) together and refrigerate for 1 to 2 hours. Then roll the mixture into oval, golf-ball-sized balls.

Heat the oil in a large frying pan until it is just smoking, then add the meatballs one at a time. Do not overfill the pan. When they are browned on one side, turn them over. Fry them up in batches until all are cooked; when they are done, remove them with a slotted spoon and place them on a paper towel to drain.

These meatballs can be served in tomato salsa, added to lunch boxes or eaten as a main with salad and chips (see page 64). Both cooked and uncooked meatballs freeze well.

Rembetika for the soul

When the cat is absent, the mice dance

Greek proverb

Dad parks the Valiant in front of the Mechanics Institute Hall in Brunswick and insists on chaperoning me to the door. The musicians are still getting their instruments out and they look up at us when we come in. Not only am I unfashionably early, but my father is standing anxiously by my side. My face burns hot.

'I'll pick you up at eleven, no later,' Dad says loudly and casts a doubtful look at the male musicians, as if they might steal my virtue in the short time I am here. If only I should be so lucky.

I slink to a chair in the corner, and only dare look up again when Dad has left. The musician with the honey-brown eyes who told me about the concert is tuning his bouzouki. He looks nervous and pays me no attention. I met him in the university caff a few weeks ago, where he was confident, charming. He is one of a group of recently arrived students from Greece who hang around the Redmond Barry building on campus. For months, I have admired them from afar, envying their ironic cool, their laid-back intellectualism. Now I have been invited to their inner sanctum ... along with hundreds of other people.

Getting the flimsy slip of carbon paper that admitted me to a Bachelor of Arts at Melbourne University was like getting the golden ticket to Willy Wonka's chocolate factory. Here was my pass to freedom, my chance to shine and grow and to escape my cloying family life. I dream of being exposed to exciting ideas, of becoming part of the heady world of student radicalism and succumbing to the seductive charms of clever, interesting men. These men will sweep me off my feet, perhaps with a little help from the house red at one of the many pubs that line the campus.

But there is one small problem: Dad still holds the keys to the Valiant, and I must beg and plead to go out at night. Whatever freedoms I take, I take in the daytime, and furtively at that. Even after months at uni, a sense of not quite belonging still clings to me like an annoying skin, stopping me from stretching my limbs. I blame my woes on Dad and lash out at him daily. In my mind, he is Patriarchy, I am Feminism. He is the Right, I am the Left. He smells Fear, I crave Opportunity.

'Just open your books and learn. Why must you get involved in so many things?' he spits out, exasperated. 'And why do you dress like a ... like a communist?!'

'You don't trust me. You still think I'm a baby.'

'It's not you I don't trust, Spirithoula. It's the people around you. Be careful.'

I got into uni. I try hard. Why can't you be proud of me? I think these things, but I can't say them to him. I fear his answer.

Even within the Greek-Australian group, there are cliques. There are those who organise Greek disco nights, which I'm not allowed to attend. There are the left-leaning, dope-smoking, Philip-Glass-listening Greeks, who get effortless As in politics and philosophy. I hang around the edges of their group, cadging cigarettes and hoping their cool will rub off on me. But they do heavy drugs and they scare me a little – my head is confused enough as it is without the help of mood-altering substances. Then there are those who simply skit in and out between lectures, attached to no group in particular. I hang around the caff because these sub-sections of my own community feel familiar and safe, but I am confused and frustrated; I hanker for an elusive 'something' outside my safety zone, a place where I might find my niche.

The government is talking about introducing student fees, which makes me angry because people who went to schools like mine might never afford to go to university. But the rallies I attend in protest often end in violence. The chaos of limbs connecting with police batons makes me feel sick. This out-of-control mess, led by a few radicals, doesn't seem likely to lead to change. The right-leaning student politicians are no better. They prance around importantly, their enunciated vowels and ill-concealed arrogance hanging off them like a bad smell. I find myself missing the more innocent student advocacy of high school, the sedate Student Representative Council and the coy regional student forums, but there is no going back. Already I feel paralysed by cynicism and impotence.

The students ingesting raw eggs and gallons of beer in an 'Iron Gut' competition make me feel even more at a loss, as they compete to see who can eat the grossest things. It's like a primal rite of passage; not surprisingly, the main players are male. I watch, fascinated, as the afternoon ends with someone vomiting into a container and drinking it. He is the undisputed winner, but not the sort of boy I'd like to kiss.

I loiter around the offices of *Farrago*, the student newspaper, hoping pitifully that someone will recognise my brilliant journalistic potential. But the students there are too busy

meeting deadlines and pasting bits of paper onto a broadsheet to take any notice of me. I pine to write but don't know how to enter their world. Everything seemed so much easier when I was the editor of our little school rag; now I need to prove myself all over again, in a much more competitive field. I pen angst-ridden poems in my journal and hide them away.

All the while, I study well into the night, feasting on potato chips and instant coffee. Despite my efforts, my English Literature tutor hands back my first essay with a big red C on it.

'Your sentence construction is muddled at times and sometimes I can't understand your argument. Is English not your first language?' she says.

I burn with shame. Despite my obsessive reading, my thirst for words and ideas, I have been exposed as the fraud that I am – a girl from a disadvantaged high school with Greek-speaking, factory-working parents. But I am also filled with anger: this woman with the plum accent is no better than I am; she has no right to patronise me. Anger and stubbornness override my sense of shame and I hone my words, spend more time carefully crafting my sentences, and reel in As in no time at all. I think back to Cavafy, whose first language was not Greek, and the widespread criticism of his poems during his lifetime. He triumphed in the end. But after my initial euphoria, there is no real joy in churning out well-constructed diatribes on Jacques Derrida and Arthur Miller, Anaïs Nin and Alfred, Lord Tennyson. How is this going to help me in life?

My sense of inadequacy continues in Modern Greek classes. I join forces with another student, George, and we sit at the back of the class, hoping to avoid the scathing comments of our tutor.

'I will now hand back the first assignment, in which there were some basic grammatical errors that you should have mastered in primary school.' He casts a look at us. We try not to giggle. Although Greek was my first language, I will never be able to compete with the native-born Greek students in the class. They in turn complain that they have to take Greek with us dummies. But still, we realise we have something to offer each other, and so we barter our skills. I help one student with her essays in English, and she helps me with mine in Greek. Thankfully – to her great amusement and that of everyone around us in the caff – she picks up an error; in writing earnestly about woman's role in society, I have referred to it repeatedly as '*yamiki thesi*' – woman's sexual position in the bedroom. My tutor would have had a field day with that one.

During my spare time I work at Coles, save my Austudy and open my 'freedom account', which will finance an extended trip overseas when I finish my degree.

The thought makes me smile as the music starts up.

The man with the honey-coloured eyes plucks at the strings of the bouzouki. His fingers move with strength and grace, and I allow myself to fantasise about what else he might do with those fingers. The bouzouki is accompanied by the higher-pitched chords of the baglama, and then the rhythmic strains of the guitar. A high, almost primal voice rises up, singing of poverty and loyalty, hashish dens and dispossession. I close my eyes and let the music seep into my skin. I become lost in the irresistible lyricism of the language. All thoughts drain from my head and my breath stills. Time seems to slow down; I feel as if my very soul is filling up with the sound of other people's pain, with their tales of redemption and love. And so it goes, song after song. I could be anywhere; the boundaries of time and space have dissolved.

I jump with a start when I feel a rough tap on my shoulder. Dad is here. The concert isn't yet over, but it's time for me to go home.

IRINE VELA ON REMBETIKA AND REBELLION

Irine Vela is a producer, composer and musician of Greek and Albanian heritage. She co-founded the Aria award-winning band The haBiBis, composed the operas Little City *and* 1975, *and has worked as creative producer with the Anti-Racism Action Band (ARAB) and Outer Urban Project (OUP). She plays the bouzouki, the Cretan laouto, the mandolin, guitar and many other fretted instruments. She talks here about the origins of rembetika and how her cultural background has influenced her own music.*

Rembetika is Greek urban popular music. It is the mother or father of modern Greek popular music, in the same way as blues, early jazz and American hymn music are to American popular music. The modes and musical language are similar to Greek folk music but, generally speaking, the instrumentation and lyrics differ. Where folk songs dealt with pastoral and rural life, early rembetika painted life on the city streets.

Rembetika started around the time of the compulsory exchange of populations following the Greco-Turkish War of 1919–22. At least 1.5 million Greek Orthodox people living in Turkey were sent to Greece, and 500,000 Muslims living in Greece were sent to Turkey. The refugees from Asia Minor brought their music, their culture and their own folk music to Greece. Some brought urban music from cosmopolitan cities like Constantinople (now Istanbul) or Smyrna (Izmir). Rembetika was a marriage of these different musics and cultures.

There were quite a few styles of rembetika. One was based on the regional folk music of Asia Minor. Another grew out of Anatolian music, which is shared by the people of Anatolia, both Greek- and Turkish-speaking; this is why you come across Greek songs and Turkish songs that are identical except for the lyrics. There was also a style called Café Aman, which is an eastern cabaret style. It's quite sexy, a bit burlesque. We're talking about music from the exotic melting-pot cities of the near east.

Following the exchange, the populations of some Greek cities and towns increased by tenfold over a short period. Some refugees had the skills to set themselves up in business, but many had to start from nothing. Aristotle Onassis is probably the most famous example of a successful Anatolian refugee.

There was a lot of chaos, hardship and social dislocation. The hashish stands, the prostitutes and the drug overdoses they sang about were real. The name rembetika comes from the word *rembetes*, which means 'vagrants' or 'rebels'. Early rembetika was often sung by people who weren't musically trained – they just played as they hung out in cafés and hash dens.

In the early years, *rembetes* were underground musicians, offering snapshots of life on the streets, in the same way that blues musicians did in the United States. They were singing it as they were living it. As it evolved, it became a much more sophisticated and self-conscious art form. It took on influences from Europe and became more mainstream. Musicians such as Vassilis Tsitsanis took it to another level. His lyrics were more romantic and more consciously poetic and exotic than those of the early *rembetes*.

Rembetika musicians used various folk instruments, but the classic pared-down instrumentation uses the baglama, bouzouki and the guitar. The baglama looks like a miniature bouzouki and is tuned an octave higher. It is often used to play rhythmic chords, but also sometimes for melody. It is the quintessential rembetika instrument, providing a high-pitched metallic pulse that completes the classic rembetika sound.

The bouzouki was outlawed at one point during the fascist regime of Ioannis Metaxas in the 1930s. It was considered undesirable simply because it was played by undesirable people. The mythology of the baglama held that it was made by people in jail. Prisoners would hollow out pieces of wood to make the instrument, and then slip it into their pockets, out of sight of prison wardens.

There are quite a few individuals and bands playing rembetika here in Australia. It's a scene that many second-generation people participate in, as well as non-Greeks. It gives you a real sense of empowerment being able to play a musical style that not everybody can play. It's a specialised music.

I myself was obsessed with music from an early age. Part of it was going to Greek weddings and Albanian functions, listening to the clarinets and fiddles. It was like a secret universe, and I had access because of my background. From age four, I wanted the guitar, not the doll. I was proud that I could offer people music from my culture, music that excited me.

I never really ran away from my roots. I was always very, very proud of my culture. For me it was a source of strength, growing up Australian as a second-generation Greek-Albanian. I never really left it, although in my twenties I moved away from home so that I could follow my passion for Greek music more openly. My mother and father, like many Greek parents, were proud of their culture but didn't want their kids to end up in the arts.

I formed bands with other people, played world music. But I was always in awe of Greek composers such as Manos Hatzidakis and Mikis Theodorakis. I admired the way they married Greek popular folk music with modern poetry to create a vibrant movement. My opera, *Little City*, was strongly influenced by Theodorakis. Even though it's not Greek music, elements of Greek music and political culture influenced the work. I aimed to marry contemporary language and ideas to a traditional base. I wanted very much to create original Australian music.

Irine's briam (spiced baked vegetables)

Serves 6 to 8

Briam is often made in the summertime with whatever vegetables one has to hand. Good-quality olive oil, slow cooking and seasonal ingredients are the secrets to its success. It can be made with herbs such as parsley and dill, but Irine adds exotic spices for a Middle Eastern take on this popular Greek dish.

Ingredients

2 medium eggplants, cut into chunks
Half a small pumpkin, cut into chunks
5 tomatoes, blanched, peeled and roughly chopped (or 1 can chopped tomatoes)
2 onions, sliced
2 red capsicums, sliced
4 medium potatoes, cut into chunks
1 teaspoon dried oregano
1 teaspoon ground pimento or ground allspice
Salt and pepper to taste
A dash of chilli
½ cup good quality olive oil

Method

Preheat the oven to 160°C.

Sprinkle the eggplant with salt, or soak it in water, for 20 minutes, then rinse.

Layer the sliced vegetables in a baking dish, preferably a ceramic one with a lid. Sprinkle each layer with some of the herbs and spices. Drizzle the oil over the top and gently toss. Cover the dish with a tight-fitting lid or foil and put it into the oven. Check after 40 minutes and add a little water if it appears to be dry. Cook for a further 30 minutes. When the vegetables are tender, sprinkle them with feta. Cover and cook for a further 10 minutes. Enjoy as a side or main with crusty homemade bread (see page 75).

Traversing difference

He who respects his parents never dies

Greek proverb

We are sitting in the bungalow, my parents and I, discussing my future.

'I'm considering journalism.'

'Journalism isn't a good career for women,' Dad says. I think he envisages me covering foreign wars; I might get killed. Or worse, I might enjoy my freedom too much and never get married.

The truth is, I am not sure what I want to do. My Arts degree is nearing completion, and the pressure to make a decision looms large.

What I do know is that I love observing people, love listening to their stories. I am interested in communities – what makes them tick and what makes them crack. I feel compelled to write, but I am not sure if I'm cut out to survive in the cut-throat world of journalism. I aced Politics and Criminology at uni. I flit about indecisively – Law? Psychology? Criminology?

I am working part-time now as a receptionist at a medical practice. In the end, a comment by the resident psychotherapist there helps me make the decision.

'Our profession needs good social workers, Spiri. Have you considered that as a career?'

I look into it and decide it's a good fit. I think about my mother and the caring role she plays in her community; I will be following in her footsteps, but with two degrees behind me. I wonder if I will ever be as good as she is.

Classes are held in a row of old terrace houses across the road from the main campus. The setting is intimate; classes are small and discussion intense. What makes a good helper? Are humans intrinsically altruistic? Have social workers helped or hindered in the past? How can social policy contribute to society?

I write yet more essays, but this time around I explore my own background: I interview my mother about her car accident, about how her lack of English made her feel vulnerable and isolated in an alien health system. I explore the reasons behind alcoholism, look at my relationship with my own father and my pressing desire to save him from himself.

I meet lots of interesting people. There's Caroline, who lives with her English boyfriend in a share house just around the corner from our place. We often talk about our families. She grew up in the country, raised by conservative Anglo-Saxon Catholics, and we are grappling with the same issues of identity, both trying to secure our independence and find our place in the world.

I get into some heady discussions with Grant, an older student who has worked in welfare. He is all experience and cynicism, in contrast to my wide-eyed optimism. Our arguments betray a thinly veiled attraction, and it's not long before he asks me out.

'It has to be lunch,' I say.

He looks confused but doesn't question me. I don't want to admit that it's hard for me to get out at night. I don't yet have a car, my father is too anxious to lend me his, and being picked up by a boy is out of the question.

We lunch at a Chinese restaurant in Lygon Street, where we pick at sweet and sour chicken and fried rice. Grant is hungry to find out all about me. I talk about my family life, about how strict my parents are. He is taken aback – this is all unfamiliar territory to him. He was encouraged to be very independent from an early age, but I suspect there is a certain exotic appeal to it all and he continues to pursue me. He calls me at home and I pull the phone with its long cord into the next room, trying to get some privacy. I whisper so that Dad doesn't hear. Before long, even before we have had a chance to have our first kiss, Grant steps back.

'This is too weird for me, Spiri. I want to see more of you, take you out, have you stay over. When are you going to stand up to your parents?'

We are sitting in a busy café on campus, students milling around us. But I feel completely alone as the implications of what Grant is saying sink in. Blood rushes to my face, a bubbling up of shame and anger. I am angry at my parents for being so protective, and at Grant for not understanding. But I am angry mostly at myself. How can I have let this go on for so long? I am twenty years old, but I still feel like such a child. I know I have been cosseted, that my most interesting experiences have been through books. I know I need to stand up to my parents and start living my life. But I've wanted to do it without hurting them. My course is teaching me that conflict is necessary, that it is healthy. But I'm not prepared to face up to them over a man. I have to do it on my own terms, in my own time.

In the meantime, we are given work experience placements. I am allocated to the Migrant Women's Learning Centre, housed in the old Collingwood Technical School down the road from my high school. This is where the tough boys used to go to become electricians, welders or petty criminals. Now, a cavernous room below street level houses a learning centre for more than a hundred women from around the world: elderly Italian, Greek and Yugoslav women retrenched from the manufacturing industry; single mums hoping to enter the hospitality trade; and doctors, psychologists and nurses who can't get their qualifications recognised in Australia and so must start again with certificate courses.

The raucous, colourful atmosphere excites me; when I sit at my little brown desk, dozens of different accents serenade me. The women bring out the voyeur in me – I love listening to their stories, tales about their homelands, about why they came to Australia and the challenges they face here. They tell of fleeing war or poverty, and of families reunited after long separations.

They are all trying to make a better life here in Australia. English and work skills will be their tickets to survival.

I feel very young in the presence of these women, but they welcome anyone who can help them. And they show their gratitude with food, bringing in treats for the teachers and tasty little morsels for me. Food is a common currency. We bond over Minh's chicken dumplings, swoon over Rosa's crème profiteroles and rave about Gisela's empanadas. We exchange recipes and trade family secrets: how to get a sauce *just right*, how to make gelato set. At lunchtime, the smell of their different cuisines wafts through the centre. This aromatic cocoon is an escape from the students' day-to-day lives, a space just for them. It is a refuge for me too – a place where I can escape my home life, where things are coming to a head.

My anger is finally spilling over. I realise I can't wait for freedom to be delivered to me; I have to take it. And so on weekends, I arrange for friends to pick me up and I go out. Most times, it is my old high-school friend Kathy, who arrives in her white Camira, usually wearing an impossibly short spangled mini skirt. All of my father's anxieties are reflected in the fabric of that skirt; its sequins represent moral decline and sexual depravity. And, of course, this is contagious, like a disease. What he has long feared has finally happened; his little girl is on her way to becoming a fully fledged slut. He seethes as we leave the house but he is powerless to stop me. I push headlong into my freedom, confident that it must be done. After all, I now know conflict is a part of life.

Crème profiteroles

Makes 12 large profiteroles

A friend's mother who grew up in Tuscany says her favourite
profiterole recipe comes not from her region of origin, but from
The Australian Women's Weekly circa 1986. Profiteroles are
often associated with Italian cuisine, but their origin is French.
They use *choux* pastry (meaning 'cabbage', as they are round
and plump) and crème or crème patisserie.

Ingredients

For the pastry
75 grams unsalted butter, cut into small, even pieces
1 cup water
1 cup plain flour
4 eggs, lightly beaten

For the crème patisserie
6 egg yolks
¾ cup castor sugar
¼ cup plain flour
2 cups milk
½ cup thickened cream
2 tablespoons vanilla extract

For the pastry
Preheat the oven to 200°C.

Place the butter and water into a saucepan and stir until the butter
is just melted. Bring to the boil over high heat. When the mixture

is at a rolling boil, add flour all at once. Stir vigourously over the heat until the mixture leaves the sides of the pan. Remove from heat and allow to cool for a few minutes. The mixture should be hot enough to cook the eggs when they are beaten in.

Transfer the mixture to a small bowl or electric mixer. Add the eggs one at a time, beating well after each addition until the mixture is smooth and glossy.

Drop tablespoons of the mixture about 5 centimetres apart onto a lightly greased oven tray. Bake for about 20 minutes, or until they feel light when you pick them up and are golden brown.

Using a sharp knife, cut the hot balls in half. Using a teaspoon, scoop out and discard the uncooked mixture from the middle. Put the balls back together and return them to the tray, cut side up. Bake for a further 10 minutes, or until they are crisp and dry.

For the crème patisserie

Beat the egg yolks and sugar in a small bowl with an electric mixer until thick and creamy. Beat in the flour.

Put the milk into a saucepan and bring it to the boil, then remove it from the heat. Gradually add the milk to the egg mixture while beating with the electric mixer at medium speed.

Return the mixture to the saucepan. Stirring constantly, heat it until the mixture boils and thickens, then remove it from the stove. Cover the surface of the hot custard with greaseproof paper to prevent a skin from forming. Leave it to cool to room temperature.

Beat the cream until soft peaks form. Fold the cream and the vanilla gently into the custard.

Just before serving, use a teaspoon or a piping bag to fill each pastry puff with a dollop of the creme, then place the 'lid' on top.

These are best eaten on the day of baking when they are crisp. If they soften, they can be dried by placing them in a warm oven for 5 minutes.

PART II
The sapling

Hope the voyage is a long one.
May there be many a summer morning when,
with what pleasure, what joy,
you come into harbors seen for the first time;
may you stop at Phoenician trading stations
to buy fine things,
mother of pearl and coral, amber and ebony,
sensual perfume of every kind –
as many sensual perfumes as you can;
and may you visit many Egyptian cities
to gather stores of knowledge from their scholars.

Constantine Cavafy

Athens adventures

Blood doesn't turn to water

Greek proverb

The man who greets me at the airport is like a younger, sunnier version of my father. I haven't seen Dad's brother since I was seven, fifteen years ago. Theio Spiro is a bit plumper than I remember, has a few grey hairs around the temples, but I recognise him instantly. He's like a life buoy in a choppy sea of Greek-speaking humanity. Everyone is jostling, carting trolley-loads of suitcases and electrical goods, gesticulating and craning their necks to look for relatives.

'*Yiasou, Theio.*' Hello, Uncle. We embrace and both wipe away tears. He takes hold of my luggage and ushers me expertly along, out into the hazy Athens afternoon.

'How is my brother? Chrysoula? My nephew Dionysios? The last time I saw you, you came to my waist. What have you been doing since then?' He fires away with questions, so many that it's hard to answer in any detail. 'Everyone is well. I have been at school, then uni,' I say. *My life is boring*, I think. I ask about his wife, the kids.

'They're well. You'll meet them soon.'

We whizz down a main arterial road, Leoforos Vouliagmenis, in Theio's little Fiat. I am struck by the light outside, which is whiter than that in Melbourne, with a washed-out quality to it. Everything seems to be covered in a fine dust – the buildings, the footpaths, the shop fronts. Motorcycles push through impossibly small gaps between cars. Every lane is crawling with traffic, including the emergency lanes, and overcrowded buses spew diesel fumes everywhere I look. It's siesta time, Theio Spiro explains, and so the roads are quiet. I balk.

We make our way towards central Athens. Theio turns into a side street and wedges his car snugly between two others parked on the footpath.

We enter the foyer of his apartment block, our footsteps echoing on the marble floor. We try to cram my suitcases into a tiny elevator but give up. Theio goes up with one case and I wait downstairs with the other. In the meantime, three heads pop out from a door upstairs. This must be my Theia Eleni and, peeking from behind her legs, my first cousins Semina and Aki.

'*Ilthe, ilthe*,' the kids whisper in well enunciated Greek. She has come, she has come.

'*Kalos lithes*.' Welcome. When I finally make it upstairs, we embrace. I am nervous.

My suitcases crowd their two-bedroom apartment. Theia Eleni has made up a fold-out couch in the children's room, where I'll be staying for the next couple of weeks.

We sit down at a table that takes up most of the space in the kitchen.

'How was your trip?'

'Good. Very long.'

'Do you want to rest?'

'No, I'm alright.'

'The family, how are they? Your father?'

'They're good. Well, you know Dad, he complains of being sick – one minute it's this, another it's that. But he's okay.' As soon as I have said it, I feel like a traitor. I can hear Dad's voice echoing in the background – '*Ta en iko mi en thimo*' – an ancient Greek saying that means 'Do not expose your house affairs in public.'

'Is he still complaining? Some things never change,' Theio says good-naturedly, but he casts an apprehensive glance at his wife, who looks away. 'So, what do you want to see? I have Sundays and Mondays off from the shop, so we can show you around.'

'Don't worry too much about me, Theio. I don't mind exploring by myself. I know you are busy. Perhaps tomorrow I will go into town.'

They look surprised, but Theio explains how to buy public transport tickets and which trolley to take.

The next morning, I make my way to the main street. I try to brave my way onto a trolley, a peculiar vehicle somewhere between a tram and a bus, but people push past me and I don't make it on. When the next one comes along I am ready and muscle my way on like everyone else. I get off at the city centre and try to get my bearings.

The first thing I need to do is exchange my Australian traveller's cheques for Greek drachma at one of the banks skirting Sindagma Square. I enter the bank and find myself in a large, smoke-filled room. When I finally make it to the front of one of the many queues, the teller takes a puff on his cigarette.

'*Oriste?*' he says gruffly. May I help you?

'*Thelo va alaxo auta ta … ta …* cheques.' I can't remember the word for cheques. My hands get clammy.

'*Apo ekei.*' Over there. He points dismissively to another queue and looks past me to the next customer.

I look at the queue for 'miscellaneous transactions', with its line of scruffy tourists. They are waiting patiently. There is no teller at the counter. It's going to be a long morning.

Half an hour later, I have my drachma tucked safely in a pouch around my waist. I buy a juice, a map and some *yaridakia* from the *periptero*, a street booth selling staples like newspapers, cigarettes and chocolates. The *yaridakia* taste exactly as they did when I was a child. I feel comforted. I am famished after my adrenalin-soaked ride on the trolley and the wait at the bank.

I try to get my bearings again, but I am disconcerted. The city stimulates all my senses at once: the smell of diesel and pollution; the honking, screaming drivers; the men who eye me with open interest. I vow to get some sunglasses as soon as I can so that I don't feel so exposed.

A businessman in a smart suit getting his shoes shined catches my attention. The quick back and forth movement of cloth on leather is mesmerising. I remember this little ritual from my childhood trip to Athens, the satisfying transformation from dusty surface to gleaming shine. As I walk, other memories come flooding back: the tourist shops selling leather sandals, along with miniatures of the Acropolis and *komboloia*, worry beads; the changing of the guard at the Tomb of the Unknown Soldier, the guards with their pompom shoes and stony faces. I put my map away and rejoice in getting lost, discovering unexpected squares, silent dead ends and hectic archeological sites. The chaotic Sindagma Square gives way to quiet cafés overhung by vines, secluded culs-de-sac lined with Cypress trees. I look up to see the Parthenon looming in the distance. It is so familiar, an image I have seen countless times in miniature in my Greek school books and reproduced in the trinkets brought home by relatives. But I am taken aback by how magnificent it looks. Its stately proportions are beyond anything I could imagine. I am tempted to visit today, but I have time; the Parthenon will wait.

I wander around the flea markets of Monastiraki, passing stalls selling brass trinkets, carpets, leather jackets. There are gypsies sitting on street corners. One holds out her palm as she cradles her limp, sleeping baby in the other arm.

'*Parakalo, kali mou, mou deineis liges drachmes yia na fae to paidi mou.*' Please, my good one, give me a few drachma for the child so that he can eat.

After giving to the fourth gypsy, I realise there is no end to the need and put my purse back in my bag. There are other beggars, too: a legless man with the hems of his pants folded up over his leg stumps; an elderly woman in a black headscarf, holding out her hand outside a Byzantine church on busy Ermou Street, a Mecca for shoe shoppers.

I come across a small tavern with a dark, cool interior. It's still too early for Greeks to lunch, but I am famished yet again. I sit down and order. My Greek seems so much slower than that of the locals, provincial now to my ears. The waiter is efficient, brusque. I'm going to need a thicker skin if I'm to cope here. When my moussaka arrives, it is too oily. And expensive. I feel ripped off. It's time to go back to the safety of my uncle's apartment.

Theio is home from work for a late lunch. He wants to hear my impressions of Athens. I tell him it's like a city on steroids; I think I like it but can only cope in small doses. I will go back again tomorrow for another onslaught. He laughs. He thinks I am a sucker for punishment. He avoids the city at all costs. He hasn't been to see the Acropolis since he took our family there fifteen years ago.

We all lie down for a siesta. I listen to cars honking in the distance, a mother on the balcony across the street calling her child, a baby crying. Then all is strangely quiet as most of Greater Athens' three million citizens lie down to rest.

Later, when my uncle returns to work, I play with the kids and try to help them with their homework. I quickly realise that my seven-year-old niece has a better grasp of Greek grammar than I have. I resign myself to reading her an English book I have brought for her. She goes to English classes after school and is keen to impress me. Her brown eyes are sharp, and I recognise the thirst for knowledge I had at her age.

My aunty potters around making dinner, a goat, pea and artichoke stew that we'll have with crusty bread from the neighbourhood bakery. It smells delicious, but we won't eat until nine o'clock when my uncle gets home again. By the time we sit down to eat I am nearly delirious, dizzy with jet lag and hunger, but this is the normal dinner time. Another thing to get used to.

The following evening, my first cousin Stathis comes by on his motorbike to take me out. The last time I saw Stathis, he was a skinny twelve-year-old running around barefoot in the village. Now he is tall and ruggedly handsome. He lives with his girlfriend and her poodle, both of whom I meet when we swing by their minimalist, modern apartment. They take me out for drinks. I find myself tongue-tied, worried that my Greek won't make the cut. But they are kind; they want to know about my life in Australia. When we've exhausted that topic, they discuss current affairs, the education system, the merits of one brand of sneakers over another, in colourful, profanity-laden Greek. I listen, entranced. We drink frappe, a cold, shaken coffee, then move on to boutique beers with a wedge of lemon stuck in the neck of each bottle. Every drink comes with a small plate of nuts. Around us, young people are talking and smoking, nursing their drinks for hours on end. Stathis works with my uncle Spiro in his book and stationery business; his girlfriend is a physical education teacher. They go out most nights each week, catching up with friends over coffee and drinks.

On the weekend, Theio's family and I take the funicular tramway to the top of Mount Lycabettus, where there are still remnants of snow. We order overpriced desserts in a hotel café and enjoy the spectacular view over Athens. The Parthenon is laid out in front of us like a glimmering jewel, surrounded by a sprawl of white buildings extending outwards as far as the eye can see. My uncle doesn't let me pay for anything. All the while, there is a running commentary about Athens, family, politics – everything is passionately explored, discussed, parodied.

The following week, Theio takes me to Marousi, a leafy outer suburb of Athens, where I will be staying with my father's sister and her family. Here the streets are lined with Cypress trees, their pine scent a refreshing change after the inner city. We turn into a smart street lined with new two-storey houses. We pull up outside my aunt's house, which is a squat, single-level building. A barking dog greets us from behind the high wire fence. My aunt comes to the door, buxom in her apron. She has Dad's strong nose and dark eyes but she is fairer, plumper.

She embraces me firmly. '*Kalos ilthes*.' Welcome. '*Pinas?*' Are you hungry?

Theio Spiro smiles. 'All you're going to do here is eat, Spirithoula. Good luck.' To his sister he says, '*Yiasou, athelfi.* Hello, sister. I'll have a coffee and be off. I've got to get back to work.'

She shows us to a tiny parlour. A massive petrol heater takes up one corner of the room and, as if to compensate for this ugly necessity, my aunt has set out neatly ironed doilies on the coffee table and over the arms of the couch. We make our way into the small kitchen. The table is laden with so much food, there's barely room for plates and cutlery.

For the next week, my aunt plies me with food. When she is not working at the nursing home at night, or cleaning houses during the day, she is cooking: trays of potatoes and meatballs, mounds of spaghetti, bean casseroles and oversized salads. Her husband and my two cousins come in at all hours from their work, open the fridge and help themselves to plates of each offering. Despite the food, they are reed thin. They say little, but my aunty talks non-stop – she wants to know every detail about our family and tells me all about hers.

'That husband of mine won't fix anything around the house, and the things he brings home – he collects rubbish, I tell you … *po, po!* Then he goes down to the village to tend to his bees and fields. And my sons – I told them to get an education. But one works in a *periptero*, stooping all day to serve his customers, and the other in a pizza shop. What sort of life is that for two young men? And when are they going to find wives? They go out every night, but no wives …'

The boys stop by the tiny kitchen and look at me sympathetically. '*Tin zalises*, Mama.' You've made her dizzy. But when they leave again, the onslaught continues. I listen politely.

Late most nights, I don jeans and a denim jacket and join my cousins on the back of their bikes to see heavy metal bands in obscure clubs on suburban side streets. Most of the men have long hair, leather jackets, tattoos. The women wear multiple earrings, shaved heads, heavy boots. We enter the clubs under cover of darkness and are spewed out, blinking, into the morning light. My cousins go straight to work and I sleep into the afternoon.

On other nights, they take me to underground venues in the city, where we listen to rembetika and down ouzo shots, sharing small plates of chips and pork, olives and feta. When we don't go out, we sit on the veranda, sometimes pulling at a sweet-smelling joint, blowing smoke into the summer night. George, the eldest, pulls back at his pony tail and makes small talk. His younger brother, Saki, is quiet, his eyes expressive. In profile, he looks like a less lined version of my father. He is philosophical, whimsical, funny.

They do as they please, these cousins of mine, ignoring their mother's nagging to settle down. My uncle Panayioti comes and goes, visiting his brother down the road, tending the bees he keeps in a lot down the street. He deflects his wife's complaints good-naturedly, breaks out spontaneously into folk songs at the top of his voice, and brings home the honeycomb to show me how the bees are progressing. I feel an easy sense of acceptance, and meld seamlessly into their eccentric family life. But soon, before I can put on too much weight from all this eating, I announce that I will be going down south, to visit the village where my father's parents live.

'They will be very glad to see you, Spirithoula,' my aunt says. 'Here's some money to help you get down there.' She hands me a wad of 1000 drachma notes. 'And I'll just pack some food for the journey.'

144

THEIO PANAYIOTI ON KEEPING BEES

Theio Panayioti speaks here about some of the more novel aspects of bee-keeping.

Bees produce from April to late May, when the spring flowers are in bloom. I collect the honey in August.

Before collecting a wild hive, I spend time near the bees; they get used to my smell and so don't chase me away. I put my own empty hive next to the wild one and drape a sheet over the top. The mouth of the empty hive has lemon juice on it, which attracts the bees.

There's a device you can use to extract the poison from bees. I've read about it on the internet. People use the poison to create medicines – it is good for rheumatism, cancer and fever, and sells for very good prices. I don't have the device but I wish I did. I do harvest the royal jelly. The queen produces small sacs of jelly to feed the young bees in the springtime; they look like little earrings on the hive. The jelly is good for rheumatism and for nervous conditions – it makes you feel relaxed. It's also good for older men, to help them perform for younger women!

I burn dried pine needles in the smoker to make the bees a bit dizzy so that I can safely remove each frame and extract the honey. I remove the wax from these with a long, sharp knife. I put the honeycomb on a poplin cloth and rest this over a basin, letting the honey drain for a day or so. I store it in a cool, dry place in glass jars. I eat it on *friganies,* dried bread crackers, or give it to my brother and his family. Although the honey is delicious, the main reason I keep bees is for the love of it.

Pastelli (honey sesame bars)

Makes about 25 pieces

Pastelli are often brought back to Australia as a gift by relatives visiting Greece. Zevgolatio, in the south of Greece, is famous for them; they are often sold at train and bus stations as a snack for travellers. They are chewy, sticky and nourishing. The type of honey you use makes a big difference – thyme honey is gorgeous – but any aromatic honey will do.

Ingredients
3 cups sesame seeds
½ cup nuts such as peanuts, cashews or pistachios
1¼ cups honey
¾ cup water
1 cinnamon stick
5 cloves
A piece of lemon peel

Method
Toast the sesame seeds and nuts under a grill or in a hot frying pan, tossing them regularly so that they don't burn. When they are golden, set them aside. Place the remaining ingredients into a saucepan and boil until the mixture has thickened (if you own a kitchen thermometer, you can remove the mixture from the heat when it reads 130°C). With a slotted spoon, remove the cinnamon, cloves and lemon peel.

With a clean, damp cloth, wet a heat-proof surface such as a glass or marble cutting board, or a metal tray. Add the seeds and nuts to the honey mixture and mix them thoroughly until all the dry ingredients are covered with honey. Working quickly, pour the mixture onto your chosen surface and smooth it with a spatula until it is about a centimetre thick. Place a piece of baking paper over the top and gently roll it with a rolling pin to create an even surface. Remove the baking paper and allow the mixture to cool thoroughly before cutting it into bars or thin strips. Stored in a glass container or wrapped individually in waxed paper, these will keep for over a week.

To Mati

No one who errs unwillingly is evil

Sophocles

'*Iegoni tou Tsintzira*.' Tsintziras's granddaughter.

'*Irthe*.' She has come.

The women's whispers reach me at the doorway. One woman, her dark eyes staring at me from under her headscarf, stretches gnarled hands to touch me. Her eyes devour me. Before I can get my bearings, the other women have come towards me; now they are all touching me, kissing me. I feel stripped bare, as if a strange energy has passed through my clothes and under my very skin. I feel their eyes are saying, 'Dionysios's granddaughter has come to the village, but our children, our grandchildren, are still in far off Australia.' Theia Kanella, Dad's sister, senses my distress and gently leads me to a seat.

My grandmother proudly sits down beside me. She crosses her ankles, showing off the moccasins I have brought her from Australia. They aren't really for outdoor wear, but she wants to make it known that her granddaughter has brought her a special gift from the *exoterico*, from abroad. She is keen for the priest's wife to notice them. As soon as we have had coffee and a sweet, she quickly bids our host goodbye. She doesn't want the women of the village to have too much of me. I am her granddaughter, and on our first day together in fifteen years, she wants me to herself.

As we walk through the village, people come and introduce themselves. My aunt patiently explains the connections between each person and our family.

The village has contracted to a few dozen elderly villagers, along with some itinerant Albanian workers. The *cafeneion* only opens in the summertime, when the families of the villagers come to visit. I tower over the counter now, where once I had to look up to see the man serving me.

Finally, we get back to Yiayia and Pappou's house. As we go up the front steps, a vivid image comes back to me: Pappou standing on this porch, shooting a rifle into the air. The first-born son had returned. Now his son's daughter has also made a pilgrimage. We have lunch. My grandparents have slaughtered a chicken in my honour; the flavour is as gamey and strong as I remember it. We wipe up the sauce with crusty, dense bread. As I eat, my grandparents look on approvingly.

'You're just like your mother. She couldn't get enough bread when she came here last. She's a good woman. I don't know what my son did to deserve her …'

Yiayia speaks of my father lovingly, but doesn't hold back when it comes to his flaws.

'If it wasn't for your mother, that son of mine would be out on the street. She looks after him, works hard, keeps him from drinking himself to death. Just because I'm far away, don't think I don't know what's going on.' She taps a bent finger to the side of her head. 'I might not know how to read very well, but I know what's going on.'

Pappou listens, amused. It seems he is used to his wife's outpourings. I too am smiling. My grandmother doesn't pull any punches. I feel at home; these people know my family. They know their foibles and love them regardless.

After lunch, it's Theia Kanella's turn to drag me away.

'The bus back to Kyparissia leaves at three o'clock. But we'll be back in a few days. Spirithoula wants to stay with you.' She looks at me. She can't understand why I want to stay in the village. She worries that I will be uncomfortable. But I want to spend time with my grandparents. I don't know when, or if, I will see them again.

We take the bus down the mountain and half an hour later we are in the cool confines of my theia's home.

'I don't feel so well. I'm going to lie down.'

I feel nauseous. My body feels heavy and my limbs ache. I can barely stand up.

My aunty takes one look at me.

'*Oh, se matiasane.*' They put the evil eye on you. She is referring to the women in the village: the way they looked at me, their energy. For the first time in my life, I wonder if there is something to 'the evil eye', the belief that people can inadvertently make you sick by looking at you with envy.

I am very familiar with the evil eye. My mother is a keeper of the incantation to 'lift' the eye once it has been cast. The incantation can be passed on, usually from an elder of the opposite sex.

Knowing the incantation makes Mum very popular. It's not unusual for the phone to ring, sometimes quite late at night.

'I don't feel well. Can you check me for *mati*, the eye?'

'Okay, just wait a second.'

Mum recites an incantation known only to her. If she starts yawning and her tummy starts gurgling, she knows her patient has the evil eye. Mum will then make the sign of the cross and the spitting sound, '*ppt, ppt, ppt*'.

'Yes, you are *matiasmeni*. Say the Lord's Prayer three times, pass your hands under your armpits three times and sniff them, and then change out of all your clothes. Have a shower if you can, so as to wash it off.'

'Thanks, Theia.'

If it isn't the evil eye, she will suggest the caller have a lie down.

As a youngster, it was affirming to have Mum stand over me and murmur the incantation. It was worth being ill just to have her pay me this sort of special attention. But as I got older, I was disdainful – the evil eye was just a silly folk superstition.

'I don't really believe in the evil eye. It defies logic,' I say weakly to my aunt.

'Oh, it's true alright. My neighbour across the road, one day she complimented me on my zucchini plants, which were thriving in the front garden. The next day, every single plant was dead. She's done it to me many times. She doesn't mean harm. It's just her eyes. People with blue eyes are the worst.'

She stands over me and mutters a prayer.

'What are you saying?'

'I can't tell you. You can only teach the prayer when it's a full moon. If you ask your mum, she might teach you.'

As my aunty continues to mutter, she yawns loudly. I can hear her stomach gurgling.

'*Po, po. Eisai poli matiasmeni.*' Oh, oh, you have a serious case of the evil eye.

She is taking the evil from my body and ingesting it into hers. I fall into a deep, dreamless sleep and don't wake for two hours. When I get up, I feel refreshed, and very hungry.

I join my aunt at the stove, where she is making calamari stew. My appetite is well and truly back. We will have the dish with rice and more of the decadent bread. I can feel my bottom expanding already.

Over dinner, we talk more about my family. I sense that I can speak openly with my father's sister. In the few days I have spent with her, she appears sensitive and loyal like my father, but she faces her difficulties stoically, with humour.

'I really don't know what Dad expects of me. We always argue. It's not like I'm doing anything wrong; I just want to go out, experience things a bit.'

'Your dad's got a lovely wife, two great kids … what more does he want?' she says. 'Things have changed here in Greece. All the *neolea*, the young people, go out now. It's not like it used to be.'

'I guess Dad's trying to hold on to the Greece that he knew in the '60s.' I feel a sudden desire to protect Dad. I am far from him, and yet so close to where he grew up – it gives me a different perspective.

My aunt doesn't complain, but I know her life has been hard. Her husband died when her children were young. She raised three boys on her own. She worked night shifts as a nursing aid in a hospital to make ends meet. And she missed out on an education, which she sorely pined for.

'I studied for the exams year after year so that I could go to high school, even after my parents took me out of school. But there was only enough money to educate one child, and that was your father. Anyway, it wasn't seen as important to educate girls back then. I guess my parents didn't know any better.'

I feel sorry for my aunt, but she is optimistic.

'It doesn't matter. My life is okay. I've got three good boys, even if they are all in Athens now. My home. Good neighbours. And you. Why don't you stay in Greece? Marry someone here? I know a good boy who's a baker. You could have all the bread you like.'

'I don't think so, Theia. It's lovely here. But my life is in Melbourne ...'

I want to joke, 'You can't live on bread alone,' but it doesn't translate.

FROM MUM TO THE MIDDLE EAST: A POTTED HISTORY OF THE EVIL EYE

The evil eye is not so much about evil as envy. But the 'envious gaze' doesn't have quite the same ring to it.

If someone says to you, 'That new coat looks nice on you,' and you are a believer in the evil eye, you might try to deflect the compliment. Why? The premise behind the evil eye is that the person making the compliment is motivated (usually unwittingly) by envy. And their envy can make you, or your children, plants or livestock, sick. In extreme cases, their envy can make things wither up and die.

Although rituals to ward it off vary, the idea of the evil eye is widespread. It is thought to have originated in ancient Sumar (modern-day Iraq). It is mentioned in the Old Testament, as well as in ancient Roman and Greek texts. Its believers come from places as far-flung as Spain and Portugal, India, the Middle East, Scandinavia, Britain and North Africa; they are Christian, Muslim, Hindu and Jewish.

If you are a believer and happen to be of Greek background, you may say '*pppt, pppt, pppt*', which is thought to ward off the eye. If your faith is Islamic, you might utter '*Mahsa'Allah*' ('God has willed it'); or if it is Judaic, '*B'li ayin hara*' ('Without an evil eye'). Talismans are often pinned onto the singlets of babies, who are thought to be the most susceptible. In Greek and Turkish cultures, the talisman is usually a blue bead or token with an eye on it. In the Middle East, an eye might be drawn onto a hand or marked on a horseshoe.

Scholars have seen the eye as a symbol of women's genitalia (the pupil being the vagina, the lids the labia, and the lashes pubic hair) or of a phallus. The Italian amulet, a horn, is more obviously phallic, as is the hand gesture, the *fica* sign (representing a phallus in a vagina). Italian men are known to touch their genitalia briefly so as to ward off the evil eye and avoid ensuing impotence. Even Freud had something to say about it: 'Whoever possesses something at once valuable and fragile is afraid of the envy of others, in that he projects onto them the envy that he would have felt in their place.'

The folklorist Alan Dundes, in his essay *Wet and Dry: The Evil Eye*, theorised that the belief is closely linked to notions that water equates to life and dryness to death. Dundes suggests that what is common to most cultures is a belief that the evil eye 'dries things up' (for example the milk from a cow's udder or a woman's breast, the sperm from a man's testes, or the water from a healthy young fruit tree). Many talismans represent water or moisture, which have a reviving effect. Dundes ends his treatise: 'I can only hope in closing that my argument holds water but that my ideas are not all wet. God forbid that anyone who disagrees with me should give me a withering look, or tell me to go dry up and blow away.'

Do I believe in the evil eye? My logical city persona scoffs at it, but my village alter ego is still undecided. One thing I am sure of: Theia Kanella's calamari stew has definite restorative properties.

Theia Kanella's calamari stew

Serves 4 to 6

The trick to creating tender calamari is to cook it either very quickly (for example, by frying) or very slowly, as in this dish, which my Theia Kanella cooks to perfection.

Ingredients
A generous splash of olive oil
1 large onion, sliced
2 cloves garlic, sliced
6 large tomatoes, cut in half and grated (discard the skins) or
1 can chopped tomatoes
3 small whole calamari, prepared as per the recipe on page 158
Salt and pepper to taste

Method
Heat the oil in a casserole dish and sauté the onions until translucent. Add the garlic and the tomatoes and cook for 15 minutes over a low heat. Add the prepared calamari. Cover and cook on a low heat for at least an hour, until the calamari is tender and the sauce thick. Add a little water if it becomes too dry. Season to taste. Serve with rice, pasta or vegetables. Don't forget to mop the sauces up with your homemade bread.

Beyond the iron gate

The apple falls under the apple tree

Greek proverb

Beyond the iron gate, the dirt road extends out to the little church on the hill, and then to the next village and beyond, winding its way further and further inland. The mountains ahead envelop me like a blanket of undulating green: solid, feminine, unmovable.

'*Se psychoplakonoune,*' Theio Spiro said about the mountains. They crush the psyche. I marvel once again at the Greek language and its ability to pin down emotion so eloquently. The word is at once simple, dark and poetic.

I wonder if my father felt the mountains pressing on him, hemming him in and trapping him. This was his home. Here he had free rein to wander the dirt tracks, to climb up trees and daydream in the fields; here he ran from his mother when she berated him. I wonder if the village became too small for him; if the mountains bore down on him as they do on me now, so formidable in their solidity.

159

The bell of Pappou's goat tinkles as he leads it up the hill towards the cemetery, where it grazes on a fresh patch of grass. I sit on the tree stump where Pappou chops wood. I am aware of my body's warmth on the cool wood. I feel my breath sink deeper into my belly, move down through my legs and into the earth below. With each breath, I imagine roots extending from my spine into the trunk, pushing deeper and deeper: past the rocks and the worms, past tree roots and coins slipped from frayed pockets, connecting me to this patch of earth. I feel fertile, fecund, my rounded hips and bottom connecting with the wood below me.

'*Spirithoula, ela na fame.*' Come and eat.

I come out of my reverie, and look up at Yiayia squinting into the sun down at me from the veranda. I stand, surprised that I am not tethered to the stump, and make my way up the stone steps. Yiayia links her arm into mine and leads me inside, past the bedroom with the single lumpy bed, the herbs hung up to dry and the plastic bags filled with miscellany, and into the kitchen.

The goat curd that Yiayia made earlier this morning is ready. I look at the creamy mass in a colander in the sink, where a trickle of thin white milk streams onto the blue and white tiles of the basin. Yiayia added *pytia*, rennet, to the boiled goat's milk Pappou brought in this morning, and soon after drained the curds through a muslin cloth to make a soft, ricotta-like cheese. Yiayia also makes a harder cheese for grating over pasta, which she hangs in a muslin cloth from a rafter for several weeks.

Yiayia sprinkles some sugar over the ricotta and watches as I taste it.

'*Mmm, oraio,*' I say. It's nice. The goaty taste may take a bit of getting used to, but it's fresher and creamier than any shop-bought ricotta I have ever tasted.

She is pleased, happy that I am willing to try everything, that I ask questions about how things are made.

'Your mother did a good job with you, bless her,' she says.

We spend the day pottering around the home. We go down to the *upoyeio*, where she has stocks of olives and oil, *pasto* (pickled pork) and wine. It is dark down there and she has to stoop; her hands are deft, expertly scooping out olives from a clay urn, pouring wine into a carafe in the half-light. We have the olives with bread, the fresh cheese and *vlita*, amaranth, a green leafy vegetable from her garden. We drink wine from little glasses. The table is silent as we eat, just as it is at home. Dad doesn't like us to speak while we are eating; he says it is bad manners. But when we finish, my grandparents are keen to find out every detail of our lives in Australia. They ask about everyone – mostly about Dad, Mum and Dennis, but also about other relations who have moved to Melbourne from the village. I tell them as much as I can, and they hold on to my every word. They are hungry for news that is not constrained by the cost of a long-distance phone call.

After we wash up, we lie down for a siesta. Yiayia is anxious that I will be cold, and offers me another itchy goat-hair blanket to add to the three already covering me. As she

takes it from the pile of neatly folded homespun blankets piled up against one wall, I remember with a smile one of my father's stories. As a young man, he found a gap between these blankets; he reached in and pulled out a wad of money his mother had hidden there. He helped himself to the notes over many months, buying cigarettes and other essentials with the family savings. When my grandmother found out, she was livid. Dad got a beating but was not remorseful.

I lie awake, still unused to sleeping in the afternoon. I've been one week in the village and have slowed down, lulled by the rhythms of eating, tending to the animals, helping Yiayia in her garden, occasionally going to visit someone. I can feel my body rounding out with the constant offers of food ('We don't want you to go back to Australia and tell your parents you were hungry!'). I feel a strange sensuality and oneness with my body, which for once is not distracted by cerebral city pursuits.

In the late afternoon, Pappou heads out to pick up his brother, who lives up the road, so that they can go to the *cafeneion* in the village square. Yiayia lets out her hair. She combs it, tantalising stroke by tantalising stroke. I have to look away. There is such an intimacy in the way she touches it, a blatant sexuality that is so at odds with her lined face, her fleshy, dark-clad body. She plaits it expertly and twists it around her head. She washes it once a week with the special soap she makes herself, and never cuts it. It comes down to her waist. I sense it is her one vanity in an otherwise unadorned existence.

As she combs, she starts to tell me her woes in a long, uninterrupted stream, rocking a little from side to side. Her voice is hypnotic; it moves and sways like a song.

'Your father was my first-born. I will never understand why he left, all the way across the world. It's not as if his family was there – all his sisters and brother stayed here. It's that Tellis, huh, the priest's son no less, who took him away from me. "Come to Australia," Tellis said. "There's money to be made. Away from this place." I still can't forgive him for that.

'I was an only child. My father died in the war with Albania in 1912, and my mother was pregnant at the time. I married when I was just sixteen; I had your father when I was seventeen. I was so proud. I didn't get to enjoy him very much when he was young – I had to work the fields every day. My mother raised him, and when she died, he was heartbroken.

'He was cheeky. He used to run riot in the village, run off when he was supposed to be helping with chores. He relied on his sisters, who worked hard.

'When we sent him to Kyparissia to study, he would barter the bread I sent with him for cigarettes. When he brought his washing home, I found condoms in his pockets. Another time, Tellis rigged up his mattress in his room, with flour on the top of it. When I walked in, it all collapsed, covering me in flour.

'But he was so smart. He would put an exercise book in his pocket, a pencil behind his ear. He didn't study hard, but he did well. We sacrificed so much for him to study, helped him to get a good job in the police force and, in the end, he gave it up for Australia.'

I watch Yiayia's gnarly fist push into the air with emotion. I sense her grief at the loss of her son, still fresh after twenty-five years. I am surprised to hear about this side of my father: a rabble-rouser, a wanderer. It suddenly occurs to me that he keeps a tight rein on me perhaps because I remind him of himself. I am always challenging him, straying dangerously from the hearth. It's a revelation.

Pappou comes back. Yiayia lights the fire and we sit around it until it burns down. When the dark blankets the mountains and the little inland villages twinkle like stars in the distance, we take ourselves off to bed, the smell of the fire and goat's cheese trailing behind us.

Fig-sap ricotta

Traditional cheese makers have long used natural coagulants to make cheese, from rennet (made from the stomachs of young calves) to nettles, thistles and mallow.

Homer, as far back as the 7th or 8th century BC, knew that the juice of figs coagulated milk: 'Even as the juice of the fig speedily maketh to grow thick the white milk that is liquid but is quickly curdled as a man stirreth it, even so swiftly healed he [i.e. Paieon, physician to the gods] furious Ares.' (*The Iliad,* Book 5, 902–904)

Aristotle (384 BC–322 BC) provided a recipe of sorts for the making of cheese using fig-tree sap: 'The juices flowing from an incision in green bark is caught on some wool. The wool is then washed and rinsed into a little milk, and if this be mixed with other milk it curdles it.'

Finally, in modern times, the New England Cheesemaking Supply Company (www.cheesemaking.com) was inspired by the ancients to provide a more detailed recipe for home cheese makers using fig sap. They can't guarantee it will work every time, but they say you'll have fun trying.

Ingredients
A few freshly cut figs
4 litres of milk
Honey or sugar to serve

Method

Put on rubber or latex gloves (the sap from figs can cause serious allergic skin reactions). Cut a few figs from the tree in the morning. The fig sap (sometimes known as latex) will seep from the tip of the fig. Squeeze a few drops directly into your milk or, if the sap is really running, rub it onto a piece of sterilised cloth and rinse this out in the milk. Alternatively, you can stir your milk with a branch cut from the tree.

Let the milk sit for up to 12 hours at room temperature, checking it periodically for the 'clean break'. When the curd breaks cleanly around your finger or knife, and does not knit back together when you remove the knife or finger, it is ready to go.

Drain the curd over a muslin cloth atop a colander for a few hours until all the excess liquid has gone. Serve with figs and a sprinkling of sugar or honey.

Sinaisthisi

Whoever holds their tongue saves their head

Greek proverb

Her blue eyes flash and her black hair swings. She gesticulates wildly.

'I love him so much, Spirithoula *mou*; how long can it go on? Sotiris and I have been living together for over a year now. If my father finds out, he's going to shoot me, literally shoot me. Sotiri's own mother says to me, "Get pregnant, trap him," but what if he leaves me?'

The question is rhetorical. I haven't yet met Sotiri, Natasha's lover. What I do know is that Sotiri is as slow in asking Natasha to marry him as he is in getting ready in the mornings. His family trades in oil; they have old money, and live in a genteel house up on a hill outside of Kalamata. Sotiri will ask my excitable cousin to marry him only when he is ready.

I've spent the last few days with Natasha in her parents' village home, with its bright geraniums and rose bushes out the front and prolific vines and fruit trees out the back. Her mother is Mum's older sister; Natasha, in her late twenties, is a few years older than I am.

We have taken up where we left off when we first met when I was seven: she leads passionately and I try to keep up, in awe of her energy. She speaks quickly, moves quickly. She walks around the garden in this house where she grew up, re-potting plants, cutting off a bud here, pruning a rose there. She works in the bank in Kalamata now, but her hands are solid, fleshy, the hands of a girl at home in the village. She smokes cigarette after cigarette, talking between puffs.

'You know Freud, he was right about the Oedipus complex. I think Sotiri is in love with his mother. I can never compete with her. But I want to have babies, Spirithoula *mou*, set up home.'

Although Natasha shares Sotiris's bed in his mother's home, she has told her father that she stays in Kalamata with her sister. If her father were to find out about her living arrangements, I wouldn't put it past him to shoot her. He is known for his violence and his staunchly traditional views.

Natasha is all feeling, *sinaisthisi*, a new word I have learnt from her. I love her passionate use of psychological language. It's such a contrast to the practical Greek of my own parents. She loves it that I take it all in like an obedient student. We sit in the front room while her dad is out in the kitchen watching television. After each cigarette, she waves her hands to clear the air; he mustn't suspect that she smokes. I smile wryly at her artifice. I am all too familiar with hiding things from my parents.

For someone so articulate about her *sinesthimatiki zoi*, her emotional life, I am surprised at how resourceful Natasha is when she engages in the daily rituals of her life here. We top and tail the string beans her mother brought in from the field this morning, and sauté them with onions, garlic and a generous helping of olive oil. When they have softened, she adds a few cups of grated ripe tomatoes, zucchini pieces and potatoes, and turns down the heat to let the meal cook slowly. She does all this with a sure hand. She reminds me of my cousin Kathy back home.

The smell of the beans fills the house. Everything in the pot has come from my aunt's fields. I can't wait to eat, but of course I must be patient; my aunt will be back from the fields after two o'clock.

Yiayia, my maternal grandmother, calls out from the bedroom. She needs her bedpan. Natasha takes it to her, then expertly empties its contents into the toilet when Yiayia has finished. Yiayia has been in bed for many months now, unable to walk with osteoporosis.

When my aunt returns, we sit around the table together. Natasha eats with passion, wolfs her food down. While her hands are fleshy and strong, the rest of her is lean and angular, all nervous energy.

When Natasha returns to work in Kalamata a few days later, I decide to go on to Petalidi, where Mum grew up. My mother's brother Nikos is living in the family home with his two girls and I'd like to see him; I want to decide for myself what to make of him, after all I have heard.

Mum's village is large compared to my aunt's; a couple of thousand people live there, most within a kilometre of the sea. The village is surrounded by farmland.

When I get to the small stone house on the incline away from the water, I recognise it immediately from our trip here when I was a child. It has whitewashed walls and an ornate iron door. But now it looks grimy, unkempt. My uncle, Mum's youngest sibling, comes to the door. He hugs me awkwardly, as if he is not used to touching anyone. He looks like an older, plumper version of my brother.

We walk through the front room and down a step into the cool, dark kitchen. I marvel that seven people once lived here. My mother used to sleep in the same bed as her sisters, and she reports that it was the happiest time of her life.

My uncle's daughters were babies when I last saw them; they are in their mid-teens now. My first impression is of a plodding solidity. I wonder how we will go, sharing this small space over the next week.

After I've put my bag down, my uncle potters about, preparing some olives and bread. He apologises that there is no meat. He is fasting.

'What can I do, Spirithoula? My wife left me. I have to fend for myself now, and look after my girls when they are staying with me.'

I look at the girls. They look embarrassed. I'm not sure what to say.

He goes on. 'How is your mother? My sisters?' The martyred tone remains.

'They're okay. They send their regards, hope you are well.'

'I'm not so well. I have my problems. I have nowhere to live now, no thanks to my sisters. This house stands empty. It's rightfully mine. They need to do the paperwork.'

'The paperwork', *ta hartia*, is something I have heard much about. My grandfather died without leaving a will. In keeping with Greek law, the property didn't pass to his wife, but to his adult children. And now these 'children' need to agree on what to do with the family home. My uncle claims it was promised to him, the only son. He has tried repeatedly to get his sisters to sign it over. But their husbands won't agree. This stalemate has been going on for many years now. I knew the subject would come up, but I didn't expect it to happen as soon as I was in the door.

'Mum is happy to sign over her part of the property, but my other aunts can't. Their husbands won't ...'

'It's your mother's responsibility to get them to sign. She's the oldest.'

I back down, unsure how to proceed in the face of my uncle's anger. I am surprised at the immovability of these old-fashioned cultural mores, this sense of masculine entitlement, sanctioned by law. My uncle was the favoured youngest child, the long-awaited son born after four girls. Everyone in the family fulfilled his every whim. Now, he's not happy that he has to compete with his sisters' husbands in far-off Australia.

The girls and I spend the week eating fruit from the abundant trees, brushing one another's hair, talking, while my uncle visits his mates at the *cafeneion* and rummages around the kitchen, mumbling. The garden is overgrown and the sense of neglect is starting to creep into the house – the unused rooms, the dust collecting in the corners. I go down to the shops for supplies, visit a few family friends from Australia who now live back in the village. Mum's goddaughter hugs me like a long-lost sister: 'Oh my God, Spirithoula, it's like I'm back in Australia seeing you! Tell me the news, I want to hear everything …'

I am restless. My cousins are not articulate; their life has been protected, even more so than mine. I feel sorry for them. My uncle won't let me take them out to the amusements that are running each night on the foreshore. He takes us to church every few days. He talks about moving to Agion Oros, the monastic community where only men are allowed. He spends long stretches of time there.

'Spirithoula!' he shouts one afternoon while we are sitting at the kitchen table. Some family friends have come to visit.

'*Ti, Theio*?' What, Uncle?

'You're crossing your legs while you're eating. It's blasphemy.'

I've spent the week listening patiently to my uncle rant about my mother, about women, about his homelessness. I've tried to reason with him, to placate him. I have tried to mediate a solution, patiently as my mother would have done. But to no avail.

'Your mother, she's the one responsible,' he says for the tenth time. Our guests look away, embarrassed. My patience finally snaps.

'My mother is a good, kind woman. It's not her fault. She has tried her best. I don't want you to speak about her like that.' I spit it out, vitriolic. I don't care who this man is, or that I'm staying in his home. I need to protect my mother from his harsh tongue.

I can see he is taken aback, but there is a new respect in his eyes. I am trembling, full of anger and frustration. I don't regret speaking up. I remember standing up to the bullies at school and how right it felt.

For the next few days, we skirt around each other. When I am ready to leave, my uncle sees me off on the bus. He kisses me on both cheeks and says, 'I'm sorry if I have been hard on my sister. I can't help it. I was upset. I have no home.'

I look into his blue eyes, into the face that reminds me so much of my own brother's, and say, '*Entaxi*, *Theio*. Okay, Uncle. I will have a talk with Mum and my aunts when I get back, to see if this situation can be resolved. But you must understand that this is not Mum's fault.'

He doesn't say anything. I climb onto the bus and take a seat. When I look down from the window to wave goodbye, I see that he has already gone, back up the hill, back to the family home.

Natasha's fasolakia (string bean stew)

Serves 6

This dish is best made when string beans and tomatoes are in season. It is a one-pot dish, like many peasant recipes. It's easy to prepare and the flavours are deliciously simple.

Ingredients

4 tablespoons olive oil
1 kilogram string beans, trimmed and cut in half
2 brown onions, peeled and quartered
2 cloves garlic
4 medium, ripe tomatoes, quartered and grated (discard the skins)
1 cup boiling water
1 teaspoon dried oregano
6 medium potatoes, peeled and chopped into large chunks
2 medium zucchini, quartered lengthwise
Salt and pepper to taste

Method

Heat the oil in a large pot. Cook the string beans, onions and garlic over a medium heat for 10 minutes, stirring regularly. Add the tomatoes, 1 cup of boiling water and oregano. Simmer over low heat for 20 minutes, checking every now and then that there is enough moisture. Add the potatoes and zucchini and cook for a further 20 minutes or until the potatoes are soft. If it looks a bit dry, add more water. Season to taste.

Serve hot as a main course or side, or cold as a salad. Best accompanied with crusty bread and a wedge of creamy feta.

Naple's finest

You could sell the whole of Naples for a dollar,
but nobody would have the dollar to buy her

Neapolitan proverb

'I have to take you there. They have the best food in all of
Naples,' Paolo insists. 'It's just around the corner.'

It's hard to imagine such a place in this neighbourhood.
We're staying at a *pensione* on a dingy lane full of backpacker
staples: pizza cafés with spruikers out the front, mini-marts and
mouldy laundromats. The houses on the street are in various
states of decay. Our *pensione* houses tiny rooms, each with a wash
basin and three sagging beds. We can hear suspicious scratching
noises at night. My travel companion Kathy, she of the short
spangly skirts that so terrified my father, is too scared to put her
bare feet down of a morning lest her toes get nibbled off.

Paolo is an Italo-Australian with a mysterious illness; he
has come back to his native Naples for treatment. We met him
in the *pensione*, where he has been staying for a few months
already. I can't even begin to imagine the state of hospitals in
this town. I hold my tongue when he waxes lyrical about the

superior quality of medical care he is getting compared to that available in Australia.

Kathy and I met up in Greece and flew together to Rome. There we overdosed on tourist attractions and art galleries. Kathy has just finished a Fine Arts degree and is determined to see every notable piece of art between here and London, where we are heading. I am happy to tag along provided I can visit a few rambling markets and have a decent coffee wherever we go.

Naples is a refreshing change after Rome. There's a sense of danger in the air, an electric energy in the seedy backstreets and derelict shopping strips. Everything feels more intense: the tomato flavour bigger, the people more generous, the colours brighter beneath the grime. And now, Paolo has led us to the rundown café. It reminds me of the dark coffee shops frequented by old Greek men back in Australia, where women are certainly not welcome. He turns to us.

'This is it.'

Kathy and I look at each other. Are we going to get mugged in there? But it's too late to turn back.

Inside, we sit down at one of the tables. At the next table is a dark-haired teenager doing her homework. And at the next, a group of elderly men, smoking and drinking coffee.

'Hello, Paolo. What will it be?' a stout woman asks in Italian; Paolo translates for us as he orders.

'Whatever you have fresh today, Sophia.'

'We have sardines today, and spaghetti puttanesca.'

Paolo nods. 'And three glasses of the house wine, please.'

Sophia places a pot of water on the stove in a corner of the room. She pulls out a newspaper-wrapped parcel, carefully tears it open, and lifts out the sardines. She runs them under the tap, tosses them in flour and salt, then switches the heat on under a heavy black fry pan. Soon the smell of frying fish fills the room. When the sardines are done, she removes them from the pan, adds a twist of lemon and brings them to the table. They taste of the sea, their flesh crisp on the outside and deliciously moist and white on the inside. She stands above us as we eat, pleased when we make sounds of appreciation.

'*Bellissimo, signora,*' I say shyly.

'*Grazie.*'

Next I watch her throw a few handfuls of pasta into the boiling water. She fries up anchovies, garlic, green olives, capers, a generous sprinkling of chilli and tomato puree. When the pasta is done, she tosses the sauce through and brings it to the table. On first bite, I know that I am tasting Naples' best. Can it be possible for a tomato sauce to taste this good, so complex and simple at the same time? The spaghetti is *al dente*; the sauce clings wetly to it. Paolo looks at me and knows I have reached a higher plane. His look says, *I told you so.* The bill comes to just over five dollars each.

After Naples, we make our way up to Florence, where there is beauty everywhere we turn: the architecture, the art, the fashion. How can I appreciate it all? I begin to hanker for less civilised pleasures; I want to get away to the countryside. But Kathy is determined that we follow our itinerary, and I don't have the confidence to go my own way. We carry on to Venice, paying an exorbitant price for a gondola ride as soon as we have put our bags down. I love getting lost in the little alleyways, relying on my instincts to find my way back to our hotel. It's hard not to get carried away by the mystery of a city built on water, like a mystical dream in a fairytale. We visit the graveyard island, Isola di San Michele, and I am moved by its eerie silence: geraniums and Cypress trees blowing in the warm breeze; the Franciscan nuns moving slowly around the austere church; the many thousands of marble and stone monuments to the dead. Like the Greeks, the Italians are practical about death, burying their dead away from the mainland for sanitary reasons.

Our next stop is Cannes, where we clamber up a tree to see famous people on the opening night of the film festival, and pay handsomely for the privilege of sunning ourselves on the beachfront. By the time we get to Nice, I am tired of packing and unpacking my bags, of eating out, of going from one beautiful site to the next. We are staying at a backpackers' hostel, and I ask the staff if I can prepare a meal in their kitchen. They are perplexed; not many visitors offer to cook their own dinners. But I miss the grounding pleasure of creating something from raw ingredients. They give me access to their freezer and pantry. It's full of frozen chicken schnitzel and chips. I am disappointed that the ingredients are not more exotic – but once I am in the kitchen, I feel at home again. The sound of the pan sizzling with oil soothes my spirit. When the meal is ready, Kathy and I eat shyly with the young staff. We are united by a shared table, but language lets us down.

Once I've seen so many Dalís and da Vincis that they could just as well be Miros and Munches, I keep track of my travels by the remembered taste of countries in my mouth: oversized lobster in a fishing village in the south of Portugal; pistachios in a bar in Seville, the whole floor covered with shells; *coq au vin* in a suburban restaurant in Paris; a glass of champagne at the Moulin Rouge. But nothing even comes close to the sardines and spaghetti puttanesca in Naples.

As we move from place to place, I become fascinated by watching people on trains. In France and Italy, commuters flirt, laugh, kiss and argue. I stare openly, entranced by how different people live their lives. Many do it passionately here, it seems. I want to stop and stay for a while, experience these lives, live as the locals do. But we have to keep moving before our money runs out. There are gypsy children and refugees who try to steal our cash and belongings. At a border crossing, we are pulled up in the middle of the night for not having a visa. But we keep our wits about us, then revel in telling these stories to our fellow travellers. I speak with my parents only rarely and when I do, they are anxious. I haven't told them that I plan to work in England, that I have prepared the paperwork to have my social work qualifications recognised overseas.

'Are you still in Europe? Go back to the village. Better still, come back home. Why are you staying so long?' Dad worries. But he also listens intently when I tell him where I have been. When I ring from Paris, he can't understand why I won't be going to the Palace of Versailles; there are so many treasures, so much history. I sense that he is envious; that he would have loved the opportunity to see some of the things I have seen. He probably would have appreciated them more, what with his knowledge of history. I want to say that my senses have been saturated by history, by beauty. It's as if my brain can't hold it all in. I think back to Cavafy:

> *… may you stop at Phoenician trading stations*
> *to buy fine things,*
> *mother of pearl and coral, amber and ebony,*
> *sensual perfume of every kind –*
> *as many sensual perfumes as you can …*

All these 'sensual perfumes' have intoxicated me, dulled my senses – I have inhaled them too quickly. By the time we get to London, I am exhausted. The weather is grim. As the ferry pulls in past the Dover cliffs, I feel a sense of déjà vu, as if I have been here before. On the train to our hostel, I get the same feeling; people are reading their newspapers, quietly going about their business as they do on Melbourne trains. At the station, a voice on the loudspeaker instructs us repeatedly to move to the left of the escalator if we are standing still, to overtake on the right.

I stay in London for two days. It's long enough for me to realise I don't want to work here. I've also made another important realisation: I can't escape myself, or my family. It's time to go home.

D.O.C.'s pasta puttanesca

Serves 4

Our family ate at Carlton's D.O.C. Gastronomia Italiana recently and I was reminded anew of eating in Italy: waiters who move quickly, flirt fabulously and down espressos speedily; simple, good-quality ingredients executed elegantly; and a pasta puttanesca that sent my tastebuds a-buzzing.

When I approached D.O.C. and explained my desire to pin down a recipe for the fiery sauce and to get the story behind its wicked name, head chef Michele Usci wrote:

'There are a few different ideas about where this sauce originated. Puttanesca means prostitute. Some say that this was a whore's favourite meal because it was very quick to make, so she could go back to work without wasting time.

'Others believe that the real story goes something like this … Late one night, some patrons showed up at their favourite restaurant in Ischia, an island east of Naples. The owner quickly explained that he was about to close and had nothing left to serve them. The clients, being hungry, replied, 'Facci una puttanata qualsiasi': 'Just cook us anything!' So the owner improvised with what he had left in his kitchen, creating the puttanesca sauce.'

Ingredients
Pasta of your choice, to serve 4
1 tablespoon olive oil
2 cloves garlic, finely chopped

1 handful Kalamata olives
1½ tablespoons small capers, drained
½ small red chilli, cut in half
2 anchovy fillets, chopped
A few tablespoons chopped flat-leaf parsley, plus extra to serve
250 grams tinned San Marzano tomatoes
Parmesan cheese, if you like, although this is not traditionally served with puttanesca sauce

Method

Bring a large pot of water to the boil and add the pasta. Heat the oil in a heavy-based frying pan. Add the garlic, olives, capers, chilli and anchovies. Reduce the heat so that all the flavours come out and the anchovies melt. Add the parsley and tomatoes and cook for 5 minutes. Remove the chilli pieces.

When your pasta is cooked, drain it, then mix through the sauce and garnish with more chopped parsley. Serve immediately.

Warragul adventures

Sit on your eggs

Greek proverb

'For the price you want to pay, you won't even get something that Aborigines would live in.'

What have I done?

I put an ad in the *Warragul Gazette*: 'Affordable apartment wanted to rent.' My budget is limited and I don't want to go through a real estate agent. Now, I'm standing in front of an elderly woman, a long-time resident of Warragul. She is the only person who has responded to the ad. I look around the room with the dark brown brick wall, the low ceiling. Her comment disturbs me, but my chances of finding another place within my budget are slim. I take the apartment.

Back in town, there are a few elderly people shopping on the main street, some teenagers smoking outside the local supermarket. I go into a café with lace curtains on the windows and order a cappuccino. The woman places a teaspoon of instant coffee into a mug and stirs in boiling water. She froths milk with a battery-operated beater and pours it into the mug. My spirits drop further.

I was offered two jobs following my return from Greece: one working with elderly dementia patients at the Australian Greek Welfare Society in Richmond; the other delivering health education programs with the Gippsland Women's Health Service. The first was just minutes from my parents' home; the second required me to move to a country town. I took the Gippsland job – omitting to tell my parents about the local offering. They were upset about my moving away, but they knew I had to start my career somewhere.

The Women's Health Service is based in Sale, but I will be doing outreach from the regional town of Warragul. I start my training at the Sale office and meet my colleagues. One woman, Judy, bowls me over in a loud voice.

'Your name is Greek. I love Greeks. So much passion, such good food. I was there in the '70s. I had a lot of fun. Have you been there?'

She's delighted when I tell her about my recent trip and insists I bring baklava to the next staff meeting, even though I've never made it before. Over the next few days, she takes me under her wing. 'Now, you'll find there is no good coffee in Warragul. In fact, there's no coffee anywhere around here like you'll find in Melbourne. Except at Coco's in Yaragon. It's run by Katya and Elke and David. You'll love it there. Just tell them I sent you.'

At the first opportunity, I drop into Coco's. There's a handsome, gentle-looking man at the counter and a tall, athletic-looking woman with a German accent making coffee. Through the kitchen window, I can see someone preparing food.

'Um, hi. A woman called Judy said I should come and introduce myself. I'm Spiri.'

'Ah yes, Judy. How is she? She hasn't been in for a few weeks. Sit down. Coffee?'

From the Gaggia machine comes the tantalising aroma of well-brewed coffee. A woman emerges from the kitchen. She's carrying a large cake plump with poppy seeds. She looks my way, smiles and comes over.

'Elke says you're Judy's friend. Welcome. I've just made my famous German poppy-seed cake, from an old recipe my grandmother handed down to me. Do you want to try it?'

I love this European way of offering food, whereby a special dish is recommended. I order the cake – it's soft and buttery, with the pleasant crunch of poppy seeds. I know I'll be back.

Over the next few days, I settle into the apartment. My cousin John brings my few belongings in his courier's truck from Melbourne. I hang bright pictures taken in Greece on the brown walls: me with a Santorini sunset in the background; on a gondola in Venice; a picture of my grandparents squinting in the sun. I cook myself a meal. And then I run out of things to do. I ring my friends in Melbourne, one after another.

'How is it there in sunny Warragul?'

'Quiet. I start work tomorrow. How am I going to get through the week? There's nothing to do here. When can you visit?'

It's the first time I've lived alone. The streets are deserted and it's only six o'clock. I've decided not to have a television. I sigh and pick up my book – at least I'll get lots of reading done.

My employer has hired an office for me at the local agricultural college. The next morning, I am greeted there by a burly, bearded man. He leads me along corridors filled with posters showing different grades of pear and breeds of cow. We pass pimply male students; there are very few women to be seen. I am taken to an office where the desk faces a large window; it looks down a hill towards a pasture dotted with grazing cows. I know I would never have an office like this in Melbourne. Maybe Warragul isn't going to be so bad after all.

My manager is in Sale, over an hour's drive away. Although I need to attend fortnightly meetings there, I am free to define my role creatively. I introduce myself to people at the hospital, at the neighbourhood house, at the migrant resource centre. I run workshops on self-esteem for women who have experienced family violence, help organise health sessions for Koori women, deliver information on pap tests and breast screening to women twice my age, and teach young girls about conflict resolution. I scream up and down the highway, from Morwell to Moe, zoom past dairies and potato farms. Most of the time I improvise, flying by the seat of my pants – but people are hungry for information and forgiving of my youth and inexperience. And because they show faith in me, I blossom, grow in confidence. Over coffee at Coco's, I tell Judy there are groups of women – Italian potato farmers, Greek fish and chip shop owners, newly arrived Filipino brides – who know very little about preventative health.

'Well, do something for them, Spiri,' she encourages me.

In Korumburra, a community worker tells me, 'The Italian women never come to anything. It's really hard to get them to leave their farms.'

'What if we gave them information in their own language? Perhaps I could invite some bilingual workers from the Cancer Council ...'

'You can try. But I really don't think they'll come.'

We organise a health day for Italian-speaking women, and there is so much interest, a bigger venue must be found. The women speak excitedly, switching from English to Italian and back again. They laugh a lot. And they bring food, cramming the table with plump Italian doughnuts, biscuits and pickles.

My days at work are full and I come home late. Every Friday, I make my way to Melbourne, where I overdose on its delights for two days. Sometimes Judy joins me. At breakfast, we all sit together and chat, Mum talking with her hands to Judy when she can't find the words.

At other times, I go away for weekends: abseil down cliffs, snorkel along reefs, swim in the sea by moonlight. I avoid being home as much as possible. My childhood room feels so small.

My father rants, 'You treat this house like a hotel. Stay home. Help your mother with the housework! You used to listen to us.'

'I've got to live my life, Dad. I'm not a child anymore.'

We are angry at each other all the time. I feel guilty, but I cling to my newfound freedoms with a vengeance. I know that, despite his ranting, Dad can't stop me going out. Mum hangs back anxiously, wide-eyed at this newly assertive daughter of hers.

When we are alone, she says, 'What will people say that you are going out all the time? They'll call you a slut. Isn't it time you settled down? Got married? So many of our friends want to introduce you to their sons …'

'I know who I am, Mum. I don't really care what people say. I'm young. I'm just having fun. I don't want to meet those men. I'm capable of meeting men myself.'

'You'll make your father sick. Can't you see how much he worries?'

'I can't be responsible for Dad. He did similar things when he was young …'

'It's different for women …'

'That was then, Mum. We don't live in the village anymore.'

Back in Warragul, I slowly start to make more connections. I play squash and create recruitment flyers to revive the flailing women's team; I volunteer at the neighbourhood house to teach Greek for beginners, making participants stomp around the room as they call out the alphabet; and I start having Friday afternoon drinks with my neighbour, a cheeky veterinary nurse who has lived locally all her life. I make friends with a naturopath in her fifties, a young gay couple and their children, and the eccentric Katya from Coco's. I'm surprised at the type of people I've met living in the country: interesting people living their own lives, unpretentiously.

Katya and I establish early on that we are both obsessed with food. 'Come over and we can have a Malaysian steamboat – we'll dip fish and vegetables into the curry. I'll show you our garden,' she says one day.

I go to the cottage she shares with Elke and David. The walls inside are painted purple, peppered by mosaicked mirrors and bright paintings. Outside, a rambling cottage garden brims with herbs and vegetables. There's a dog, three cats, and Coco the galah. The home is warm and relaxed, the hospitality generous. I recognise in Katya the urge to feed, to nurture, to create a home. I have a hankering to do the same, and wonder when I too will be able to make a real home for myself, one where I truly belong. But I don't reflect for too long; I am brought back to the here and now: Ella Fitzgerald plays in the background; Coco squawks loudly; and a divine-smelling Malaysian steamboat beckons.

Katya's poppy-seed cake

Serves 8

Katya has fond memories of visiting her grandmother Charlotte in Berlin on Sunday afternoons. They would sit on her balcony surrounded by the geraniums and eat Charlotte's delicious poppy-seed cake. Katya remembers that the cake was usually still warm and always accompanied by a rich cup of hot chocolate.

Equipment
1 x 26-centimetre *gugelhupf* (ring) tin

Ingredients
300 grams unsalted butter, plus extra for greasing
A pinch of salt
250 grams sugar
6 eggs
150 grams plain flour, sifted
150 grams ground almond meal
200 grams poppy seeds
½ vanilla bean (seeds only, scraped from the pod) or 1 teaspoon vanilla essence
1 tablespoon icing sugar, to garnish

Method

Preheat the oven to 180°C. Grease your gugelhupf tin with
butter. In a large mixing bowl, beat the butter with a mixer
until it is white and fluffy. Add salt and sugar and mix until
combined. Add the eggs one at a time and beat each for 1 minute
on a low setting. Add the flour and almond meal and beat for
another minute. Fold in the poppy seeds and vanilla seeds or
vanilla essence.

Pour the mixture into a cake tin and bake at 180°C for
50 minutes. When it is cooked, remove from the tin and place on
a cooling tray. When the cake is completely cool, sprinkle with
icing sugar.

My language on Homer's shores

The way of speaking honours the person

Greek proverb

'*M*e lene Spirithoula. *Eimai apo tin Australia* ...' I stutter. My name is Spirithoula. I am from Australia ...

What am I doing here? I cannot be sure of my place and I sit down, red-faced.

I'm in the epicentre of Minoan civilisation, where the palace of Knossos, legendary home to King Minos's mythical Minotaur, gleams majestically in the summer light. But I will barely have time to explore its wonders – I'll be spending the week with the people in this room, learning how to engage kids in meaningful discussions about drug and alcohol use, even though all I want to do is drink at seaside bars and dance on tables.

I've managed to secure a scholarship to Greece to research her preventative health programs. I am twenty-six and have been working in the health sector for a few years now. The scholarship represents a professional milestone, but more importantly means a four-month Greek sojourn, which I have craved. I've been living with my parents again, and although I come and go as I please now, I still can't seem to make the break from my parents' home into my own. Being in Greece is a chance to get lost again in chaos and passion and beauty, to view my life anew through a different lens.

Greece's innovative health programs are few and far between. I visit the health department in Athens, where a heavy-lidded, chain-smoking bureaucrat laughs sardonically at me – *You're here from Australia to research* our *systems?* – but I doggedly persevere, in between clubbing in Athens with cousins and planning which islands to visit.

Finally, I connect with a well-spoken educator who invites me to participate in a one-week program on drug education. If I cover the cost of my own flight and accommodation, she'll cover the cost of the course.

'We've just run one in Athens. The next one is in Heraklion, Crete.'

I can barely contain my excitement. My goddaughter, Chrysoula, whom I baptised in Albury when I was ten, now lives in Chania, a mere two hours from Heraklion. Another family friend, who grew up in Melbourne but now lives in Greece, has suggested we hire a car and go exploring. I imagine rocky beaches and *retsina*-fuelled taverna meals. I just need to do a little work before I can start my holiday proper. How hard can a one-week course be?

I am the youngest person in the class. When the teachers start speaking their lingo, I am painfully aware of my inarticulateness, my lack of anything to contribute. The course is based on a psychotherapeutic model: we are challenged to face our own fears, unpacking what makes us uncomfortable, what personal barriers stop us from talking about difficult things. I start to think the organisers must be sadists; even if we reach the elusive nirvana of self-awareness, we will be shrivelled shells of our former selves, bled dry by all this self-examination. We break off into small groups to brainstorm and take notes. This feels too much like my work life in Melbourne, except that it's all in Greek, spoken at top speed.

I can name all the herbs in my mother's garden, the most obscure vegetables. But translate 'subconscious', 'archetypes', 'collective consciousness'? We never spoke of such things when I was young. I discovered them for myself as a young adult through Jung and Freud – in English. I am astounded at the level of consciousness in the group and begin to understand what it means to be an educated Modern Greek speaker. I feel out of my depth, a fraud. Everyone is kind, but I know I've got to step up if I'm going to survive the week. I can't skim the surface here.

Early in the first day, to break the ice, we are paired up and told to explain the meaning of our names to one another. 'My name is Spirithoula. "Spiro" means to sow; "doula" means slave, or a handmaiden or midwife. Together, these words might mean a giver of life – a facilitator of sorts, perhaps?' I feel proud of myself – what a clever interpretation.

The woman I have teamed up with promptly refutes my theory. 'Spiro does not mean to sow – that word is spelt differently.' She stops short of saying that my name means nothing.

The next day the onslaught begins again – this time, we are required to look at our own upbringings and how we deal with conflict. I think back to accompanying Dad to the pub; to family arguments when I slunk back, wishing for peace. I think about my own desire for self-determination, the battles I still have with Dad on a regular basis, even though I am twenty-six. It occurs to me I can't keep blaming Dad for my woes – I too have to take responsibility. It's a confronting thought, one I will need to digest. As the week progresses, I begin to talk about my fears and concerns, my family life and my role in it. I start to feel safer as, in pairs and small groups, others divulge their innermost thoughts too.

Back at the hotel each night, the middle-aged hotelier is very attentive; he has no idea of my existential angst, nor does he really care. He is more interested in luring me into his bed. He takes me to a tavern on the outskirts of town, where we drink Campari with orange juice from long glasses and feast on pickled octopus and sea urchins. I am not sure if I like their salty sea smell, but there's something undeniably sensual about them. At least here I can lose myself yet again in the decadent pleasures of food. It's a contrast to the bland offerings at the workshop: sandwiches and packaged juices, ubiquitous conference food, even in this little Minoan oasis.

Every morning, I sit through the agony that is 'circle time', when we spontaneously share our insights from the previous day. Sometimes we sit in silence for minutes on end. I try to melt into the background, become as inconspicuous as possible. But on the last day, before I know what I'm doing, I find myself standing.

'My name is Spirithoula,' I announce to the group. 'At the start of the week, I wasn't sure why I was here. I was scared, not sure what I had to offer. I have learnt a lot about myself through this program, and how I might become a better practitioner. Thank you.'

My voice bounds across the room, clear and strong. I can barely contain it. Where is it coming from?

I sit down. The organiser smiles at me. The workshop has shifted something in me. I feel very still, very calm. This is my voice. It doesn't matter if I don't get all the words right in my kitchen Greek: it is mine. Unbidden, a strand of poetry comes to mind:

> GREEK the language they gave me;
> poor the house on Homer's shores
> My only care my language on Homer's shores.

Later, I ask one of the teachers about it, and she tells me it was written by the Greek poet Odysseus Elytis; it is from his epic poem *To Axion Esti*. She recites the rest of the fragment in Greek and I am mesmerised.

There bream and perch
windbeaten verbs,
green sea currents in the blue
all I saw light up in my entrails,
sponges, jellyfish
with the first words of the Sirens,
rosy shells with the first black shivers.
My only care my language with the first black shivers.

That night, the participants and teachers all meet at a local taverna for dinner. We sit outside under a grape vine. A balmy breeze moves across its leaves. Our work is over and we laugh and gossip about the week's events. The facilitators make light of their heavy-handed tactics. They worked, didn't they? The

local priest has been invited along, as has his daughter. When the shared plates of calamari, *horta* and chips, fried fishes and *tzatziki* are finished, the priest's daughter stands and we all fall silent. She starts singing a song made popular by Greek singer Eleftheria Arbanitaki. In a clear, high voice, the young woman laments that she needs to be touched, kissed, loved; treasured like old wine; embraced as one might their homeland.

I feel shaken by the beauty of her words, by the depth of meaning she has managed to convey. I try to stop myself from crying, but tears roll regardless. Everything that has happened during the week – the bubbling up of my voice, the breeze, the music – it all connects me to a bigger presence, brings me closer to myself. I reflect how far I have come in just one week on Homer's shores.

Heraklion octopus salad

This 'salad' is more of a pickle. The cooking time will depend on how well the octopus has been tenderised. Traditionally, this was done by fishermen at the port by hitting the octopus against a stone. This dish is best served as an appetiser with *tsikoudia* (a Cretan grappa) or ouzo.

Ingredients

1 whole octopus, about 1½ kilograms, washed and dried
1 cup olive oil
1 cup red wine vinegar
1 cup dry white wine
1 bay leaf
6 black peppercorns
1 teaspoon dried oregano

Method

Place the octopus in a heavy-based pot, tentacles first. Pour in ¼ cup oil, ¾ cup vinegar and all the wine. Add the bay leaf and peppercorns and simmer over a moderate heat for 40 minutes or until the octopus is tender. Remove the octopus and place it onto a platter. While it is still hot, sprinkle it with oregano. Allow it to cool, and then cut it into bite-sized pieces.

Place the pieces in a clean glass jar, add the remaining oil and vinegar and mix carefully. To serve, drizzle with a little oil and a few drops of vinegar. This will keep for up to 10 days in the refrigerator.

Cafeneion laments

Better a drop of wisdom than an ocean of gold

Greek proverb

I spend the next day exploring Crete's Rethymno, walking along the café-lined port. I find myself at the Fortezza, a castle built in mediaeval times. It feels barren, forgotten somehow. There aren't many tourists on this windswept day. I wander into the newer parts of town where the locals do their shopping and come across a thriving town square. Young people nurse their iced coffees, laughing and smoking. I grab a piece of spanakopita from a bakery. The pastry is golden, the spinach and cheese fresh and creamy. I sit on a bench and revel in my simple feast, watching the passing parade.

When I get back to the hotel, there is a message waiting for me. It is Theia Kanella, my father's sister. I ring her back immediately. She is the only person who has my phone number at the hotel. She wouldn't ring unless it was an emergency.

'Theia, is everything okay? You sound terrible.'

'Pappou died last night.' She waits. I say nothing, shocked. 'Are you able to fly back for the funeral? It's tomorrow. I've been trying to ring you all morning.'

I shift into autopilot, thinking about the logistics of what I must do: make my way to Heraklion's airport, find a flight to Kalamata, and take the bus to Kyparissia a few hours away. There is no way I'll make it back in time.

I arrive soon after the funeral. My aunt and grandmother are still in shock. I think back to the first time I met my grandfather, a dapper man with a trim moustache, the mayor of the village. A man who was generous, who pushed his new daughter-in-law on a homemade swing under the mulberry tree. The next time I saw him, he was still regal, sprightly, even in his early eighties. The last time I visited him, just before the workshop, he was quiet, removed; his spirit seemed to have receded to some deep, inaccessible place.

I ring Dad and he can barely speak. I feel his angst at being so far away, and imagine how unreal it must seem to him. It's so much easier being close, being able to speak about Pappou, to cry and reflect.

My aunt and I stay with my grandmother in the village. The back window looks onto the cemetery where my grandfather is buried. We all avoid sitting in the chair where Pappou used to sit. I stand on the veranda and remember him smoking his pipe, his eyes twinkling with mirth.

We fall into a rhythm over the course of the week: cooking, cleaning and sitting by the fireside at the end of each evening.

Theia Kanella is concerned for her mother – how will she cope here on her own? – but Yiayia is stubborn. This has been her home since she married; it is where she had each of her children, where her husband died. She is not leaving. The goats are long gone, so she can't make cheese anymore, but she still has a few chooks. She can still bake. She still has her garden. She agrees to my aunt sending supplies on the twice-weekly bus service from Kyparissia, but this is her only concession. She holds up a familiar clenched fist, and my aunt knows this is a battle she cannot win.

In preparation for the memorial service to be held on the ninth day after Pappou's death, we make *kolliva*, boiled wheat mixed with pomegranate seeds, sesame seeds, almonds, cinnamon, sugar, raisins and parsley. After we boil the wheat, my aunt lays it out to cool on a clean tablecloth in the parlour. Then we mix it with the other ingredients and place the mixture in a long tray, fashioning it into the shape of a grave. We sprinkle it with powdered sugar and decorate it with raisins in the form of a cross and Pappou's initials. In the middle, we place a candle.

At the *mnimosino*, the memorial service, the priest prays for the departed and blesses the *kolliva*. He offers comfort to those of us standing around the grave, reminding us of our own mortality and the brevity of this earthly life. '*Eonia I mnimi tou*' – may his memory be eternal – he chants over the grave, swinging the censer filled with incense. Everyone in the village who is not bedridden has come to the service. The small graveyard fills with dark, weathered faces in headscarves and woollen caps. Yiayia wails, a long, primal lament – she has lived with Pappou for close to seventy years. The villagers cast looks at me every now and then, watching to see if Panayioti Tsintziras's daughter will cry for her Pappou. I do. They look down, seemingly satisfied.

Afterwards, we gather in the village *cafeneion* for coffee and liquor. The priest lights up a cigarette.

'I remember your dad. I was just a kid when he left the village.'

'I will tell him I saw you. He is very sorry that he couldn't make it to the funeral.'

'It's a long way to come. It's lucky you are here.'

'Yes, it is ...'

Everyone wants to talk to me. After expressing their condolences and asking how my parents are, they want news of their relatives in Australia. I get confused – which elderly face belongs to which family back home? In some cases, I haven't seen their relatives since my early teens. I meet a writer who has written a history of the area and regularly contributes to the village newspaper – the tiny village seems to have a few creative sorts, including my aunty, who fills little notebooks with poetry. I wonder if the compulsion to tell stories runs in my blood. Despite the professional path I have chosen, I still feel the need to write, to record my own experiences and those of others in a bid to honour them. The writer remembers my father and speaks fondly of him. Everyone laments that Dad is so far away. My aunt is competent as always – she serves coffee, speaks to everyone and then whisks me off home. Perhaps she is worried I will be struck by the evil eye again.

There will be another memorial on the fortieth day and another after one year. I reflect on how affirming it is to have such markers on the grieving journey, a time to reflect and to check in with other mourners. A sensible, practical ritual.

A few weeks later, I go back to my aunt's home. When I tell her I'd like to return to Crete, she gives me her blessing. I fly back to Heraklion and make my way to a tiny village outside of Chania to visit my goddaughter, Chrysoula. Our families connected when I was a child in Narrandera, and when I was ten her parents asked my dad and me to be her godparents. They returned to Greece when Chrysoula was a little girl; she is thirteen now.

When I arrive, I find that she has grown into a slender, dimpled young woman with long dark hair. She and her brothers are delighted to see me and bombard me with questions about Australia. It hasn't been easy adapting to life back in the village, they tell me. It's a very small, conservative place, where everyone knows your business. In the tiny village square, men in *tseberes*, traditional black-fringed headscarves, sit around drinking coffee. It's like a scene out of *Zorba the Greek*. They watch silently as the *Australezi* walk past. I feel trapped by their gaze.

That night, we manage to get away with a few older cousins to a bar in town with gleaming fluorescent lights. Men swarm around my goddaughter and I squirm, knowing how her protective father and grandfather would react.

Back at my goddaughter's family home, I am fed until I am bursting: pickles to stimulate the appetite; onion and rabbit stew; lemony roast potatoes. Chrysoula and her brothers are keen to speak in English, having missed the Australian way. And yet their town is so picturesque, their lifestyle seemingly so easy. Their parents, after working exorbitant hours in fish and chip shops in Albury and Narrandera, can finally relax and enjoy their family. But the kids are finding it hard to settle into school. The system is so different here, the language not their own. I realise they are facing the same problems as many migrants face in Australia.

The family humours my desire to walk the Samari Gorge, a sixteen-kilometre hike across the island, from the village of Omalos all the way down to Agia Roumeli on the shores of the Libyan Sea. Not deterred by my lack of suitable footwear, I buy some cheap sand shoes from a shop that trades in sun hats, inflatable toys and flippers.

We set off soon after sunrise the next day. The rocks beneath our feet are round and slippery. The kids run on ahead, but I quickly realise that I have made a serious mistake in skimping on shoes. Once in, there is no way out of the gorge except by retracing your steps, or finishing. Pride does not allow me to back out. I persevere, all the while marvelling at the towering stones on either side of the thin path. By the midway mark, my toes are in excruciating pain and I join the queue at the medical station to get them bandaged. I limp along, finally making it to Agia Roumelli as the sun begins to set. The twinkle of blue water around the final corner is like a mirage. I take a quick dip in the sea. The immersion is akin to a baptism, a cleansing of the body and soul, but I can't revel in it – we practically have to run the next three kilometres to catch the boat across to Hora Sfakion, so that we can make the last bus back to Chania.

A few days later, my blackened toes and I bid my goddaughter and her family goodbye. We promise to meet again, either here or in Australia. I feel sure they will somehow find their way in this magical little paradise. For me, it's time, once again, to return home.

Asimina's sfakiano (Cretan rabbit stew)

Serves 6

This stew is deliciously rich and tender. It marries well with a side of rice or pasta, with homemade bread to wipe up the sauces. My *koumbara* Asimina notes that it's also best accompanied by her husband Andrea's homemade wine.

Ingredients
1 whole rabbit, skinned, cleaned and cut into pieces
4 bay leaves
½ cup olive oil
6 whole cloves
6 black peppercorns
6 allspice berries or ½ teaspoon ground allspice
1½ cups red wine
Salt to taste
8 large onions, peeled and cut into quarters
500 grams ripe tomatoes, peeled and grated (or 1 can diced tomatoes)
½ teaspoon each of paprika, dried oregano and cumin
5 whole cloves garlic
1/3 cup white vinegar

Method

Put the rabbit, bay leaves and salt into a heavy-based pan and lightly brown. When the rabbit pieces have taken on a light smoky aroma, add the oil, cloves, peppercorns and allspice berries (or ground allspice). Cook until browned. Add half a cup of wine. Simmer for about half an hour, or until the liquid has reduced. Remove the rabbit from the pot.

Add the onions to the pot and cook on a low heat until translucent. Remove half of the onions. Return the rabbit portions to the pot, arranging them on top of the onions, then cover the rabbit with the remaining onions. Add the grated tomatoes, paprika, oregano, cumin, garlic, the remaining wine and the vinegar. Put the lid on and simmer on low heat until the sauce is thick and rich and the rabbit pieces are tender. If it requires more liquid, add additional wine (not water). Serve with rice or wedges of crusty bread.

The road trip

The stone that rolls never gets mouldy

Greek proverb

Backlit by the setting sun, the 'Welcome to Coober Pedy' sign finally appears. We are relieved to see its rusting, bullet-holed surface. We get out our cameras. Another sign warns 'Beware of mine shafts', with a picture of someone falling into a hole while taking photos. We put our cameras away.

Adelaide, which we left early this morning, feels like a distant memory. As we made our way north from the city outskirts, the landscape fast became a mass of burnt-orange earth. Soon we were passing rusting petrol bowsers at isolated truck stops, swerving to miss dead kangaroos and disturbing eagles feasting on road kill. My new friend Katerina had never driven a manual car before, but felt confident enough to drive after a quick lesson at a roadhouse on the way – so long as she didn't have to make any right-hand turns. Thankfully, there haven't been many of those. The car shakes every time a lorry passes us, and we can almost feel our parents breathing over our shoulder: *Be careful.*

The 800-kilometre journey has been a chance for us to get to know each other better. One thing we knew at the outset was that we both love eating. In the three days since we left Melbourne, we have already shared several memorable meals. In Kingston on the Great Australian Bight, home to the Big Lobster, we ate roast beef that fell off the fork, rich and flavoursome. When we asked the waitress how it had been cooked, she drawled laconically, 'There's no fancy formula. It's just aged beef from a local farm. The cook hangs it out to cure. Then he seasons it with salt and pepper and cooks it to buggery.' I'm sure she was thinking, *Stupid city tourists, with their la-di-dah questions. It's just food.*

Then there was the laksa in Adelaide: thick noodles, tender pieces of chicken and crunchy vegetables in a creamy, aromatic curry. Perfect comfort food – but twelve hours later, it is still wreaking havoc on my bowels. I've let off a few in the car.

'This is a whole new level of intimacy,' I say after another. 'I guess now that I can fart in front of you, we're officially friends?'

Katerina laughs. 'Yes, definitely.'

We laugh a lot, sing at the tops of our voices and talk about anything that floats into our heads. We discuss the frustrations of living back home after extended trips overseas, of the pressure to get married. We are both living with our parents and longing to escape.

The idea to come to Coober Pedy was born a few weeks back. It was the first time I'd been out with Katerina, although we had crossed paths occasionally at uni and sometimes run into each other at the Retreat Hotel in Brunswick, where we danced to Greek blues music and shared cigarettes. And then there we were in a little bar off Lonsdale Street, raising our voices over the music to plan an adventure.

'We should go on a road trip. Go somewhere warmer.'

'Let's go to Sydney for the weekend. We could drive up, stay the night and come back the next day,' I posed.

Katerina hesitated. 'Sydney's not that much warmer. I've always wanted to go to the desert. What about Coober Pedy? My friend Maria knows someone there. We could drive up and head back through the Grampians.'

The idea excited me. I imagined Coober Pedy as a kind of Aussie Wild West, a place where people go to escape and make their fortunes. Tellis, the son of the priest in my dad's village and now a close family friend in Melbourne, once lived there. He has tattoos running up his arm, salacious portraits of his wife. It is whispered that he 'stole' her at gunpoint from her first husband. He has great stories to tell about his time mining in the desert. I must admit, I like the idea of hanging it on the patriarchs in my family, two women on an adventure.

We nutted out the logistics on the way home from the bar in my Valiant. We entertained driving to Coober Pedy in the Valiant, but only briefly. That would be suicide. By the time I dropped Katerina off, we had a starting date and a time limit:

ten days to get there and back, before I have to go back to work. We'll sort the rest out as we go.

A few weeks later, we joined a three-day backpacker bus tour that took us the long way to Adelaide. We stayed overnight at a sheep station, ate homemade scones for afternoon tea, raced up massive sand dunes and visited Aboriginal rock art. And now, the Thelma and Louise of the Greek-speaking community have finally arrived in Cooper Pedy in a boxy blue hire car, the *Priscilla* soundtrack playing on repeat all the way. Our vehicle is hardly the outrageous bus of the movie, but it got us here.

'Shall we try to find Maria's friend, and then book into the hostel?' Katerina says.

'Yes, but first, do you mind if we get some supplies? I think I've had enough of pies and chips, Coke and instant coffee. I need something fresh.'

'Good idea. We can ask about "G" at the shops.'

We are in a strange town in the middle of nowhere. We have no accommodation booked. We have one contact in town, a friend of a friend, but we don't even know his real name. We are hungry. I try to smile reassuringly. Everything will seem better once we've got some real food into us.

We make our way down the main street and call into the supermarket. The pickings are slim when it comes to fresh produce: a handful of browning apples, a few shrivelled oranges and some green-skinned potatoes. We're told there hasn't been a delivery of fruit and vegetables for days. My shoulders slump.

I browse the shelves while Katerina asks where we might find the mysterious 'G'. I am surprised to find jars of Kalamata olives on a dusty shelf, as well as the fat Volos variety from central Greece and stuffed green ones from Spain. There's sleek sheep's-milk yoghurt and creamy feta in the fridge, and packets of slippery sauerkraut and dry kabana on the counter – a little bit of Europe in the Australian desert. It strikes me as funny that people in this dusty town of forty-five nationalities can make do without fresh fruit and vegetables, but can't forego the pantry staples of their homelands.

We are told that we will find 'G' in the Ampol diner we passed on the road into town. Inside the diner, there's Greek music blaring and a Harley parked in the middle of the floor. An Aboriginal man is smoking at one of the tables and

213

exchanging banter with the man behind the counter, a stocky bloke in his early thirties. This is 'G', George, the owner of the roadhouse. We introduce ourselves as friends of Maria and tell him we have just driven up from Adelaide in a day.

'We do that trip all the time,' he says, unimpressed. Still, he looks at us with interest – two young women who have strayed into the desert, dusty, tired and probably hungry. I expect him to say, 'Come into my lion's den.'

He does.

'It's nearly closing time. I have a few friends dropping in for pizza. Join us ...'

Like most locals, George lives in a dugout. The caves are like cool cocoons in the unforgiving heat. George's dugout is sparsely furnished, with an industrial brick 'bachelor' bar in the living room. He tells us about the sizeable Greek-speaking community in Coober Pedy, and the many busloads of Greek-Australians who came from Adelaide and Sydney for the recent Glendi Greek Festival. He is charming and sexist in equal measure. Katerina and I sneak glances at each other – we are not quite sure what to make of him. I suspect he is hamming it up for us, but I could be wrong. I am tired and I don't trust my usual instincts.

A Ukrainian man, his Romanian wife and their son soon arrive, along with a miner from Croatia and her Finnish husband. A ferret sits on the Finn's shoulder and a bird squawks from a cage in the corner. Soon a guitar materialises and the Ukrainian man starts to sing in Hebrew, then Greek, then

Russian. Gypsy songs, quirky jigs and sad laments echo off the red earthen walls. We eat pizza from George's shop and drink homemade port that someone has brought in a gallon jar. We feel as if we've stepped onto the set of a strange movie. We drink glass after glass of the sweet port. It gets late.

When we try to take our leave, George tells us that the reception area at the hostel will be closed at this hour. At any rate, the owner has been caught perving on young women in the showers through a hole he drilled into the wall; we wouldn't want to stay there. George offers us his spare room. The alternative is to sleep in the car. We stay.

Katerina and I lie cramped together on the double bed, whispering. Katerina is uneasy about sleeping at George's house – she feels we are vulnerable. I am too uninhibited by the alcohol to worry much. I wonder whether I would have allowed myself to be charmed into George's bed had I been alone, a natural progression of the night. The thought both mortifies and amuses me. George is exactly the sort of macho male I generally avoid. At any rate, I am here with Katerina. Sisterhood trumps stupidity any day.

The next morning, we wake with throbbing headaches. George has left for work already. We call in to the roadhouse to thank him for his hospitality. He insists he will see us for dinner back at his place, and suggests we drive out to see the Breakaways, the bizarre moon-like landscape in *Mad Max III*.

Once there, like children, we slide down a hill into a barren valley, taking photos that will do no justice to the majesty of the place. Later, we drive down a dirt track along the dog fence that stretches 5,300 kilometres across three Australian states, to see the sun set over the hills. We finish off the olives, feta and bread we bought the day before: a Greek feast in the Australian desert.

Back at the roadhouse, George apologises that he is unable to join us for dinner at the dugout after all; he has to work. Instead, he cooks us an oversized chicken schnitzel and chips at the diner. We listen to Greek blues and share a bottle of *tsipouro*, a strong, grappa-like spirit. We stay at George's place again. By now, we feel like old friends.

The next day, George puts us on to his friend Yiannis, who shows us around his reproduction opal mine, a shrine of sorts. He serves us Turkish coffee and invites us back to his dugout for dinner. More lions, more dens. Except this lion is lankier, expensively dressed, with a thin gold chain around his neck and a wedding ring on his finger.

When we arrive at Yiannis' place, I take off my dusty travelling boots. His dugout is opulently furnished, the carpets pristine. This is clearly a family home, although he tells us his wife and daughters live in Adelaide. Coober Pedy is not the sort of place you want to raise a family, he says. George joins us and we drink yet more *tsipouro*, this time in elegant glasses. They regale us with wild stories from the recent past, tales of fights in bars and shootings in the street, drunken parties and violent feuds. They lament that there are now more tourists in the town than outlaws. But still, they manage to have fun. I'm still wondering what the intentions of these two men are, their expectations for the night, but we get back to our bed safely, waking without anything more than a hangover.

I promise to make George a meal to thank him for his hospitality. It becomes apparent he is never going to leave work early enough to eat it, so I suggest I cook for him in the diner. I feel quite nervous – an interloper in the functional industrial kitchen, without the luxury of familiar ingredients. I decide to keep it simple, preparing fettuccine tossed with olive oil, feta and sun-dried tomatoes, accompanied by garlic bread and a salad. When I begin to cook, I start to feel at home. I move into that comfortable space where I can chop and simmer, improvising with base ingredients. As I serve George and Katerina, I realise I can't avoid channelling my mother, no matter how far I travel. Even in this godforsaken place, I share her impulse to nurture with food. I briefly entertain the fantasy of working full-time in the diner, serving up utilitarian staples to the miners, the red earth of the desert perpetually under my nails, my skin burnt by the harsh sun. It's an intriguing idea, but I know I would miss my friends, decent coffee, city bookshops. And, dare I say it, my family.

The next day, we must leave. A few days of almost constant drinking make for a late start. We buy a very expensive bottle of aged port as a gift to thank our host. He tells us that this wasn't necessary, and that at any rate we should have bought it from him, not his competitor. Still hung-over, I drop the port on the floor as I hand it over. I am mortified. Our goodbyes are awkward, but we promise to come again with a busload of musicians for the Greek festival the coming year.

Our next stop, William Creek, is an easy 167 kilometres away, a mere centimetre on the map. But we don't bargain on the unsealed road, its rocks scraping the underside of the car all the way. The edges of the road are fuzzy, the same colour as the desert sand. The going is painfully slow. We play 'Eye Spy' for the sheer joy of spotting something, anything – 'e' for endless blue sky, 'h' for haze, 'r' for rocky road. We laugh and sing and talk more about food.

'I love that you enjoy food, Spiri. That eating doesn't worry you.'

'I can't help it. I've always loved it. Perhaps it's even an obsession.'

'Yes, I know about obsession. Sometimes I can't stop thinking about food. And I know I use it to push down feelings that are uncomfortable.'

I look at Katerina, and realise it's hard for her to speak in this way. I nod, and she goes on.

'When I was a kid, I used to hoard food. My hunger felt bottomless. Even now, there are times when I can't control my eating.'

I listen, sensing her anxiety. I see something of the vulnerable girl she must have been. It's as if she is saying, *I hope you can accept me now that you know.*

'Katerina, you are a funny, adventurous, clever woman. By the way, did I mention funny?'

She looks a bit bewildered. 'I don't always believe that of myself.'

'I believe it. I'm really enjoying your company. I am loving getting to know you more.'

She looks relieved, as if I might have run away. But she needn't have worried. I'm not going anywhere.

When the odometer hits 1000 kilometres, we stop to take a photo. But we don't dawdle, lest we get stuck out here after the sun goes down, unable to distinguish the road from the vast desert.

Tired and thirsty, we drive into William Creek as the sun casts its final rays. The town has a pub full of people and the basics: water, food, beds and copious amounts of beer. There are more light planes parked outside the pub than cars.

In a dormitory out the back of the pub, we drop our bags onto two single beds. Through the thin plywood walls, we hear bed springs rhythmically bouncing up and down. A walk is in order.

Katerina goes on ahead into the darkness and I find myself wanting to call out, 'Don't go.' What would I tell her family if she didn't come back? That I lost her in the desert?

She disappears into the black night and I wait on a wooden bench, just outside the circle of light that emanates from the pub. I look up into the mass of stars overhead. I feel very small, like a speck of dust. The endless landscape, stretching out as far as the eye can see, takes hold and doesn't let go. Where my skin ends and the landscape begins becomes blurry. This is a place to get lost in, a place to make me forget I ever lived in a city, had a job, had a family. My smallness is both confronting and comforting. Anything is possible out here. I sieve the red earth through my toes; it is still warm from the day's rays.

When Katerina finally returns, I am relieved. But she looks spooked.

'I heard something strange.'

'What?'

'The sound of sticks being played. You know, Aboriginal rhythm sticks.'

Her declaration hangs in a void just beyond understanding, beyond tangible explanation. We are silent. There is nothing to do but return to the sweaty embrace of the pub.

The next day, we make our way to the dry salt bed of Lake Eyre. We pull into a roadside café in the tiny town of Marree. 'Greek souvlaki' is chalked up on the board. Curious, we order one each. The owner pulls a souvlaki-shaped package out of the freezer and puts it in the microwave, wrapper and all. We laugh. Predictably, it tastes disgusting.

We make our way to the Grampians, detouring down a rough track that has our hire car bucking and jolting. There are more pub meals: seafood cocktails smeared in cheap mayonnaise, a poor imitation of spaghetti carbonara, flour-thickened pumpkin soups. In one small town, we play pool and barely escape the advances of some over-enthusiastic local boys. I steal a butter knife from the pub and sleep with it under my pillow, in case they decide to look for us in the middle of the night.

We imagine more shared adventures. I think about travelling around Australia, eating country food and writing stories. *Yarns and Yabbies* I will call it. I declare my intention to Katerina, who supports me wholeheartedly. We'll go together, of course.

The *Priscilla* soundtrack plays all the way home. We've learnt the lyrics to 'I don't care if the sun don't shine' by the time we hit the 2000-kilometre mark, where we stop to take another photo. When we finally reach the sobering city skyline of Melbourne, we've clocked up over 3000 kilometres. Before we can return the hire car, we hose off the red earth that still clings to the car's underside and watch sadly as it washes down the drain.

Spiri's improvised fettuccine with olive oil, feta and sun-dried tomatoes

Serves 4

Ingredients
500 grams fettuccine
200 grams sundried tomatoes
200 grams feta
A drizzle of olive oil
Salt and pepper to taste

Method
Cook the pasta in salted water until al dente and drain. Break up the sun-dried tomatoes and feta with your hands and toss through the pasta, along with a generous drizzle of olive oil. Season and serve immediately.

Baring my skin

Whoever did not walk in a moonlit night, and in the morning with the dew, did not enjoy the world
Greek proverb

The Big Fish is still here. It has cast off its cage and oversized boomerang, its fibreglass scales are peeling, and it's not as big as I remember – but it's still here, welcoming visitors to Tidy Town Tocumwal.

When I was a kid, seeing the Big Fish was the highlight of the drive from Melbourne to Narrandera, a few hours west of Sydney, where Theio John and Theia Sophia had their fish and chip shop. When I was little, we spent holidays here. Later, my parents bought into the shop and we moved to Narrandera for the first few years of my schooling. No one bothered to change the name – 'John's Fish and Chips' remained. Of course, fish and chips were the main event: thousands of plump packets wrapped in butcher's paper passed over the counter in the shop's heyday. But the *pièces de résistance* were the battered savs, pink sausages fried in batter and pierced with an ice-cream stick. Out the back, grease-stained walls were stacked high with boxes of Smith's potato crisps and Schweppes Passiona. I remember being impressed that my cousin Kathy would sit on the counter and take orders from the customers, skipping school to help while her dad blew the shop's profits at the races. She was six.

I think guiltily that Kathy, now in her late twenties, would have passed through Tocumwal today too. She is on her way to Narrandera for the Easter long weekend, taking a nostalgic trip through our childhood. I was supposed to join her; we have been planning it for months. The idea was to walk through Narrandera, starting at the shop, passing each of our former houses, the park and, finally, the train station, where our mothers used to treat us to raspberry icy poles and the chance to see the once-a-day train scream past. Instead, I have ditched her to go to a festival with a couple of Melbourne acquaintances. When I told her, she wasn't happy.

We arrive at the site of the festival, just a few kilometres from Tocumwal, and stop to pay our entry fee. I spot a man with a money belt covering his loins. When he turns around I can see his bare bottom, wrinkling into folds where cheeks meet legs. My eyes travel up to the tattoos lining his arms, the ink crudely applied, the images faded. He takes our money with a smile. 'Welcome to ConFest.'

We drive through a dusty expanse of land, perhaps once a grazing paddock. It is overrun with tents, fire twirlers and more dreadlocks than I've ever seen in one place. The smell of campfires and dope wafts on the warm breeze and makes me queasy. I can't stop the memories of Narrandera flooding in. My aunt looked after us six kids while my mum and our dads worked in the shop. She would make us drink a cup of overheated milk when we arrived each morning. The cartoon characters on the tall, gaily coloured cups seemed to mock me. We weren't allowed to go out and play until we had drunk it all. The smell of burnt milk still makes my stomach turn.

I wonder what cousin Kathy would make of all these unclad bodies. She would give me a look, flick her long hair and turn on her heel: *Cous, what are you doing here?*

But she's not here. Our paths diverged at Tocumwal — mine leading to sagging scrotums, hers to memory lane. I try to shrug off these thoughts. I think of the smorgasbord of adult things I might experience this weekend. Welcome to ConFest indeed.

We find a space overlooking the river and start to set up our tents. We heave the Esky out of the boot. Once we've set up, I go exploring. I sit to the side of the fire twirlers, watching their colourful bellbottoms sway as they move. I watch people swimming nude in the river and wonder if I will be brave enough to peel my layers off in public. Locals ride past on speedboats, calling out, 'Hey, pooftas!' and 'Great tits!' Maybe not just yet.

Back at the campsite, I meet our neighbours. There's Ruth, all soulful eyes and flowing skirts. She's here with her friend George, a tall man eating olives. George looks at me shyly from under his woollen beanie. I can't read his dark eyes behind his glasses, but his gaze lingers for a few moments too long.

To hide my discomfort, I blurt out: 'Are you Greek?' How idiotic. He's from Malta, it turns out. His family came out when he was two. He offers me an olive and asks what brought me to ConFest.

'A friend of a friend invited me. I was supposed to be somewhere else …' *I broke up with a man eight months ago* is what I don't say. *I'm finally getting over it. I am here to have fun. Re-join the world. Swim in the nude. Flirt.*

George wasn't supposed to come either, he tells me. He tagged along with Ruth at the last minute.

In the next half hour, I learn that he lives in Balaclava, near Melbourne's St Kilda. He loves photography. He dances. He makes maps for a living and has a cat called Sydney. I notice his strong chin, his full lips. He is softly spoken and seems a little nervous.

'In Greek, George means "tiller of the soil".'

He laughs. 'I enjoy tilling the soil.'

The olives are finished and there's a lull as our conversation reaches its natural end. I wander off to the massage tent. A volunteer masseuse crudely runs his hands over my body. I notice that nearly all of the volunteers are men and wonder who gets the most out of the service.

Later, George is sitting by his tent. He looks up as I approach, then quickly averts his eyes. I'm confused. How can he be so distant after our earlier conversation? I don't worry about it for too long – there's a flirting workshop on soon.

At night, we sit by the fire. My friend Nick has made a delicious vegetable curry, which we eat with crusty bread and a bottle of wine. The group waxes and wanes as people wander in and out as the night progresses.

'I want to fall in love,' I say wistfully into the fire. I say it despite myself. It seems to bubble out of some deep place and surfaces without my wanting it to.

Ruth laughs. George looks at me silently.

Later that night, George and I follow the sound of drumbeats like kids searching for hidden treasure. We tiptoe around the campsite, edging towards the sounds as they get louder. I look at him – he is crouching like a tiger, listening intently – and I laugh. Here is a man who is even daggier than me. When we find the beats, we dance to tribal African rhythms, drumming up the dust at our feet. Magic crackles in the air.

Over the next few days, I take myself off to singing workshops and meditation. I cower nude in the sauna tent. I immerse myself in mud under moonlight. I swim with only my undies on in the river. I push myself to bare my skin in the interests of 'getting into it', but I can't quite pull off even partial nudity with as much panache as that ageing hippy. The locals screaming insults doesn't help. Part of me understands their point of view – how ridiculous all these feral city folk must seem.

I share meals with a passing parade of new friends. We talk about the important p's: politics and pasta; peace and passion. We converge at the fireside to eat baked beans and porridge and lentil soups cooked in a kettle. Days pass and I find myself getting into a rhythm of simple, sensual pleasures. I sing and eat. I daydream, read and swim.

George goes into town each morning to buy the *Age*, and I watch him leaf through its pages. He has nice hands. Mostly we do different things, but I look forward to seeing him at the daily choir session.

At the end of the long weekend, I seek him out to say goodbye. I am leaving early to get back to work. He hands me a card from Zara's restaurant in Coburg. He has written his phone number on the back.

'I've really enjoyed your company. Would you like to catch up for a coffee back in Melbourne?'

He looks me in the eye. He's nervous and earnest and in my hand is his premeditated act of ink on card.

'Thanks. That would be nice.'

Back in Melbourne that night, I feel lost. I crave the fire, the big sky filled with stars, the company. I call George and leave a message on his answering machine, knowing that he will still be at the festival; I imagine him sitting by the fire.

He rings back the next day. We talk about ConFest, about what a magical time we had and what a grind it is to go back to work. We arrange to meet at Readings bookshop in Carlton in a few days' time. Now I am nervous.

On the day we meet, I wear my Melbourne clothes: my favourite red coat that I bought in Greece, a black skivvy, a short skirt. We make our way to Tiamo for dinner. I find myself talking more than him, divulging intimate details about my life, my thoughts, my fears. He listens generously. He gives me a whimsical children's book, *Song of the Earth: The Magic of Earth, Fire, Water and Air,* as a gift. He tells me shyly that he saw 'two full moons' one night at ConFest – my bare bottom by the river and the full moon in the sky. I feel my face flush.

At the end of the night, he walks me to the Valiant. Before I know it, we are kissing. I feel a hot twist of fear in my belly. I think I'm falling.

George on preserving olives

Equipment
Sterilised glass jar or jars, to store

Ingredients
2 kilograms small fresh olives
1½ cups salt
2 cups vegetable oil
10 cloves garlic
1 handful of whole black peppercorns
Dried oregano to taste
1 small chilli (optional)
1 cup white wine vinegar

Method
Wash the olives and place them in the glass jar(s). Cover with cold water and salt and shake well. When the olives have settled, add 2 tablespoons oil to the top of each jar to make a thin film over the water. Store them in a cool, dark place such as a kitchen cupboard for 1 month, shaking occasionally.

After a month, discard the brine and rinse the olives in fresh water. Return them to the cleaned and sterilised jar(s) along with the garlic, peppercorns, oregano and chilli. Add vinegar and oil, ensuring that the olives are completely covered. Stored in a cool, dark place, they will keep for over a year.

The smitten series

A woman and a horse want a worthy rider

Greek proverb

'Is it possible to fall in love by the third date?' I ask tremulously.

'Oh yes,' he says, his eyes bright.

Noses touching, George and I are sitting on a couch in Fitzroy's Night Cat. There are people dancing, smoking, but they are merely a backdrop to the small drama playing out on the couch. A first kiss. A second date. And now … I am head-over-heels, can't-get-the-smile-off-my–face, floating-off-the-ground in love. It's very inconvenient.

The next day, by email:

Dear Mr Mifsud,
I am writing to inform you that you have committed a serious
misdemeanor of the highest order, which can only be described
as being SMITTEN (adj.): loving, adoring, amoroso,
devoted, fond, tender, erotic … This is a serious crime and

*should be punished accordingly. I thus impose the penalty of
one lunchtime rendezvous with myself, at a time convenient
to both.*
Spiri Tsintziras

Dear Spiri Tsintziras,
*I plead guilty to the offence as stated above. I believe I have
an ongoing problem with this issue of being 'smitten'. To be
honest with you, this problem doesn't seem to be going away.
I can only concur with you that the first step in the corrective
program would be to arrange a lunchtime meeting with you. I
am sorry for my crime, but I can't help it!*
George Mifsud

Of course, I fight it. I am terrified. In the past, I've been
attracted to men who are transient, wild, interesting: penniless
out-of-work actors; waiters who drink well into the night.
There was always a part of me observing, analysing, *distancing*
myself so as not to lose my hard-won independence. Now I've
met a man who is smart, creative, attentive – and very, very
funny. My protective barriers, which I have been building up
for so long, are falling with alarming speed.

My first serious relationship was with a sultry Greek man
on holiday in Melbourne – his name too was George. Next
there was a long-haired George on a motorbike. I tease this
new George that he is not the first George in my life. 'Perhaps
I'll be the last?' he says.

I try to jeopardise the relationship with my 'what ifs' and 'buts' but George refuses to run away. He stands steadfast. He listens. He holds me tight and makes me laugh. Damn it, he *trusts in us.*

So, what is a girl to do but leap into the delicious abyss?

From the Night Cat, it is a whirlwind of dinners and circus performances. Pumpkin soups and coffees in bed. Weekends away and picnics by country roads. Lengthy partings on street corners late at night, when we must finally go back to our respective homes. And afterwards, on the phone:

'I had a lovely time tonight.'

'Me too. Now say goodnight. It's late. And I saw you forty minutes ago.'

'Goodnight, my love.'

'Goodnight.'

'One more thing …'

Three weeks after we meet, George wants to show me the house he has bought in Preston. It's five hundred metres from the rambling, raucous Preston Market, where we pick up tomatoes, crusty bread, dolmathes and plump olives. He doesn't yet have the keys; settlement is weeks away. But we decide to have a picnic in the back yard and face the consequences if we get caught. We are lovers, untouchable.

I bring some herbs from my father's garden as a housewarming gift. I have never planted anything for anyone before. Pulling the herbs out of the ground, shaking the dirt from their roots and replanting them in pots – it feels good. My father watches me, amused and surprised. Perhaps he wonders if his daughter has finally met a man who will be able to tame her.

At George's new home, I water the herbs at the tap beside the house. We spread our picnic blanket on the lawn and eat our little Mediterranean feast. We lie back and dream of all the things we might do to transform the back yard from scraggly lawn to magic garden. The clouds chase one another in the sky, framed by the tan brick walls around us.

The next day, we trade emails that build on the dream, sentimental brick by sentimental brick:

Ah Spiri, my beautiful dancer … A dream … Our garden will flourish and be noisy with boisterous bees and sensual smells as our kitchen will be generous with tall tales and arousing aromas …

Oh George, we have to make a start to all this delightfulness by building our mural – and from its branches will extend all these wonderful things. Today, I daydreamed about our seat, fantasising about ochre colours as a backdrop, perhaps a big pot of aromatic basil. A delightful peasant garden. I daren't even think these fantasies, much less tell you about them, but here we are.

A few weeks later, George's family and friends help him move into the house. I hang back – shifting his things seems too intimate somehow, when I haven't yet met his family – but drop in late in the day. I bring a chocolate cake with a plaque that reads, 'Hello, George's home'. His mother, Dolores, sneaks me a look as we plate it up together. Does she think, *Now here is a woman who will make a warm home with my son?* His father, Alfred, laughs contagiously. He dusts a chair for his wife and lets her sit down first. I can see from the way he touches her shoulder that he is still smitten. We sit on chairs and boxes, eating our chocolate cake from paper plates. George's sister Josephine gives me an encouraging smile. It says *everything is going well.*

I, on the other hand, take months to introduce George to my family. I have rarely spoken to my parents about my relationships. It is understood that the man you bring into the family home is the one you intend to marry. I have only ever brought one boyfriend home before. The next morning, my mother came into my room, crying that I had brought a 'martian' home – he was bald, short and flat-footed – and offering to pay my fare to Greece if I would leave him. When he left me some months later, they could barely contain their delight.

For years, they have proffered single men as suitors: accountants and lawyers and electricians; tall ones, short ones, fat ones – all of them sons of Greek-speaking neighbours and friends. I have always declined to meet them. Now, I am twenty-eight, and my parents have almost given up hope of my ever settling down; I am altogether too outspoken, too outgoing, too independent.

George is confused and hurt by my hesitation to introduce him to them. 'It's not you, it's me,' I assure him. I'm not ready to expose him to their scrutiny. But I desperately want their approval, too. I trust their judgment, harsh as it is. Once again, I feel the push and pull of independence and connection; I want to please yet I want to *do as I damn well please.*

After four months of whirlwind courtship, I finally agree to bring George home. I am terrified. George is nervous. My parents are reserved. Will I be bringing home another martian?

George arrives on the designated day. When my father shakes his hand, I see him glance up at George's receding hairline. I cringe. Everyone in the Tsintziras clan has a spectacularly full head of hair. It's going to be a long afternoon. We sit down to coffee in the formal dining room, where a lace tablecloth has been laid out for the occasion.

'What do you do?' my father asks George.

'I'm a cartographer.'

Dad looks to me for a translation. *Typografos.* He nods. An old, respectable profession. 'And where is your family from?'

'Malta.'

'Malta is very close to Greece.'

They start talking history and geography, and I breathe a sigh of relief. At least Dad won't be asking, 'What are your intentions for my daughter?' before the coffee has had a chance to cool.

My mother doesn't say much as her English is limited, but she watches shrewdly over the rim of her coffee cup. I will no doubt get her full assessment later. Soon, Cousin Kathy arrives with her husband, Terry. They are loud and boisterous for us, breaking the tension. Then the doorbell rings again; it's a neighbour from across the road. Then Cousin George *happens* to be driving past with Mum's sister, Theia Sophia. So much for an intimate meeting of shy suitor and stern father; soon we have a room full of people, all talking at once. George smiles nervously, answers questions, drinks more coffee and eats everything that is offered to him. We hold hands under the table.

Finally, the evening is over. My father seems impressed. George is tall. He has a good government job. And he clearly loves me. I think he has passed the test. Now he can visit whenever he likes. As we spend more and more time together, George even stays the night, sleeping in the single bed in the bungalow in the back garden. I sneak out after everyone has gone to bed, and creep in again before dawn. We maintain the charade for my father's sake, out of respect, although *we* know that *he* knows what's going on. And the emails continue, from George to Spiri:

> *And so*
> *Slowly, slowly*
> *Your story unfolds …*
> *Gently, gently*
> *My story unfolds*
> *And we sit and listen*

As our stories catch up
With one another ...
hold hands,
and embrace.

A few months later, George and I talk of having children. We decide we'd like two. A boy and a girl. We will call them Dolores and Emmanuel, after George's mother and grandfather. When George goes away to map fires in Gippsland, the 'children' write him a letter:

Daddy, come home, we need you. Mummy said you were fighting fires and we got all excited like, but we want you to come home in time to read us a story.

I write their names with a label maker and stick them onto two egg cups. I put these up on a high cupboard. We don't want to tempt fate too much.

How is it possible that a whole year passes? We go to an Italian restaurant, Marchetti's Latin – a Melbourne institution – to celebrate our first anniversary. Its understated elegance and attentive, witty waiters are as far from our first meeting at ConFest as one can get. At the end of the night, I present George with 'The Smitten Series', 150 bound pages of our emails from the past year. Already we have created a past together. We hold hands across the table and gaze at each other, wide-eyed and optimistic about our future.

Baked lima beans
(Spiri to George via email)

Dear George,
The following recipe can be made in the company of lovers and
friends. Two crucial ingredients are the laughter of children and
the strains of Latino music.

Ingredients
250 grams lima beans
1 handful of fresh herbs from the garden (parsley, basil, thyme)
A drizzle of olive oil for frying
A few cloves garlic
1 onion, finely chopped
2 or 3 cups tomato salsa (Spiri can provide passata, made
lovingly)
Salt and pepper to taste

Method
Soak the lima beans overnight in cold water. In the morning,
discard the water, put the beans into a pot and cover them with
cold water. Bring to the boil and simmer until the beans are
tender but not soft. Towards the end, add a teaspoon of salt. Of
course, kiss your lover as the beans boil.

Preheat your oven to 200 °C.

In a frying pan, heat a little oil and sauté the onions, garlic and herbs for a couple of minutes until the kitchen fills with their aroma. Add the salsa and simmer for about 15 minutes.

Strain the lima beans and transfer them to a baking dish. Cover them with the tomato mixture and stir to coat. Bake for about ½ an hour or until the beans are soft (a second opinion may be required here and so Spiri will be available on a consultancy basis. Fees include tender kisses, laughter and maybe a few cuddles as an extra incentive). Serve with crusty bread and good wine.

Love, Spiri

This one is better looking

It's better to lose an eye than to get a bad name

Greek proverb

'She is just like a Maltese girl.'

It's the ultimate compliment from George's Aunt Gracie. Our heads are bent over a tub of marrows. I help scoop the flesh from their insides. We will fill them with a mince-meat mixture and bake them. I try to learn the words for the ingredients we are using. *Aribali*: zucchini. *Qarabagħli mimli*: stuffed marrows. Aunty Gracie loves that I like to cook, that I am curious about the kitchen, about her language. She doesn't speak more than a few words of English, and we communicate with our eyes and our hands. We are in Hamrun, in Malta, where George's mother grew up.

Aunty Gracie's kitchen is no bigger than our bathroom at home, but her generosity is boundless. She has moved out of her bed and into the lounge room to have us stay with her.

Her plush leather couch is covered in plastic, and there are gilt-framed photos of her children and grandchildren all over the house. There are pictures of George and of his father and grandfather.

George hasn't seen his extended family since he was two. His mother's sister Polly has come all the way from England to see us. The whole clan was at the airport when we arrived, ready to hug and kiss us. George is still taking it all in, having grown up knowing only his immediate family in Melbourne. He is disconcerted to discover first cousins who look like him; he meets people who grew up in the same house as his mother and father, and others who remember him as a baby.

Aunty Gracie gives us a guided tour of Hamrun. We visit the church of Saint Gaitano, where George's parents married, and walk past the club where his father played cards. Carmena, an old friend of George's mother, cries when she sees George. She remembers him sitting on the step as a toddler and sobbing when it was time to go to Australia.

George's cousin Charlie makes *fenech* for us: rabbit cooked in a whole bottle of white wine. It is tender, deliciously moist. We wash it down with Cisk, a Maltese beer. Others take us out to lovely restaurants with balconies overlooking the Sea. Everyone is very generous and it's impossible not to be enamoured with this new extended family of George's.

When we're not cooking and eating, we explore the stately capital city of Valetta. George is particularly taken by the expansive Grand Harbour, with its pivotal role in so many battles and historical moments. I'm impressed by its majestic beauty, but am more inclined to wax lyrical about the *kannoli tal-irkotta*, fried pastry tubes filled with ricotta, for sale at the chaotic bus terminal. We take day trips to Mdina and the Blue Grotto and the island of Gozo, where we eat *lampuki* (fish pie), *toumpana* (a baked pasta dish) and countless *hobz biz-zejt* (bread rubbed with tomatoes, drizzled with olive oil and filled with tuna, olives and capers).

We are taken aback at the piles of rubbish; on one of our walks we encounter a dead horse on the path. With 380,000 people crammed onto an island a third of the size of Melbourne, sanitation is a challenge. It gives us a new appreciation of the systems back home.

George and I travel companionably, much to my relief. Perhaps if we can survive a nine-week trip together, we can manage a lifetime.

After farewelling George's relatives, we head to Greece. We barely stop in Athens, but make our way down to Kyparissia to meet Theia Kanella and my grandmother and start our one-month trip around the Peloponnese. I'm nervous about introducing George to the family.

My yiayia, who is now living with Theia, looks up at George and doesn't say much at all when she first meets him. I sense she is a little disappointed. Could it be the thinning hairline?

George goes out to the shops and comes back with a fisherman's cap on his head.

When Yiayia sees it, she exclaims, 'Who's this? Did you get a new man? This one is better looking.'

I translate for George and he laughs. He wears the cap for most of our stay, even inside.

Theia shows us to our double bed; it goes without saying that George and I will be sleeping together. I thank her gratefully; my parents were so concerned about what the family would think of us travelling together, but no one has batted an eyelid.

Theia and I take up where we left off. It's as if I haven't been away.

'You said that next time you came to Greece, you would bring a man with you, and you did. *Bravo.*'

During the day, George and I explore the town and swim in the sea. In the evenings, I cook with Theia. We visit my father's village home, which has been locked up now. Inside, everything has been left as it was, as if someone might return any minute and start living here again. My aunt opens the blue shutters that look out onto the cemetery, letting in some air. When we walk through the village, no one comes out onto the road. We make our way to the graveyard and light a candle for Pappou. I walk past the headstones, noting the familiar names of my relatives: *Vlahos, Tsolodreas, Tsintziras, Flindissis, Kolokotronis.*

On our last day, George and I go to a café in Kyparissia. We are inundated by the smell of cigarettes, the din of soccer finals on TV, the click of dice against a backgammon board. We drink cognac as the rain pelts the muddy potholes in the square outside, shielded by the plastic walls that extend from the café proper. We lean together and kiss, still deliciously smitten.

When we have said our teary goodbyes to my grandmother and aunt, promising to come again, we make our way inland to Kalamata. My cousin Natasha is now married with young children; my mother's sister Pipitasa is living with her other daughter, Smaragdi. Pipitasa invites us to use her empty house in the seaside village of Analipsi and we gratefully accept. Nothing has changed there since Natasha and I sat in the front room some eight years ago. George and I are delighted to have the place to ourselves after spending so much time with family. We don't do much at all: we sleep in until late, read, cook and watch television at night. The people in the village leave us alone.

One night a torrential rain pours down and water comes in under the doors, flooding the floors. The wind howls and the trees outside bend dangerously back and forth. The phones are cut off and we wonder if this is it: perhaps the roof will cave in and we will die here.

My aunt is on the phone the next morning, mortified. How could she have left us on our own? What sort of host is she? What will her sister say? I reassure her that we are fine, that it was all a big adventure. When she comes to check on us the next day, George helps her to prune some branches from the fruit trees. She takes us to her fields, where we collect oranges and potatoes. Although she is nearly seventy, she is still robust, still able to carry buckets on her shoulders after a lifetime of working the fields. She reminds me of my mother in so many ways: her generous laugh, her warm eyes.

We visit Mum's village, Petalidi, together with Pipitasa and Natasha. They open up the house where my maternal grandparents lived. Many things have been left as they were when I visited Mum's brother, Theio Niko, some years ago: there are bottles of ouzo and oil on the table, a dated calendar on the wall. I remember when I met my grandparents on our first trip to Greece, how surely they moved around this home, how vibrant it seemed. So much work went on in these old village houses and now they stand empty. I feel a sense of loss, a dull ache that doesn't go away for days. I think about my mother, about how hard it would be to see her family home devoid of life.

George and I take off on our own, travelling around the Peloponnese for a month. We play noughts and crosses on the paper tablecloth at a railway-station café somewhere between Diakofto and Kalavryta, eating fish and fried potatoes and *horta*. We buy a *candili*, a votive lamp, in the fortified mediaeval town of Monemvasia. We swim in the sea at Nafplion and climb the 999 steps to the castle above. We stop off at Gytheio and eat grilled octopus at a seaside taverna. George basks in the glory of every ruin, every castle, every historical landmark. I bask in the translucent Mediterranean waters, in not having any responsibilities and in being in love. I think back to Cavafy's 'Ithaka' and revel in this journey with George, rejoicing that this is just the beginning.

Gracie's qargha baghli mimli bil-laham (marrow stuffed with meat)

Serves 4

Ingredients
4 large marrows or long zucchini
Olive oil, for frying
1 large onion, diced
1 clove garlic, sliced
500 grams mince meat
1 tablespoon tomato paste
2 eggs
3 tablespoons grated parmesan cheese
1 handful of chopped parsley
Salt and pepper
1 kilogram potatoes, sliced

Method
Cut the tops off the marrows and set them aside. Using a small knife or teaspoon, scoop out the flesh from each marrow and chop it up. Set the marrow skins aside. In a heavy-based pot, heat a little oil and fry the onion and garlic. Add the mince meat and tomato paste and cook until the meat is browned. Add the marrow pulp and cook for a few minutes. Remove from the heat and allow to cool, then add the eggs, cheese, parsley and seasoning.

Preheat the oven to 180°C. Fill the marrow skins with the mince-meat mixture and put the marrow tops back on. Arrange the sliced potatoes in the bottom of a shallow baking dish. Place the stuffed marrows on top and drizzle them with olive oil. Bake for 1 to 1½ hours or until the marrows are browned and cooked through. If they appear too dry, pour a little hot water into the sides of the pan. Season to taste and serve.

PART III
The fruit

Keep Ithaka always in your mind.
Arriving there is what you are destined for.
But do not hurry the journey at all.
Better if it lasts for years,
so you are old by the time you reach the island,
wealthy with all you have gained on the way,
not expecting Ithaka to make you rich.

Ithaka gave you the marvelous journey.
Without her you would not have set out.
She has nothing left to give you now.

And if you find her poor, Ithaka won't have fooled you.
Wise as you will have become, so full of experience,
you will have understood by then what these Ithakas
mean.

Constantine Cavafy

The wedding dance

If you join the dance-circle, you must dance.

Greek proverb

'What makes a successful marriage?' I ask George's mum on her fortieth wedding anniversary.

She answers without hesitating: 'Patience.'

Not long after that, George and I are sitting at the formal dining table, facing my own parents. Our hands are held tightly on the table. 'We're getting married.'

'When?' Dad asks.

'Next year. In February.'

'That's too late.'

I can feel my excitement draining away – as usual, I can't seem to please him.

'Too late for what?'

'You're practically living together. What are you waiting for?'

To do it when we choose.

'We can have a small engagement party if you like in the meantime.'

He seems placated by this. On to the next point of order.

'Where will you get married?'

By this he means, *Will you get married in the Greek Orthodox church?*

At least we're prepared for this one. George and I had this discussion early on: the children would get their names from his side of the family, and we would get married in the Greek church.

'We'd like to go to the church in Red Hill.'

Red Hill is a small bayside village south of Melbourne on the Mornington Peninsula. The grounds of the church are beautiful. There's a big tin shed where they make lamb on the spit. I fantasise about dancing amongst the pines and olive groves that the priest has planted during his long tenure.

'That's too far. What if people get drunk – how will they get home? They might have an accident.'

It takes all my willpower to hold back tears.

'George and I will talk about it.' I get up from the table. This was not the response I was hoping for.

George and I considered getting married while we were overseas, at the church where Dad was baptised, with a feast in the village square afterwards. When we hinted at this plan to our respective parents, they made it clear that they would not come. My parents had not been to Greece since our trip as a family in the '70s. And my soon-to-be in-laws had never been back to Malta. *It's too far. Too hard. And what about our family and friends? Most of them are here.*

Now, we are being asked to compromise again. Part of me wants to rebel. But my parents are, as always, practical. And, in the end, George and I want to make a commitment to each other – the finer details do not matter so much.

We decide to have the ceremony at the Holy Monastery of Axion Esti in Northcote, on the rambling grounds that also house the Little Sisters of the Poor St Joseph's home – a symbolic melding of Orthodox and Catholic faiths, we like to think. I feel drawn to the church rituals that were such a big part of my childhood. I won't feel properly married unless I exchange rings with George and don the *stephana*, two crowns linked together by a ribbon. We have asked Katerina to be the *koumbara*, our maiden of honour, and a long-time friend of George's, Hugo, to be our best man.

I shop with Katerina for wedding dresses. In the fitting rooms, we giggle at the expanses of taffeta and tulle and silk I am offered to try on. I'm wearing the wrong shoes and we have *altogether the wrong attitude*, the shop assistant's glare seems to say. I am horrified by the huge, outrageously expensive gowns. Attending bridal fairs and poring over wedding magazines doesn't interest me in the least. In the end, I head down to a tiny fabric shop on Brunswick's Sydney Road and buy myself a length of fabric whose sheen doesn't hurt my eyes. As a concession to my mother, I order some organza for a veil. I deliver the fabric to a dressmaker, along with instructions for a simple gown. A friend loans me a necklace. George and I breathe a sigh of relief as each wedding task is ticked off our list; now we can go back to making our home in Preston, where we have been living together these past few months.

The day before the wedding, I say goodbye to George and head back to Mum and Dad's house. A group of girlfriends joins me and we paint our nails, give each other massages. Mum brings out an oversized platter of fried eggplant in rich tomato sauce, along with bread and cheese. Dad sits at the head of the table and we dig in. The conversation turns to my decision not to change my surname. My name is part of my identity, my cultural heritage – I've had it my whole life and I don't want to let it go.

'Do you think you will be able to do what you want when you get married? Things will change, Spirithoula,' Dad says.

His warning is sobering. Will I still go out with my girlfriends, still do things I enjoy? I know some things will change, but I tell myself that marriage isn't the same as it was in my parents' day, in the village. I shrug off Dad's polemic and turn to the eggplant, which is rich and almost meaty in its thick sauce. I put slippery pieces of it onto a thick wedge of bread and bite into it. *Take that, Dad.*

Family and friends drop in for cognac and nibbles on the morning of the wedding. We form a circle and dance around the living room in a *kalamtiano*, a folk dance from Kalamata. I start the dance, holding my dress so that it doesn't drag on the ground. Dad takes my hand and looks at me proudly. Afterwards, he takes the lead and does some *fiyoures*, fancy moves: turning and squatting and jumping. He holds the hanky that distinguishes the leader from the followers, and my uncles lift him up. There is a sense of continuity. I have danced this dance with my family since I was a child. It's been around for a long time; my parents danced it in their villages. Dad once told me that Homer, in the *Iliad*, describes similar dances around the spear of Achilles. Here we are in our suburban home, continuing the circle.

I get dressed and then Mum comes into the bedroom; she holds me and cries. Even though I no longer live at home, this is a symbolic parting – her daughter is leaving the family home to start her life as a married woman.

We leave for the church in a convoy, cousins and uncles and friends. At the door of the church, Dad clutches my elbow tightly. He is nervous; the corners of his mouth are turned down.

'Don't worry, Dad. It's going to be alright.'

'Hrrmmmpp.'

We wait for a long time for the signal to go forth. An usher finally comes and apologises: the priest has been caught up in traffic following a funeral at another church. It's another twenty minutes before he arrives, his robes ballooning out behind him. We can start.

I walk slowly up the aisle. George looks strapping in his suit, smiling nervously. I take his hand. The priest starts chanting, wielding the censer filled with incense. Soon, Katerina is given the go-ahead to switch the *stephana* back and forth three times. This represents the joining of two souls, and our commitment to creating our own 'kingdom'. Then the priest leads us around the altar in the dance of Isaiah, which symbolises the eternity of marriage, with no beginning and no end. Before long, we find ourselves signing the paperwork and it's done. I am elated. We made it.

Outside, the music has already begun. My male cousins throw *koufeta*, sugar almonds, which land hard on George's head. Katerina's brother Zois has taken up his *toumbeleki*; his mates yield a clarinet and trumpet. They are playing a traditional song, '*Na eixa ta niata mou thio fores*' – 'If only I could be young twice'. People start dancing. Someone pours whisky and port into tiny plastic cups for a toast. Theia Georgia is handing out *thiples* – thin, sweet pastry, fried and dipped in honey syrup and sprinkled with walnuts. She knows *thiples* are my childhood favourite and has made more than 200 for the wedding. The sun is glorious and the only thing missing from my fantasy village wedding are a few lambs on spits.

Ecstatic, I eat more than my fair share of *thiples*. I don't know it yet, but baby is hungry too.

Chrysoula's eggplant in tomato sauce

Serves 4 to 6

Mum often makes this dish when friends and family gather together, particularly when eggplants are in season. It is rich and comforting – perfect for pre-wedding nerves. It can be served as an appetiser or a side dish.

Ingredients

4 large eggplants
Olive or vegetable oil for frying
2 large onions, diced
1 clove garlic, peeled and sliced
375 millilitres passata or 1 can diced tomatoes
Salt and pepper to taste

Method

Slice the eggplants longways into thick pieces and salt liberally. Set them aside for 30 minutes, then rinse them and pat them dry with kitchen paper. Heat a little oil in a frying pan and fry the eggplant in batches, setting each piece aside to drain once it is golden on the outside and soft in the middle. In a separate pan, fry the onions and garlic for a few minutes, then add the passata. Simmer for 15 minutes or until the liquid has reduced. Add the fried eggplant to the sauce and simmer for 5 minutes. Serve hot or at room temperature.

Growing a watermelon

The hungry bear doesn't dance

Greek proverb

'I need watermelon. Go and buy me some watermelon, George.'

'It's late, Spiri. And it's the middle of winter. Where am I going to find watermelon?'

'I don't care where you get it. Just get it now, *please*.'

George gets up from the movie he is watching and slips out of his flannelette pajamas. He puts on his jeans, a jumper and a jacket, and goes outside to heat up the Camira. It's been raining, and I know there will be water puddled at his feet, where the rain gets in through the rust. We really are going to have to get a newer car; something safe for baby. I feel sorry for George as I wave him off into the night, but a craving is a craving.

He brings me a whole, out-of-season watermelon from Preston's Safeway. I almost berate him for the expense – a good-sized wedge would have been fine – but stop myself. Hormones can only excuse so much. George watches me as I eat like a woman possessed. The watery sweetness sates me, at least for now.

After the first few weeks of pregnancy, when I craved pasta and potato chips – in fact anything high in fat and sugar – my appetite goes. I vomit each morning as soon as I get up, in gutters on the way to work and in the toilets when I get there. Most days, all I'm able to keep down is watermelon and Vegemite toast. The vomiting continues for five months, all day and every day. As my belly grows, a tight drum in front of my body, the rest of me thins out. It's as if the stored fat in my bottom and thighs is finally being put to good use growing baby.

George wants to track the pregnancy with his camera, but every time he suggests a photo, I resist. I'm nauseous and irritable. When I do sit for him, he marks the baby's growth with things we find in the garden: a turnip at twelve weeks; a pomegranate at eighteen weeks; a quince at twenty-four weeks. He tempers my ill mood with patient good humour. Even in my hormonal state, I know I have married the right man.

At times, I imagine I am growing a watermelon, I have eaten so many of them during this pregnancy. But the first scan proves that we are indeed having a baby, with all its fingers and toes. As the foetus moves in a swishing sea of fluid, George and I hold hands, marvelling at what we have created. When baby kicks inside my belly, it's confirmed beyond a shadow of a doubt: I'm growing a life.

As the time for the birth draws closer, our families rally around to offer the things baby will need. Mum and Dad give us money for a cot, and my in-laws for a wardrobe; my brother pays for a sturdy, old-fashioned pram; and my cousin lends us the basinet that both her children slept in.

It's overwhelming what one can purchase for a baby, but our two-bedroom home won't allow for excesses. We clear out the detritus from the spare room and create a nursery. For the first time in my life, I get obsessive about cleaning, sweeping aside cobwebs from corners and dusting every surface.

This is the first grandchild on both sides and all four grandparents-to-be are delighted. One day, after lunch at my in-laws' house, they call us into one of the bedrooms. They present me with a suitcase they brought with them from Malta in the '60s. Inside are tiny singlets, cloth nappies, body suits, hand-knitted booties and woollen jackets, all knitted by an elderly neighbour to my mother-in-law's instructions. There are woollen blankets and a sheet set. Everything is neatly folded and wrapped in tissue paper. The smell of baby soap wafts up. I burst into tears, overwhelmed by their love and generosity.

I am not particularly worried about the birth. I feel my body will do its thing, as women's bodies have been doing for thousands of years. For once, I am grateful for my generous hips. I am keen to give birth with as little intervention as possible, and feel sure I won't need pain relief after dealing with chronic migraines all my life. I am reassured by the fact that my mother reported easy births. We have booked into a hospital birth centre with paisley bedspreads and mood lighting. At our birth classes, we sit on our bean bags and titter at the earnestness of some of the younger participants.

I am more worried about bringing baby home. Will I be able to decipher its cries? Will my maternal instinct kick in? It is barely two years since George and I were nuzzling at the Night Cat; am I ready to be a parent? But we are as ready as we will ever be: the pram is in the hallway, all the tiny clothes have been washed and ironed, and I am unable to sleep for the bulk in front of me. This is a baby we have both wished for and dreamt about, a baby we created together. Soon we will be able to bring the egg cup down from the high cupboard.

Early one morning, I feel water gush down my leg and onto the mattress. I go to the toilet and my undies are drenched. I wake George.

'I think my waters have broken.'

George jumps out of bed, tells me to lie down, checks that everything is in the overnight bag in the hallway and hops into the shower. Within ten minutes, he is ready for action. We ring the hospital.

'Any contractions yet?'

'No.'

'If you don't get any, come in this afternoon and we'll see what's going on.'

The contractions don't come. We go into hospital, clutching our bag. There, the nurses are kind but firm.

'You can do a number of things to bring the contractions on. Walk up and down stairs. Have curry. Go for a walk around the block.'

I get up from the examination table, disappointed. I was hoping my body would do its thing by itself.

Over the next day and a half, we do as we are told, but I only get a few fluttery contractions. We are admitted, and after a few hours, it is suggested I be induced to avoid infection. We are transferred from the birth centre to a grim room downstairs. Gone is my fantasy of massage oils and music. I am strapped to a machine and injected with oxytocin. Within minutes, my contractions start properly, waves of excruciating pain that rocket through my body. I forget to breathe, start to panic. I wonder how long I can take this pain; I pull at the gas mask like a drowning woman, sucking desperately for air.

Before long, George and I get into a rhythm: every time I have a contraction, I breathe and push down, my arms braced firmly around his neck. The pattern is comforting; my body has taken over. George's eyes, his voice, the gas mask are all that matter. The nurse checks in every now and then. She looks at the monitor but doesn't interrupt us. Have I been here minutes or days, I want to know.

'A few hours,' George grimaces as I push down on his shoulders yet again.

Finally, I bellow for the birthing stool; I have the urge to bear down. The nurse comes in, tells me what to do, but I ignore her. *I know what to do*, I want to scream. I crouch down. I feel as if I am standing at the junction between life and death, between darkness and light. As I push down, I call out in pain, in joy; a long primal scream. Our daughter comes out in one slippery gush. I look down to see her land safely in the nurse's arms. Her mucus-covered arms and legs are flailing, the umbilical cord a bloody line still attaching her to my body. She is made of flesh and blood, fattened mostly by watermelon and toast. I am relieved to see that she seems to be a decent weight, and that she is not green and round.

George snips the umbilical cord and the nurse takes the baby while I am led to the bed. I lie down and the nurse brings me our daughter. She places her on my chest and I feel a fierce, tender love. I know beyond a doubt that I would kill to protect this child. The thought both shocks and placates me. I know now what it means to be a mother.

As I deliver the placenta, the nurse hands Dolores to George and I feel a sudden jolt; I don't want to let her go. George looks scared he might drop her, but once he is holding her the look in his eyes is one of pure adoration. I want to enfold the three of us in my arms.

The nurse offers me tea and toast and after six hours of labour, I gratefully accept. She comes back with a mug of sweet black tea and white-bread toast lathered in butter and Vegemite. It is by far the best thing I have ever tasted. Just as I am starting my tea, Dolores starts to howl.

'This is as good a time as any to try breastfeeding,' the nurse says wryly.

I put my tea down on the table, well away from baby, and look at it wistfully. It occurs to me – not without a pang of loss – that from now on, my child's needs will come before my own.

Katerina's watermelon and feta salad

Watermelon sustained me through two pregnancies and is still my very favourite fruit. Katerina had been suggesting for a long time that I try it with feta, which seems an unlikely combination. But the watery sweetness of the melon contrasts beautifully with the creamy saltiness of the feta. The amounts should be 5 parts watermelon (cut in chunks) to 1 part feta (crumbled). For an additional burst of colour and flavour, scatter mint leaves over the top.

265

The king of the beefsteak tomato

The drowning man grips to his own hair

Greek proverb

He holds out a beefsteak tomato, which fills the palm of his hand.

'*Na, vlepeis. Auti einai domata!*' Look at this. Now *this* is a tomato!

He passes the tomato into my hand. It is ruby red and feels heavy. I bring my nose down to it. It smells faintly of earth, and of sweet tomato nectar. The alchemy has happened yet again: a seed has become fruit. Dad complains each year that growing tomatoes is too much work, that he won't bother next year; but the next season rolls around and he plants them again.

He builds little makeshift hothouses from recycled glass and plastic, and places small pots inside. In the garden bed that runs beside the bungalow, he prepares the soil with sheep's manure, digging it in. He makes *aulakia*, ridges, so that the water can soak well into the roots of the plant. When the seedlings have matured, he transplants them from the pots. He watches them grow from the bungalow window, until the view of the garden is overshadowed by the tall vines. Then they bear fruit, and he gives away more tomatoes than he keeps. He now has the luxury of a bigger yard in the middle-class suburb of Kew, no longer a patch of dirt in Collingwood. His tomatoes finally rival those of Vlahos and Tasiopoulos.

Dad turns to three-year-old Dolores, who is sitting on a blanket under the orange tree.

'Look what Pappou grew,' he says. 'A tomato.'

She touches the tomato. He places it in her plump little hands. It's all she can do to hold it up. She looks up with her serious brown eyes.

'I'll wash it and we can eat it.'

He pulls it apart with his fingers and they eat it. Juice runs down Dolores's chin and onto her dress. My mother – her Yiayia – clucks, berates my father, and runs to get a tea towel to place over Dolores's clothes, but it's too late. I laugh. Yet more washing.

When they have finished eating, Dad makes a fist, covers it with his other hand, and snaps his fingers to make a clicking sound. This never fails to elicit a delighted laugh from Dolores. His fingers are stiff now, like those of his mother, but the skin is still smooth, the nails rounded. I suddenly remember his fingers snapping to the music, keeping time to his favourite song at a family celebration; a tune about an overcast Sunday that resembles his heart, which is always cloudy. When the melancholic tune ended, my cousins would pick Dad up onto their shoulders and dance around the room with him, he with a glass of beer in his hand. The challenge was to avoid spilling the contents of the glass. Dad revelled in the attention of his nephews.

I smile at the thought. It's been a long time since we've been to a dance. My cousins and I all have young families now, and our parents are getting a bit too old for dancing – or at least for sitting on people's shoulders.

Dad reaches into his back pocket. He closes both hands into fists and presents them to Dolores.

'*Pou einai I karamella?*' Where's the lolly?

Dolores picks the wrong hand, but he gives her a second chance and she gets it right. Dad tries to lift himself from the blanket. I help him up.

'These bloody knees. They're killing me. I'm going to bed.' He makes his way to the bungalow, where the old single bed George and I shared during our courtship still sits. This is where Dad spends a lot of his time these days, smoking, chatting to neighbours who drop in, and napping. Mum is worried.

'He keeps grumbling about his knees. Some days he can barely walk. And he's stopped drinking.' This last fact shocks her most of all. She's never complained about him not drinking before. Dad always seems to have some ailment or other, and we've already been to the doctor about this. Nothing appears to be wrong.

I nod, but soon my attention is diverted by our son, eighteen-month-old Emmanuel, who tries to waddle down the porch steps and lands on his face.

A few days later, Mum calls an ambulance; Dad can't walk at all.

That night, the kids stay with George and I meet Mum at the hospital. Dad is lying between white sheets and looks a little relieved to be here; finally someone is taking him seriously.

The doctors run a battery of tests over the next few days: knee X-rays and ultrasounds and blood tests. They can't find anything. And yet Dad still can't walk; he's not eating. Mum takes him to the toilet in a wheelchair. The doctors start to look elsewhere in his body: his lungs, his brain. There is a suggestion that his problem might be neurological. I visit as much as I can, trying to catch the elusive doctors.

The days turn into weeks and still, one test after another comes back negative. In the meantime, Dad keeps losing weight. He can't turn his body in the bed; he's in pain. A steady stream of visitors comes to comfort Mum and sit with Dad. They bring fruit from their gardens, chocolates that Dad can't eat. They all say the same things: *Kouragio.* Courage. *Ipomoni.* Patience. *Persastika sou.* May it pass.

Finally, with no clear diagnosis, they decide to transfer him to a rehabilitation hospital. Two orderlies lift him from his bed to a trolley. As the sheet slips away, I notice how thin his legs have become. They look like twigs that might snap in half at any moment.

At the rehabilitation hospital, a doctor makes an initial assessment and calls me into his office.

'I'm very surprised they've sent your father here. He is very ill. He should be in palliative care. He is dying.'

My mouth opens. This is the first time someone has said the word, although it has hung in the air, unspoken, for the past few months.

'Has anyone talked with you about this?'

'No. Oh. I'll have to tell my mum. And my brother. Oh.'

'Yes. I'll organise a transfer back to hospital in the next few days. I'm sorry.'

I stumble out of the room and bump into my godmother in the corridor; she's come to visit Dad. I weep on her shoulder. 'Oh my God. He's dying. How am I going to tell Mum?' She holds me tight, comforts me.

When I tell Mum that afternoon, she bursts into tears.

'We have to get him home. I don't want him to die in hospital. He has to see his garden again. And we mustn't tell him he's dying.'

'Mum, we can't do that. He has to know. Maybe he has something he wants to do, or say …'

'Please, Spirithoula, he mustn't know.'

I try to spend even more time with Dad. I badger him to retell me stories I have heard countless times before. I press him for details, and he is glad to take his mind off his ailing body. He tells me tales of deceit and fun, poverty and resilience, tales drenched in rosy nostalgia: of racing with donkeys down the hills of his small village; of shooting bits of paper at his teachers through his makeshift gun; of being a laconic student with an exercise book in his back pocket and a cigarette in his mouth; of life as a young policeman, his trusty typewriter keeping him company on the rocky outcrops of Rhodes. And when he came to Australia, working in factories; drinking beer at lunchtime at Carlton United Breweries, or joking on the production line at Vickers Ruwolt ammunitions factory. 'Thirty-three jobs, I had,' he says proudly. 'If some boss gave me the shits, I would leave.'

'*Pan metron ariston*.' Everything in moderation. 'That includes work.' He laughs.

One day, I take a deep breath. There are things I must say before he goes.

'Have I done anything to hurt you?' I ask, a lump in my throat.

'Only you know that,' he says. His eyes are clear. They look at me directly.

I'm a little angry. I had been hoping for absolution, a cathartic talk perhaps. But I have to laugh, too. He's telling me that I've got to live with myself, with my own conscience. It doesn't matter what he thinks, what might have happened in the past.

'I'm sorry if I have. I love you, Dad.'

'I love you too.'

One day, I wait in his hospital room while they take him for yet another scan. He nearly chokes when they lie him down. They quickly wheel him back up to the room. His dark eyes look panicked, sunken in their sockets. *Why are they doing all these tests? Is there hope?*

Five and a half months after Dad is admitted to hospital, the doctors call a family meeting. Dad is lifted out of his bed with a harness and put onto a trolley. He is wheeled into the room.

Through a translator, he is told: 'Mr Tsintziras, we've confirmed that you have Motor Neuron Disease. We think the best place for you right now is in a palliative care hospital. They will look after you there, make sure you are not in pain.'

'Is there no cure?'

'I'm afraid not. Your case has progressed very quickly. This is why you have had trouble swallowing in the last few weeks.'

Dad seems resolute, as if he has been waiting for this day for a long time.

'Maybe we could take him home, look after him there … the garden …' Mum says.

'I'm too tired to go home. I want to stay at the hospital.'

Mum starts to cry. It wasn't supposed to go like this. He wasn't supposed to know. My brother blinks, looks lost. The doctor and physiotherapist and social worker look away. Someone shuffles their feet.

Dad doesn't talk about dying to us. He tells my cousin's husband, a policeman, that he wants a policeman's funeral, an acknowledgment of his time in the force all those years ago.

He is transferred to a palliative care hospital. All around him there are thin forms beneath white blankets who mostly sleep. He still manages to click his fingers for Dolores when she visits, and I pass Emmanuel over his bed for a kiss, but otherwise he lies still.

When we are alone, I hold his hands, massaging them. It makes me uncomfortable to hold my father's hands like this – it's so intimate – but I don't know what else to do.

Two weeks later, a room full of family and friends stand around his bed. We have been told his death is imminent. His breath is laboured, strangely reminiscent of my own breath when I was giving birth. The nurses ask us to leave the room briefly so that they can make him more comfortable. I return just in time to see him take his last breath. Just like that, he is gone. I no longer sense him in the room; only his wasted body remains in the bed. I wonder where he has gone, if he is finally home at last.

The hands that created the larger-than-life beefsteak tomatoes lie strangely still on the white sheets. In the dim light of the hospital room, I can almost hear the words of the Greek poet Seferis:

I have seen in the night
the sharp peak of the mountain,
seen the plain beyond flooded
with the light of an invisible moon,
seen, turning my head,
black stones huddled
and my life taut as a chord
beginning and end
the final moment:
my hands.

NIKOS ON GROWING TOMATOES

Nikos Vlahos grew up in the same village as Dad. They raced donkeys together, stole watermelons together and went to school together. And they came to Australia within a short time of each other.

They also shared an aunt, Tasia. Nearly fifty years ago now, Tasia met my mother in a factory where they both worked. Tasia was impressed with the young woman who had recently arrived from Greece. She said to her, 'I have two nephews. One is tall and dark, the other is shorter and fair. Who do you want to meet?'

'I'd like to meet the tall, dark one.' Mum, who is fair and blue-eyed, always coveted olive skin.

Mum went on to meet and marry Dad. As for the fairer lad, the other choice, Nikos, he went on to marry Panayiota, my cousin Tina's mother. Our families are still very close; I was the maid of honour at Tina's wedding and godmother to her daughter Johanna. As I'm no longer able to ask my father for his tips on growing the best tomatoes, Theio Nikos said he would be honoured to step in. He too grows a mean tomato.

You will need
Tomato seedlings
Seedling pots, 5 centimetres in diameter
Potting mix (1 cup per plant)

Mushroom compost (1 handful per plant)
Organic pest-control spray, such as pyrethrum*
Mulch, such as pea straw
Garden twine
2-metre wooden stakes (1 per plant)

*There are homemade alternatives to commercial pesticides.
Mix 2 cups water with ¼ cup oil, a few cloves of garlic, or several
crushed chillies. Strain before using.

Towards the end of spring, when the mornings are no longer frosty, half fill the seedling pots with potting mix. Place one seed into each pot and top with soil. Place in a warm spot (for example, on a sunny windowsill) where there is good air flow. If you wish, you can place them in a small hothouse or rig up a piece of glass on a wooden frame and place the pots underneath. The biggest threat to the plants at this stage is morning frost. Keep the soil moist but do not overwater.

When the plants reach a height of 20 centimetres, prepare a garden bed by digging holes about 15 centimetres deep and 40 centimetres apart. Dig into each hole a handful of mushroom compost and water well. Leave to settle for a day or two.

Remove the seedlings from their pots and plant one in each hole. Fill the hole with dirt then place mulch around the base of each plant to aid with water retention.

Water the seedlings every 2 or 3 days. Once the first small tomatoes appear, the plants need a good soaking every 8 days, or more often if it is very hot. Keep the hose very close to the root and avoid watering the leaves. You can dig little aisles alongside each row of tomatoes and fill them with water if you wish to give the roots a good soaking.

When the plants have reached a height of 30 centimetres, place a stake close to the vine and tie it loosely, so that it still has some room to move but not too much. As the tomato vine grows, continue to stake the plant upwards. Some tomato varieties can grow to more than 3 metres.

After a few weeks, clip the shoots from the bottom of the vine, leaving only 1 or 2 of the upper shoots. This gives the plant a chance to strengthen and increases the chances of the flowers cross-pollinating.

During these early stages of growth, spray the leaves with the organic pest-control spray. This will not eradicate all bugs (you may have to don a pair of garden gloves and pick the larger bugs off) but it will deter them. Cultivating companion plants such as basil and amaranth (see page 289) also helps to keep pests away.

Ideally, pick the tomatoes when they have ripened on the vine. However, you may find that birds or other animals such as possums get to them before you do. In this case, once the fruit start to redden, you can pick them and allow them to ripen at room temperature indoors.

Remember, at the end of the season, leave your best tomato on the vine and allow it to redden. When the plant has dried up, pick this last fruit and save the seeds (see page 41).

The spring garden

The woman who doesn't wish to bake bread,
spends five days sifting the flour

Greek proverb

Emmanuel teeters on a chair, little hands trying to work the latch on the screen door so that it stays wedged open. I resist the urge to say that the flies will come in and help him with his balance instead.

'There,' he says when it's done, expansively gesturing with both arms in a wide arc. 'Now we can see the garden.'

And so we can. The view is uninterrupted by the grey mesh of the flyscreen, by the cobwebs that have collected in the corners over winter, or by the dust and fingerprints that sully the glass.

Emmanuel is proud of his efforts, as if he himself, by some miracle, has conjured up the colours of spring: the lushness of the new pink flowers on the branches of our peach tree; the shocking red stalks of the silverbeet; the bright orange head of a tulip, which sways, as if in coquettish discussion, with a couple of daffodils.

The calendar announced spring a little while back, but I feel as though I have only just woken from a long winter's sleep. I feel my soporific body – plumped with too many roast dinners, chunky casseroles and Tim Tams dipped into hot chocolate – stretch towards the sun. A body sedated by early nights, hot-water bottles, mindless detective novels and the limbs of my husband wrapped around mine. The closed-up house reverberating with children's footsteps as they run up and down the hall, bickering and watching too much television as winter has settled over us like a grey blanket. The ducted heating running almost non-stop, so that the only clean air we breath is in the mad dash to the car each morning. The kids standing over the heating vents to put on their clothes; damp sheets slung over the backs of chairs to dry.

Grief has clung to me since Dad's passing; the initial feeling of being hit in the chest has given way to a cloying sadness. I feel untethered by the loss of Dad's strong presence. I wonder where he is now. One night he comes to me in a dream. We are in a house with many rooms.

'It's good here, Spirithoula. Mama is here. I'm alright.' He touches my hair gently. 'I have to go. They are waiting.'

I speak with Mum, who for the first time really understands that she too will die one day. Both her parents died in Greece – perhaps she subconsciously feels that they are still alive, still tending their gardens. Dad, on the other hand, is most definitely not here. The finality ages her. The ever-growing band of Greek widows in the neighbourhood rally around her,

bearing gifts of fruit and sweets. My brother, Dennis, who lives with her, takes on jobs Dad used to do: he mows the lawn, tries to fix things around the house.

Time doesn't slow down to give my grief the space it needs. There is the relentless march of domestic life and a demanding job. I find myself forever squeezing in another load of washing, mopping another floor, before wearily picking up a novel; eavesdropping on strangers' conversations on the train to work, eyelids drooping with sleep; jostling with humanity at the Saturday markets, a frenzy of boxes and sweaty armpits; the endless churn of dinners and guessing games, school drop-offs and pick-ups, lunch boxes and broken crayons and crumbs and fingerprints; wet tiles at bath time, stories at bedtime, cuddles in the morning. Placating little bodies with their indefatigable frustrations – 'It's not *fair*' sprouting from four-year-old lips.

Today, I see the garden as if for the first time in a long time. Insects buzz around the sage and rosemary bushes. The tag on a young apple tree flicks about in the breeze. The kids are bare-footed, jumping over a fledgling redcurrant bush. Clothes flap on the line and, inexplicably, I can smell chamomile flowers.

The kids find a tub full of forgotten toys in the garage. They pull out a kickboard, an old floaty, sand-encrusted goggles and a few beach toys. They want to have water fights, spray each other with a water gun. After a firm *no*, they discover a shade shelter. George helps them erect it in the garden. Emmanuel bashes the pegs with an old hammer and the job is done.

Dolores brings out a misshapen pram and a dolly that hasn't seen the light of day for a few years. Emmanuel carts out boxes of activity books and a dump truck full of textas. He places his hammer carefully in a little compartment in the shelter and proceeds to work through the books.

'Mum, Lilly's hot,' Dolores complains after a while. 'Maybe she needs ice-cream.' The sun is hitting Lilly the doll full in the face, as well as our two children.

I am reading the weekend papers, all the while thinking that I should be doing something about those cobwebs. But the sun is making me lazy. And magnanimous.

'Go and get Lilly and yourselves some ice-cream,' I call out. 'And maybe you could get me some, too,' I add as an afterthought.

I can think of no better way to celebrate the opening of the double doors onto spring.

CHRYSOULA ON DRYING HERBS

Mum grows and dries her own herbs so that she has them available all year. This air-drying method works well with low-moisture herbs such as Greek oregano, thyme, savory, dill, bay leaves, rosemary and marjoram.

Hose down the herbs in the evening and cut them the following morning. Divide them into handfuls and tie these with garden string. Hang them in the shade where there is good air flow – under a veranda or in a shed is ideal. Or, for small-leafed herbs such as mint and oregano, place the cuttings in a tray and leave them on a windowsill until they dry. This will take around a week, depending on the herb. Check them periodically, as the leaves can get brittle if they are left too long.

When they are dry, put the sprigs in glass jars and store them in a cool, dark place. Alternatively, rub the dried cuttings between your palms and collect the leaves in a bowl. Remove any stalks or woody stems and store the leaves as above.

Where the wild things grow

Hunger fights castles and hunger surrenders castles

Greek proverb

Dolores comes running as soon as I come in the door, bowling me over before I can put my bag down.

'Mama, Mama, look what I brought home. *Mousmoula.* Yiayia taught me how to say it.'

Dolores eagerly holds out a large branch full of plump, orange cumquats. She snaps one off the branch and carefully peels it. She nibbles at the juicy flesh, working her way around it until only the brown seeds and their translucent membrane remain.

Mum is sitting on the couch, her chin dribbling with the juice of the fruit. She looks at me sheepishly.

'Your neighbour, the Italian man down the street, said we could cut off a few branches. He's a very nice man.'

I feel briefly mortified. I imagine Mum complimenting

283

Mario on his cumquats, and him generously offering her the bounty.

While I've been at work, Mum and Dolores have been on one of their walks. I can envisage their trajectory. They might have strolled past the pomegranate tree at the local park to check if it was bearing any fruit, turned into our back lane to see if any of the overhanging trees had edible gifts to offer, and finally made their way past Mario's. My brother would have been watching television in the lounge room with Emmanuel. He is happy to stay safely indoors and avoid these 'village walks', as he calls them.

Mum has always been a forager, ever since she searched for mushrooms and wild snails in the hills near her village in times of poverty. Back then, she would not have taken anything from overhanging trees – the owners didn't look kindly on children taking their fruit, as they would preserve any excess for the winter – but Mum is disturbed that in Australia, many people let the fruit drop and go to waste. Dolores is a most willing accomplice.

I feel a mixture of pride and dismay. I know that the fruit they collect would otherwise go uneaten, and I am glad she is handing down her knowledge to Dolores. But still I feel self-conscious that my mother and daughter are walking our suburban street, foraging for food while I am at work.

All the while, Mum will be talking to Dolores in Greek. Mum keeps reminding me to speak Greek with the children, but I find it difficult. More often than not, I lapse back into

English after only a few minutes. Although Greek was my first language, it is in English that I am most comfortable.

When I was about Dolores's age, I too would set off with Mum. We always took a plastic bag and a knife to pick *horta* from a hillside in Collingwood. As my mother cut the greens on the lower slopes of the hill, she patiently explained why we shouldn't pick them from the flat land, where passing dogs might have urinated on them. I remember her bent back as she cut the greens at the root with a deft sweep of her hand. On the walk back, my thongs slapped the hot bitumen, the plastic bag brimming full.

At home, she would wash and boil the *horta*, draining and then dressing them with olive oil, salt and lemon juice. We often had them with fish and *scordalia*. At other times, we would eat them cold as a salad. Some were bitter, some sweeter, depending on the variety. When I was older, I refused to go with her on these excursions. I imagined my friends looking on and laughing, although I needn't have worried – our suburb was filled with new migrants with equally novel rituals. Gradually, the areas where she could find wild greens disappeared, replaced by freeways and new apartment blocks, and she had to go further afield to suburbs like Epping and Thomastown, blissfully far from my self-conscious gaze.

Now I think what a shame it is that there are very few places to pick *horta*. Mum mostly grows her own now, but insists it is nowhere near as good as the wild ones. I love these bitter greens, but I only have them at her house. I can't imagine my children ever eating them, and the fleeting, sad thought hits me that I may never eat them again after my mother passes on.

My reverie is broken when Mum shows me a pot full of beef casserole, and another of rice.

'The kids are probably full.' She looks away, sheepish. This means they have eaten the potato chips and chocolates she brought with her as treats. 'But I've made this for dinner. Maybe they could have it later.'

'Thank you, Mama. That looks lovely.' I give her a kiss, grateful that I won't have to cook tonight after a big day at work.

'The kids are fine. Dolores said she had a good day at school. And Emmanuel has been playing quietly since he got back from kinder.'

I know she probably wouldn't tell me if they had been badly behaved. I feel the familiar tug of guilt about leaving them with her a few days a week while I work.

She picks up her bag and calls out to my brother.

'Come on, Dennis. Spirithoula's home now. Let's go.'

MARK DYMIOTIS ON WILD GREENS

Mark Dymiotis has been growing fruit and vegetables in his Melbourne garden for over thirty-five years. He is a passionate proponent of the traditional diet of Greece and shares his skills – growing fruit and vegetables, bread making, building wood-fired ovens and wine making – through his writings, and through courses at the Centre for Adult Education. He speaks here about his passion for wild greens.

The Mediterranean diet is based on simple, unrefined, unprocessed and unpackaged food that is 'of the season'. This way of growing and eating food is good for our health and good for the environment. The traditional, everyday Mediterranean diet was mostly made up of locally grown, seasonal food, of which wild greens were an important part. These were a staple of the Greek diet and were collected from fields or grown in gardens.

Some of these are self-sown. In Australia, such greens can be found in untended lots, beside railway lines or even in back yards – purslane, stinging nettle and dandelion, for example. Others can be grown from seed. I sometimes source these seeds from elders who produce fruit and vegetables in their home gardens using traditional methods handed down by family and friends – these people are the master practitioners of Mediterranean cuisine. Some greens, such as chicory, sorrel, radiccio, rocket, endives, mustard greens and beetroot tops, can be bought at markets.

To wash greens, remove any old- or sick-looking leaves and immerse the remaining greens in plenty of water. Change the water until no dirt is left in it. As with mushrooms, it is best not to eat wild greens that you do not recognise, or that grew in a polluted area. With some varieties, only certain parts of the plant can be eaten.

Many of these greens can be added to *hortopita*, a pie made from greens (see page 55 for *spanakopita*). Another way of eating wild greens is simply to cook them in boiling water and dress them with olive oil and lemon juice. They go well with bread, olives or a little cheese. They are high in nutrients and fibre, often rivalling their more 'civilised' sisters such as spinach and silverbeet. They have also been associated with other health benefits, such as the low incidence of cardiovascular disease amongst Greek migrants. What's not to like about wild greens?

Wild Greens: A Whirlwind Tour

Sow thistle (*Sonchus oleraceus*)

Commonly known as *zohos* in Greek, this plant grows everywhere. It is best eaten young, when the shoots are bright green and can easily be snapped by hand from the bush. According to myth, the hero Theseus ate a dish of *zohos* before taking on the bull at Marathon.

Season: Winter through spring

To cook: Boil until tender. Add salt at the end of the cooking process. Drain and dress with lemon juice and olive oil. Also good in pies.

Amaranth (*Amaranthus spp.*)

Commonly known as *vlita* in Greek, this plant generally doesn't grow wild, but you can harvest the seeds from a very mature plant. The young shoots are harvested before the plant flowers. Amaranth is coveted for its sweet flavour.

Season: Summer

To cook: Boil until tender. Amaranth is not often used in pies, except in small quantities.

Stinging nettle (*Urtica dioica*)

Commonly known as *tsouknida*, stinging nettles can grow to three- or four-feet tall. The young leaves are snapped by hand, preferably well before the barbs, which can irritate the skin, have had time to develop. Nettles grow wild, often in untended lots, or may appear in gardens where they were left to seed the year before.

Season: Winter

To cook: Nettles are beautiful in pies. They can also be boiled with other greens or used as a tea.

Mallow (*Malva parviflora*)

Commonly known as *moloha* ('to soften'), the young shoots of this plant can be eaten, as can the immature seed pods.

Mallow is considered a common weed and grows widely in neglected lots and gardens. The ancient Greeks used the leaves as a substitute for grape leaves for making *dolmathes*.

Season: Winter

To cook: Sauté with olive oil, garlic and chilli to lift the flavour; include in salads; or add to soups as a thickener.

Purslane (*Portulaca oleracea*)

Commonly known as *glistrida* or *andrakles*. The young leaves or shoots are used in salads – for example, combined with tomato and cucumber. They have a succulent texture and peppery taste.

Season: Summer

To cook: Use raw in salads or sauté lightly, dress with lemon juice and olive oil and serve as a side dish.

Fennel (*Foeniculum vulgare*)

Commonly known as *marathos*. The fronds of the fennel are used as a flavour enhancer.

Season: Winter and early spring

To cook: Use small amounts as an aromatic in pies, or to flavour fish.

Dandelions (*Taraxacum officinale*)

Commonly known as *radiccia* or *agriohorta*. The roots, leaves and buds of this plant are all edible. Cut the dandelions just below the base.

Season: Winter

To cook: Boil as for thistle or *amaranthos*, or sauté with olive oil.

Cat's ear or flat weed (*Hypochaeris radicata*)

Cat's ear is similar in appearance to dandelions and is even more widespread. These hairy leaves can be found in pastures and lawns, and along roadsides. Cut them just below the base.

Season: Winter

To cook: Boil, then dress with olive oil and lemon juice.

Chicory (*Cichorium intybus*)

Chicory plants grow along roadsides and fields and look similar to dandelions. They have blue (or sometimes pink or white) flowers. The leaves are eaten before the plant flowers.

Season: Early spring

To cook: Boil, then dress with olive oil and lemon juice. The roots can be used as a tea.

For more information about wild greens and the Mediterranean diet, see www.markdymiotis.com.

A very helpful booklet about identifying edible weeds is Doris Pozzi's *Edible Weeds and Garden Plants of Melbourne.* Or, check out the many foraging sites online.

The forest sighs

The uphill road is followed by a downhill road

Greek proverb

'We need to have a trip without a map,' Katerina says. 'I'll ask George to look after the kids. Let's book in a date.'

It's not quite Coober Pedy, but it's still an adventure. We'll follow our noses, see where we end up. It captures *something* of the women we were ten years ago. Admittedly, our escapades have been more sedate of late: Udon soups in Brunswick, sitting cross-legged on red cushions on the floor; bowls of *phó* in Preston, our elbows vying for space amongst the functional containers of chilli, soy sauce and chop sticks; reception-hall dinners at each of Katerina's siblings' weddings.

Katerina pulls me away from the family for our monthly dinners out, where we speak Greek the whole night, reveling in words picked up on the streets of Athens and Salonika, hamming up our accents and making up words when we're not quite sure of the real one. She keeps abreast of Greek music events, often inviting our family along. Whenever 'our' song comes on – 'Enteka', Eleven – Katerina and I get up to dance to its lyrical rhythms. We are still Thelma and Louise, just a little older, a little tamer.

We never did get back to Cooper Pedy. I have the children to think of now, George and our home; I can't just take off on a whim. As for Katerina, it's not easy to get away on long trips either; there's her neurotic cat, Spicy, who doesn't like to be left alone, a mortgage, and the small problem of the cancers that keep coming back.

'I've been diagnosed with a rare, aggressive lymphoma – more common in older African men than young women of Greek heritage,' Katerina quipped when she first found out a few years back. Her finely tuned sense of irony is still her greatest asset. 'At least now I might lose some weight.'

But it hasn't all been jokes and laughter. For the past few years her cancer has been like a shadow, following her wherever she goes. The treatments are relentless: chemotherapy, bone marrow transplants, blood transfusions. There are conversations about low blood counts, diarrhea and exhaustion. Her long, curly hair falls out in tufts onto her pillow; there are tears over the phone, and then the subdued chatter of family and friends as we gather in her back yard under moonlight and help her shave it off.

Today, I happily leave the street directory on the bench top, strewn amongst school notices, bills and the morning's breakfast dishes. I place guilty kisses on George's lips and the children's heads before heading off, giddy with anticipation.

We let the car guide us, heading roughly northeast. We leave the suburbs behind and the landscape gets hillier, the air fresher with the smell of pines and gums. We stop at a small shop selling crafts and Devonshire teas, where we finger purple crystals and dusty postcards. We debate whether it's too early for scones. Yes, it is, but the smell is too delicious to resist so we buy some to eat later.

'There's a rainforest about 200 metres down the road,' says the woman at the counter when we ask her what we might do locally.

We make our way along a muddy track to the forest floor and sit on a wet seat.

'It would be nice to meditate here,' Katerina says.

'I'll try not to fidget.' I'm not good at meditating.

'Just let the thoughts flit in and then out of your head, like we learnt at the Ian Gawler workshop.'

I close my eyes.

What will the next stop be? Will we be home by dark? I shouldn't have left the chops out to defrost … it's turning out to be a warm day …

The noises of the forest gradually drown out the incessant clatter of my thoughts. I hear the chirp of rosellas, the drip of moisture somewhere far away, the rustle of huge gums as their leaves stretch up to the sunshine, the wet foliage underfoot shifting and moving. It's as if the forest floor is sighing, resigning itself to the relentless activity.

As the moisture from the mossy seat on which we sit seeps into my pants, the fog in my head begins to clear. I feel Katerina shift next to me as she makes herself more comfortable, her eyes closed too. I feel my breath slow and move down lower into my abdomen.

I am transported back to the memory of another seat, dry and hard, its legs embedded in baked red soil. Even now, I can almost feel the warm desert sand as it tickles between my toes. That self seems eons away in space and time; we were unencumbered then, sleeping in strange men's caves and blissfully unaware of what lay ahead.

The forest breathes and sighs, breathes and sighs.

I wriggle, uncomfortable with the moisture on my skin. I wait for Katerina to open her eyes. When she does, we shift easily back into conversation.

'It's hard to place the sounds of the forest – where they're coming from at any given moment,' I say, disconcerted.

'I like that. It reminds you that there are some things you can't control.'

'Yes, but there are some things we can control. Like my bum getting wet. Should we head back to the car?'

We walk back slowly. Inside the car, our conversation moves to more serious terrain. The lymphoma has come back. The prognosis is not good; Katerina's doctors are saying that palliative treatment for controlling the pain is the only option left.

'Spiri, I'm not ready to die. I will miss seeing my nieces and nephews and godchildren grow up, my friends and family ...'

It feels like we are talking about someone else. A sense of unreality pervades the conversation. Katerina presses on.

'I'm scared about what comes after, about not being here … will people remember me five or ten years from now?'

'Of course we'll remember you, you dill. How can you doubt it?'

We talk about things she wants to do, now that time is limited. Collate her poems and blog entries. Write letters to her nephews and godchildren. Update her will. Perhaps even organise a small fundraiser for the Leukemia Foundation – to give back to those who have helped her.

The car leads us to a small winery looking down onto a hill of grapevines. We order a ploughman's lunch of creamy blue cheese, prosciutto, crusty bread and impossibly small tomatoes that look like grapes. I have a glass of wine and a coffee to finish. The smell of the coffee makes Katerina feel sick; I drink it quickly, guiltily.

We continue the conversation as if we hadn't left off.

'When I *do* die, I'd like you to call a few people to let them know. I have made a list.' She dips into her bag and hands over a piece of paper.

I look down at the vines. The dark green and brown patterns are comforting in their simple, symmetrical beauty. It's unimaginable, Katerina not being alive. It's surreal to think about telling her friends, telling our children, that she has passed away. *Died. Gone to heaven,* perhaps. I'm not sure I'll be able to find the words. Katerina looks at me.

'I know it's hard. And, who knows, it might not happen for a long time. But I just feel I need to be prepared.'

On the way home, we stop at a deserted roadside stall and buy some lemons, leaving our money in a tin. We move away from the sticky terrain of life and death as we leave the countryside, and slip back into comfortable banter. Little roads feed into bigger ones lined with massive homewares stores and hardware barns, service stations and takeaway food chains, marking the way home.

At the door, the kids jump on us as if we have been away for a month. There are toys and books strewn on the floor and they've turned the kitchen table into a cubby house. George has put the chops into the fridge. I kiss him gratefully.

Katerina sinks into the couch, tired from the day's adventures. The kids clamber onto her lap, nestle into her bosom. She plays word games with them and listens to their stories. I take out the scones, lather them in jam and butter and put the kettle on.

Tina's scones

Makes 14 scones

Tina Tasiopoulos is a school counsellor and scone connoisseur.
She is also the mother of my goddaughter, Fransene. Whenever
our families go away together, Tina is attracted to every little
Devonshire teahouse and country fair. She always asks them for
their scone recipe, and has consequently tried making scones
with everything from butter to beer. She assures me these are
the fluffiest and tastiest.

Ingredients
3½ cups self-raising flour
75 grams caster sugar
200 millilitres cream
250 millilitres milk
A pinch of salt

Method
Preheat the oven to 180°C.

Sift the flour. Mix all the ingredients together in a large bowl
until the dough is light and fluffy. Do not over-mix. Place the
dough on a lightly floured board and gently flatten it with your
fingers or a rolling pin until it is about 3 centimetres thick. Cut
out the scones using a scone cutter, clean glass or biscuit cutter.
Arrange them on a baking tray 2 centimetres apart.

Brush each scone with milk. Bake for 15 to 20 minutes. Enjoy
with jam and cream.

The Arrival

Age brings experience, and a good mind wisdom
Greek proverb

A s we approach the island, I remember …

Keep Ithaka always on your mind
Arriving there is what you are destined for …

It is now the eve of my fortieth birthday. It has taken me this long to reach Ithaka's shores. I feel overcome with emotion and relief. We are finally here.

Except it is not Ithaka we are approaching, but the nearby island of Kefalonia. The ferry docks, slowly unloading its cargo, and we realise we have got the wrong island.

My husband laughs at my mistake. I too am amused. I remind myself that Cavafy was speaking metaphorically. I check my high expectations, protecting myself from disappointment – but Cavafy has already been here too: *If you find her poor, Ithaka won't have fooled you …*

When we finally approach Ithaka, she stands before us like a beast jutting out of a sullen sea, her 800-metre tip nestled in dark rain clouds, mist clinging to her sides. I think of a line in Arnold Zable's book *The Sea of Many Returns*: 'Ithaka. I cannot recall the first time I heard the word. It has always been there like an ancient longing welling up from the sea.' I imagine Zable penning that line as the ferry approached Ithaka's shores, the physical reality of the island converging with a more primal longing. His need, like that of many before him, to capture the idea of Ithaka in words, to immortalise it on the page.

The ferry pulls in at the small harbour of Pissoaetos – the 'eagle at the back'. We find a taxi and the driver, Theodoris, immediately asks where we are from. Once this might have raised my hackles, but now the question makes me feel at home. I have been asked the same thing my whole life in Australia: by other Greek-Australians wanting to know which part of Greece my parents were from, and by Anglo-Australians wanting to know my origins on hearing my name. It's a question that seeks to place and define.

I tell Theodoris we live in Australia, that my family is originally from the Peloponnese and my husband's family is from Malta. He tells us he has travelled all over the world with the navy, but has regrettably never visited Australia. He reaches into the glove box and pulls out a tourist brochure with a kangaroo on the cover – he really would love to visit.

We cross the island, passing moody cypress forests glistening with rain. We round Vathy Bay and wind our way up the

mountain to our accommodation, the Odyssey Apartments —
what else? Theodoris hands us his card: if we need anything —
anything at all — please to give him a call.

The view from our apartment takes my breath away.
The dark mountain opposite the bay, a sprinkling of houses
dotting its side, is framed in the doorway. Fishing boats bob
in the water below. Even though it is still drizzling, we put
our luggage down and sit on the balcony. I breathe deeply, and
the stress of travel — of catching early-morning ferries and late-
night planes, being delayed by strikes in Athens and carting
luggage through grimy port towns — dissipates.

At times in the past four weeks, I have felt like one of the
harried wooden puppets we saw in a Sicilian museum. The
challenges of travelling with children are fresh in my mind:
sheltering in a wind-blown restaurant in Malta, just off the
plane, jet-lagged and cold; lost in the rough-looking streets
of Catania, my heart beating fast and the children's hands
clutched tightly in mine; tussling with George about who will
piggy-back Emmanuel when he refused to walk any further.
Without the structures and routines of home, we have had to
learn anew to be a family. Now, I sit on the balcony and put it
all behind us. We have finally arrived.

The next morning, I can hear George and the kids blowing
up balloons in the room next door. I pretend to be asleep,
feigning surprise when they bring me coffee and cake in bed.
Once the kids have delivered their birthday blessings, they

quickly want to know how soon they can use the pool. Would I like to come with them, since it *is* my birthday?

I watch them splash about in the freezing pool, the first we have come across so far in our travels. Not for the first time, I wonder whether we should have planned a more sedate holiday – Surfer's Paradise or Fiji, the sort of trip I hankered for when I was a child. Instead, we have made them traipse around Europe, meeting relatives, exploring our family history, visiting enough ruins to tire even the keenest archeologist.

While they are swimming, I go for a walk to get supplies. I make my way along a *monopati*, a small path down the mountain. It is lined with fig and olive trees; their roots twist into the earth. Sage and fennel bushes blow in the breeze. Fat grasshoppers and bumblebees fly above bright green lizards. Everything is glistening, larger than life, bombarding my senses and filling me with joy. I am finally here, and I am not disappointed.

At the end of the path, steps lead down to a tavern that juts out into the sea. It is called the Paliocaravo – the old ship. Fishermen untangle their nets nearby and yachts with English and Australian flags are moored in the port. After the pollution and din of Athens, I had nearly forgotten that such places still exist in Greece.

Young guns on mopeds zip across the main road that rounds the port, while old men drink coffee in waterside cafés and women cart food back home. I bump into the owner of our apartment, who recommends the best places to shop for food and offers me a lift back up the hill when I am finished.

Later, we head to the taverna for lunch. We are welcomed into the dark interior and choose *barbounakia*, red mullets, and *yopes*, minnows, which are whisked off to be cooked. The kids add chips and calamari and I order *horta*. George and I toast our arrival with *retsina*. When the food arrives, the kids loyally pronounce that the chips are not as nice as Yiayia's, but manage to finish them regardless. The fish has a perfectly crisp golden skin; the flesh in the middle is white and moist. We sit for hours as the children play at the water's edge. We drink too much, just as Odysseus did on arriving at the shores of his homeland after his long absence: *When they had poured libations to the blessed gods, they drank the wine as sweet as honey – just as much as each one willed.*

The next day, I join a walking tour led by a stout Dutch guide, Ester, who has lived here for years. We start at the north side of Vathy Bay, walking past vineyards and olive groves. We soon leave the smart homes that line the port and climb the mountain, where the landscape is lush with spring growth. We pass a field of yellow asphodel flowers, their fleshy stalks bending in the wind. Ester explains that in Greek legend, the asphodel is one of the most famous of the plants connected with the underworld. Homer describes them covering the great meadow, the haunt of the dead: *The disembodied spirits of common dead dwell, in the field of these fragrant pale yellow flowers, weeping, wandering around like phantoms, being confused like dreams.* The ancient Greeks planted asphodels near graves, as it was thought they were the favourite food of the dead.

Further up the mountain, the ground is littered with collapsed stone fences. Outside one rundown house, a large dog is tethered to a stake and growls at us as we pass. Finally, we reach a one-room chapel, its whiteness a stark contrast to the grey detritus surrounding it. We sit on benches outside and eat our packed lunches, our backs against the chapel's cool walls. Someone starts talking about metaphysics and the existence of God. We debate the issue, our English and German and Australian accents mingling against the ancient landscape. The sun beats down on us as we make our way back to the town. We have met no one in the four-hour walk. Back at the bay, we rest in an expensive café and I look at my feet. They are not clad in stout boots like the rest of the tourists. I order my drink in Greek. My parents were born not far from here. But still, I too am a mere tourist in Ithaka. I try to ignore the stares of the locals as we speak loudly in English.

Over the next few days, we are lulled into a soporific rhythm. We swim each day at a secluded back beach; we eat at the taverna. I feel like we are being seduced by the goddess Circe, who fed Odysseus's men to keep them from returning home: *On thrones she seated them, and lounging chairs, while she prepared a meal of cheese and barley and amber honey mixed with Pramnian wine.*

For the first time on this holiday, there is no pressure to go anywhere, to see anything in particular – no ruins or relatives, museums or markets.

By the fifth day, we snap out of our stupor and decide to see a bit more of the island before we have to leave. I ring

Theodoris the taxi driver. He quotes us a price for a personal tour of the island.

The taxi ride is like a potted lesson in the history of Greek-Australian migration. Did we know that since the late 1800s, more Ithakans have migrated to Australia than live in Ithaka now? He points to houses belonging to expatriates who return year after year to the island, in some cases third and fourth generation Australians.

He takes us to an outdoor folk museum set up by the late Stathis Raftopoulos, who emigrated from Ithaka to Australia in the 1930s but returned to the island many times. The display includes olive and wheat presses, towering obelisks and statues. A small plaque states that the museum is dedicated to 'the memory of past generations who for a thousand years cultivated the soil of Ithaka, to remain here until the end of time'.

'The island bewitches you,' Theodoris says matter-of-factly as we twist and turn along steep roads to isolated monasteries and windswept bell towers. We stop at a *cafeneion* and go inside to borrow the key to an old church next door. The elderly café owner asks where we are from. Theodoris offers to shout us a coffee and a treat for the kids. I am reminded of the Greek word *filotimo*, which translates loosely as honour, generosity, pride. Theodoris is doing all he can to show us his love of his island home, and of those who have left its shores.

A few days later, we embark on the next leg of our journey, visiting my family in the south of Greece. When we say goodbye to the owners of our apartment, they give us a metal cast of Odysseus's boat, decorated with ribbons and beads. Down at the tavern, the owner invites us in for syrupy baklava and tells us to look up her sister, who lives near my aunty in the Peloponnese.

On the last day, Theodoris drives us and our luggage down to the port in the early hours of the morning. He waves away our offer to pay him. I hand him our contact details back home and say, 'If you come to visit Australia, look us up if you need anything. Anything at all.'

Taverna-style fried fish

Serves 4

Ingredients

1 kilogram small fish, such as whiting or sardines, and/or squid
3 cups plain flour
1 teaspoon salt or to taste
2 cups olive or vegetable oil for frying

Method

Clean the fish by slitting the underside of each and running a finger along the spine to remove the innards. Remove the scales by running a sharp knife against the sides of each fish, working from tail to head. This is best done outside, as it is a messy business.

Prepare the squid by holding the body firmly with one hand and pulling off the intestines and the cartilage that run down its length. Discard these. Cut the tentacles off (retain them) and discard the head. Peel or scrape the mottled skin back from the body of the squid and discard it. Pull away the flaps on the side of the body and slice these thinly. Slice the body lengthwise into 'rings'. Rinse the fish and squid pieces and pat them dry with a paper towel.

Combine the flour and salt in a deep bowl or clean plastic bag. Toss the fish and squid in the flour mixture and shake off any excess.

Heat the oil in a frying pan; if you are using both fish and squid, use separate pans for each, as the squid will cook more quickly than the fish. When the oil is very hot, fry the fish and/or squid in batches until they are golden. Between batches, add extra oil if required. Serve with thick wedges of lemon, a garden salad and Chrysoula's *tyganites patates* (page 64).

Stathi's souvlaki

The house is small, but the heart is big

Greek proverb

Theia Kanella won't hear of us staying in a hotel.

'Remember when you stayed with us when you were little? Your father got so angry at all the racket the kids were making that he threw a mattress down the stairs?' she says fondly. 'They were good times.'

I remember the stairs, and my dark, skinny cousins, but not the mattress coming down at us. My three boy cousins were like a pack of wild animals and they teased my delicate brother mercilessly. Now, they are men in their forties. Stathi lives with my aunty and works down the street, managing a cavernous two-dollar shop. Dionysios has divorced from his Swiss wife and he is also staying with my aunty while he builds his own home. His three children stay with him every weekend.

I can hear Emmanuel fighting over the PlayStation with Dionysios's son Odysseas in the other room. Emmanuel speaks hardly any Greek and Odysseas hardly any English, but somehow they manage to negotiate a solution. Emmanuel is picking up Greek words with amazing speed, no doubt out of self-preservation. *Thelo* – 'I want'. *Thiko mou* – 'mine'.

George has gone with Dionysios to buy meat for a barbecue, perched on the back of Dionysios's motorbike. He has no helmet; as they pulled off, I could see the trepidation in his eyes. Stathi is already outside in the tiny rectangle of yard, tending to the fire. He happily dons an apron and waves an Australiana tea towel my mother once sent him under my nose, laughing.

My aunty is now seventy-one. She looks weary. At this age, she didn't expect to have her two grown sons still living with her. Her son's divorce was a big blow. She is also worried about the diving economy and how it is affecting Stathi's business.

'Oh well, Spirithoula *mou*, we'll survive – we've been through worse than this. Greeks are survivors. We still manage to have a good time.'

George and Dionysios finally come back with the meat and a dozen bottles of beer.

George grins and whispers to me, 'We went up the mountain to see the land where Dionysios will build his new house. I was holding the meat in one hand and the beer with the other. We'd had a few beers at the *cafeneion* beforehand. It was fun, but I'm glad to be back here in one piece.'

I'm glad too. My cousins seem as wild as I remember them, despite the middle-aged spread around their tummies and the fact that Dionysios is now the father of three children.

My aunty and I prepare the souvlaki meat and cut a salad. Stathis brandishes his tongs and cooks it all up. A few friends of Stathis drop in and we sit around the kitchen table, picking at the food and talking about the state of the economy. The situation is getting dire in Greece. As they talk about the broader political and economic forces at play, I have very little to contribute; my Greek is nowhere near good enough to keep up. George, even more at a loss, just knuckles down and has another souvlaki.

After lunch, we gather bathers, towels, goggles and floating devices. Stathis arranges four plastic garden chairs in the back of his work van and the kids pile in.

'Hold on to the rail and don't let go,' he tells them sternly.

I would never allow this in Melbourne, but we're in Greece and it would seem prudish to put up a fight. As I close the van door, the scent of dope wafts out. Did Stathis sneak a joint earlier, as well as the beers over lunch? The beach is two kilometres down the road. I pray silently that everyone will be safe. George and I hop into Stathi's sports car, along with Dionysis and his eldest son, Achilleas. The car is a reminder of more affluent times; there are no buyers for such things now.

At the beach, my cousins tumble through the surf with the children, showing them how to dive into the clear waters. Stathis would have made a nurturing father, I think. He is smart, generous and articulate. I am fond of this charming cousin of mine. Before long, he whips out a bag of souvlaki wrapped in foil and we dig in yet again.

I swim out much deeper than I ever would in Australia. The waters are still and I can see the bottom even at a depth of eight or nine metres. I let go of my conscious mind and focus on the sensation of salt on skin, of water and sun, of my limbs floating without effort.

When the kids are back on the sand, their bodies limp with exhaustion, Stathi suggests we visit the tiny chapel of Saint Yioryios, up behind the town's mediaeval castle. The kids and their garish, oversized floaties are crammed back into the van and we set off up the hill on an unsealed road. Halfway up, I look back and see the van stopped on the side of the road, smoke billowing up from behind it. We pull over and walk back down to see what's wrong.

'I think there's too much strain on the engine. I'll give it a rest and try again in a little while.' Stathis doesn't seem too concerned. The kids are having a great time in the back, delighted by the novelty of it all.

Eventually, the van starts up again and we reach the little chapel behind the castle, set amongst olives groves. The township spreads out below us. We light a candle, take a photograph, finish the rest of the souvlaki and make our way down the hill again. Finally, we arrive at my aunt's house, salt-encrusted, sandy, but still alive. I breathe a sigh of relief. Saint Yioryios must be looking over us.

Stathi's souvlaki

Here is Cousin Stathis's insider advice – a treatise of sorts – on how to make the perfect souvlaki.

The skewer

Souvlaki literally means 'little skewer'. Anything that can be skewered can be turned into souvlaki: pork, beef, lamb, kid goat or fish. Various vegetables can also be used: carrots, potatoes, peppers, fennel, eggplant, artichokes or zucchini. Simply remember that the pieces must all be approximately the same size, so that they cook evenly.

The marinade

For the best flavour, marinate your meat in the fridge for at least 12 hours. The marinade I make for all meats has a base of olive oil, crushed garlic and finely chopped spring onion. I don't add salt or pepper at this stage, as salt saps the meat of moisture and pepper interacts with the olive oil and gives a flavour to the meat that is not at all pleasing. Certainly you can add any fresh herbs that you like – rosemary, thyme, savory or oregano, for example – but they are best fresh, not dried. Lemon, salt and pepper can be added once the meat has been cooked and removed from the fire.

In Greece we say *'Peri orexeos kolokithokorfathes.'* This ancient Greek saying literally means, 'When it comes to taste, anything goes, even eating the zucchini plant tops.' You can add to the marinade whatever you or your invited guests like.

Fish is best with a light marinade of olive oil and lemon, added 10 minutes before you grill it. Saltwater fish has very sensitive flesh. It doesn't like too much moisture once it has been removed from its natural environment.

For vegetables, I use a marinade of olive oil, balsamic vinegar, freshly grated tomato and sugar (1 tablespoon of sugar for each litre of marinade). Marinate your vegetables at least 2 hours before cooking.

The barbecue

The barbecue should be placed in a spot protected from the wind. To this end, it helps to have an enclosed barbecue, and one that you can move around. The taste of food cooked over wood cannot be beaten. Avoid using wood that has that white stickiness to it, such as eucalyptus or any other wood that has a resin that makes your hands sticky.

The salad

The salad that accompanies souvlaki should include whatever you and your guests desire. Personally, I prefer a Greek salad of sliced tomato, sliced onion, fresh parsley, *tzatziki* (yoghurt and cucumber dip with garlic – but not too much garlic) and paprika.

The pita

Pita is a companion to souvlaki. The bready taste of pita – be it Greek, Arabic, Indian, American or Russian – makes for a more filling souvlaki. Ready-made, frozen varieties of pita are full of preservatives and indifference. If you can't make your own pita, a few hunks of freshly baked bread (see page 75) will do nicely.

The secret

Finally, there are two simple ingredients that are present in every Greek recipe: love and instinct. When you include these ingredients in your dish, it will not only be tasty, but also *hilionostimo* – a thousand times tasty.

Psaria, freska psaria!

If you cannot catch a fish, do not blame the sea

Greek proverb

'*Psaria, psaria, freska psaria!*' Fish, fish, fresh fish!

The boats are coming in. They circle the small bay and drop their catch off near the makeshift stalls on the foreshore.

'They're not bringing much in today,' Mum's cousin Theia Magda whispers as she inspects the calamari, small fry and a few *yopes* that have just been laid out onto blue plastic sheets. It's early, but already it is hot and the flies are out.

'Let's go and buy the bread and we can come back later. Maybe by then another boat will have come in.'

We've been in Mum's village for four days now, and this daily morning walk with Theia Magda is fast becoming my favourite part of the day.

Many other women are out picking up supplies for the day's meals. In the *fourno*, the bakery, the baker piles crusty loaves from wicker baskets onto the shelves. The smell almost

316

makes me faint with desire, just as it did all those years ago from my grandmother's oven down the road.

At the greengrocer, we fill a paper bag with brown lentils. My aunt eyes the tomatoes. They are too ripe for a salad, but they are perfect for the lentil soup. As I know my kids won't eat lentils ('Spirithoula, you've got to teach them; my grandkids *love* lentil soup!'), I go into the butcher's to pick up some mince for a Bolognese sauce. There is a whole lamb and what looks like a young goat strung up from the rafters, and an animal spread out on a cutting bench behind the counter. The butcher cuts pieces from the carcasses to order. I notice that people ask for small portions; each customer walks away with a petite package or two. Meat is so much more expensive than in Australia. There are a dozen women in the small shop, greeting one another and gossiping. I daresay there won't be much meat left by mid-morning.

Should I just ask for *kimas*, mince, or will I need to specify from which part of the animal? My aunt is suddenly by my side and after a few quick words in Greek, my package is handed over the counter.

We walk around the foreshore, past the *vrissi*, the tap spurting fresh water from a deep well, and past Theia's *patriko spiti*, her father's home, where she grew up. As we walk, she reminisces about the good times she had in that house. It's a two-storey *archondiko*, one of the stately old houses on the water, and once had a café out the front. I never thought of my mother's village as having a middle class before, but Theia Magda's family would

317

have been described thus. Her father worked in the United States and returned to Petalidi with enough money to send his three daughters overseas to study, at a time when educating girls was unheard of. He taught himself French, practising new words in a notebook every day. Theia Magda has a masters in education and speaks a quaint, formal English, also rare for a Greek woman in her seventies. But still, she had to work in the fields as a child. She fondly remembers working alongside my mother, laughing and singing. Her own laughter is contagious, loud and musical. In my mind's eye, I can see Magda and Mum giggling together. I have never met anyone quite like Magda – she is a delicious combination of city civility and village earthiness.

We wind around the big house and enter the one behind it, where Magda now lives during the summer. On the TV inside, Tom and Jerry race across the screen, babbling in dubbed Greek. The kids eye the fresh bread and George cuts them a few thick wedges, which he drizzles with olive oil and oregano. My aunt and I put away our shopping and prepare the lentil soup and Bolognese sauce. Finally, I put on a pot of Turkish coffee and mix in a spoonful of tahini, a habit my aunt remembers from the Depression; she has now got me adding the nutritious sesame seed paste to the thick brew.

Today we plan to visit Mum's old home. I have been avoiding this, for fear of the state it will be in.

'It's a shame, Spirithoula *mou*, what's happened to the home. It's falling down. I've tried to ring your uncle, but he never picks up his phone.'

I too have tried to contact my uncle, but on the one occasion he did pick up, he hung up on me. I was trying for my mother's sake, but I am proud for her sake, too. I don't plan to ring him again.

We walk up the hill to the old house. A friend of Theia Magda's, who is lame in one leg from a childhood disease, limps along beside us. We help her with her shopping. Her goat trails behind us, bell clanging. The kids are delighted; they've never walked a goat before. We wave goodbye when we reach her home and keep going up the hill. Magda tells me her friend looks after her bedridden father, who is now in his nineties.

The front courtyard of my mother's old home is covered with debris and weeds. We pull them away from the doorway to get in. I put the big metal key into the keyhole. After much tugging and pulling, the door finally opens.

Inside, it is dark and cool. There is dirt all over the floor and fallen plaster on the faded nylon bedspreads. I step down into the kitchen. The table is covered in rubbish: a Raki bottle; a packet of flour eaten through by mice. An old calendar shows the year 1993, just a couple of years after I visited my uncle and his girls here. One wall has collapsed outwards; I can see a patch of yard through the gaping hole. In the bedroom, a black woollen coat hangs on the wall and I recognise it as one my mother sent to my grandmother many years ago. I recall my grandmother tending the wood-fired oven, my grandfather in the garden drying grapes, and I ache for them. My aunty looks at me sadly, as if she were to blame for the wreckage.

'Perhaps the will is hidden somewhere here? Maybe we should look?' Her big brown eyes dance. She really wants to see this home belong to someone, to see it brought back to life. But my grandfather died in the early 1980s. It was rumoured he made a will, but no one could find it. Surely my uncle has searched here already?

Still, we have nothing to lose. We look under lumpy mattresses, in cupboards and musty suitcases. I find old clothes ruined by mould, newspapers dating back to the '80s, a thin gold ring tucked inside a black wallet. As we hunt, I feel a pang of guilt; it feels like we are disturbing something we shouldn't. When we don't find the will, I am disappointed but not surprised.

We lock up and go back to Magda's house. For lunch we eat silky lentil soup with tomato, carrots and celery. We pick at olives and feta and wipe our plates clean with the bread. The kids eat spaghetti. My aunty berates me good naturedly for giving them too many choices. And she tells me again that I must make more of an effort to teach them Greek. I shrug. *I know, I know.*

After lunch, we go upstairs to have a siesta. There is no breeze. An electric mosquito zapper *pzzts* intermittently. The kids read and I close my eyes; sleep does not come, but it's nice to be still.

In the afternoon, I tell Magda I'm going back to Yiayia's house to clean up.

'I feel I need to do it, for my grandmother.'

I buy a hardy broom and industrial garbage bags from the hardware shop. On my way back to the house, I can hear voices from the porches I pass, feel eyes following me up the street.

I start with the weeds out the front, filling a black garbage bag to the top. I am interrupted by a neighbour, my mother's cousin, Theio Panagioti.

'*Spirithoula, esi eisai?*' Spirithoula, is that you?

'Yes, Theio. We're here with my husband and two kids, staying with Theia Magda. It's nice to see you again. I've come to clean up.'

'What a shame the house has come to this. It was so lovely when we were kids. Now, I'll expect you and your family and Magda will come for a meal before you leave, yes? My girls and wife would love to see you.'

'Yes, Theio, thank you.'

Mum often tells me stories about her cousins next door, of the good times she had here growing up. She will be pleased I have seen Panagioti.

Inside, I collect all the musty clothes, the newspapers and anything else that has no value, monetary or sentimental. Into the bag it all goes. One by one, black bags pile up by the front door. I daren't go into the kitchen for fear that the stone roof will collapse on me, but I clear every other room of debris. I sweep the floors, tidy the beds and arrange the scattered chairs. Finally, I salvage what hand-woven mats I can, shake them onto the road and lay them out on the floors. I leave the black coat hanging where it is. It has taken a few hours, but I feel my grandmother would be pleased.

George, Magda and the kids come up the hill to check on me. They are back from a swim in the sea. I ask George to take photos so that my mother can see her old home. No doubt she will be upset, but I feel a pressing need to record this for posterity; who knows what will be here the next time we visit?

Magda's fakes (lentil soup)

Serves 6

Ingredients

3 cups brown lentils
1 cup olive oil
1 bay leaf
1 sprig rosemary
2 medium carrots, sliced
2 sticks celery
750 grams fresh tomato pulp, or 1 can diced tomatoes
4 or 5 cloves garlic, finely sliced
1 brown onion, finely sliced
Salt and pepper to taste

Method

Wash the lentils in cold water and discard any that float to the top. Place the lentils in a large, heavy pot with 2 litres of water and turn on the heat. When the water comes to the boil, skim the surface of the frothy grey scum that comes up. Add the oil, herbs, carrots and celery. Cook on a low heat until the lentils and vegetables are nearly soft. Add the tomato, salt and pepper, and cook for a further 20 minutes.

Psarosoupa

In the cauldron of pain, everyone gets their share

Greek proverb

Since our forest adventure five years ago, it has been a rollercoaster of hope and disappointment for Katerina: the unexpected offer of a trial treatment that kept the cancer under control for a few more years; periods of low immunity and hospital stays, followed by surprising comebacks. She manages to claw through each day, mostly keeping the black dog at bay. Rumi and Paulo Coelho and Kahlil Gibran help. So does her priest, who lets her ask the hard spiritual questions that plague her. She sees her counsellor, Felicity, regularly.

'I'd love to meet this Felicity one day. She sounds lovely,' I say.

'Probably you'll get to when I ...' She lets the sentence trail off. We both know what she means.

Not only has Katerina ticked off everything on her list since our trip without a map; she has also organised annual fundraisers for the organisations that have helped her. And she has stubbornly reminded all of her friends and family to keep it real, to be present, to enjoy every day. To me she says, 'Keep writing, Spiri. Don't worry too much about the mortgage. Have regular massages; you deserve them. Floss your teeth – it's more important than brushing.'

'If you had only five days to live, what would you do?' she asks me one day.

I think for a while. *I would spend time with family and friends. Hold my husband and children close. Write letters to those I love. Cook and eat. Read. Write. Swim in the sea.* Now that I work from home, writing for a living just as I've always wanted and spending time with my family, there is not a great deal more to yearn for.

'Probably the sort of things I'm doing now,' I say. 'I don't have a pressing need to do anything differently.'

She looks at me quizzically. 'Not many people I know are doing exactly what they want.'

I've lost track of how many times we've talked about death since that day in the forest. *Death is a part of life. We have to face it. If we bring ourselves to talk about death, we can live a better life.* These are her mottos, and she feels them keenly.

'If I reach my fortieth year,' Katerina says, 'I will celebrate with a massive party. A bit like the wedding I never had.' She smiles wickedly.

It seems like an impossible goal but, amazingly, after a terrible prognosis in her early thirties, the day comes. We gather to eat and drink in her honour, dressed in extravagant hats. She is the shining star of the show, our very own 'Kat in the Hat'. The food is generous, the mood festive. The children win prizes for the best hats and slide across the dance floor. As we toast Katerina, I think back to that day in the forest and how far she has come. She is positively glowing, and I think to myself that those phone calls to announce her passing might still be a way off.

A year later, Katerina invites me for a weekend away in a fancy house on the water. She insists on paying: *What else am I going to do with my money? I'm not going to take it with me.* We luxuriate in the decadence of it all – huge glass windows overlooking a moody sea, gleaming open spaces, a glimmering heated pool. We swim and lie on deck chairs, talking non-stop and laughing and crying and singing as the mood takes us.

In the state-of-the-art kitchen I cook salmon on a bed of bok choi and a bastardised version of *phở*. Katerina delights; she hasn't eaten this much in weeks. She is back on chemotherapy and I joke tentatively that, with luck, we will have a vomit-free weekend. *We.* As if I am in control of this too – a cooperative effort to keep the contents of Katerina's stomach down.

I eat so much more than Katerina does. I pick furtively between meals: handfuls of nuts and chips and sultanas. It's an anxious eating, to fill up the silences when Katerina sleeps. It's as though I am stocking up – for what, I wonder.

We have a Scrabble marathon, putting all our energy into it. I cheat by looking at Katerina's letters; we both refer to the guide for two-letter inspiration; and we tease each other mercilessly – about how competitive we are, about how cancer isn't an excuse for playing badly – trying to distract each other. When the game finishes, late at night, we sit back exhausted on the oversized couch. We talk about everything, as we always have. About my concern that my kids don't eat enough vegies. About the spots in Katerina's lung that have shown up in the latest scan, and the three-centimetre growths in her liver.

In the morning, I whip around and tidy up – pack away the Scrabble game, wash the dishes, wipe down the bench. I tidy with a nervous energy. The many windows of the house let in the early morning light, and the clean, modern surfaces disarm me – I prefer the rustic surfaces at home, the peeling plaster walls and the well-loved kitchen table.

It's during the quiet of the morning, while Katerina sleeps until the sun is high, that I realise how much energy I have, and how little she has. How much harder it is for her to get up, to carry herself up stairs, even to swim; her muscles hurt, her breath is short. I wipe around the big bag of medicines she has brought with her – drugs for pain, for nausea, for constipation, drugs that contra-indicate one another and set one another off – and I wonder when it will end. After eight years of treatments and fatigue and nausea, Katerina tells me her body is tired. She wonders when she will say 'no' to more treatment. I imagine how hard that will be. I sit there, feeling helpless, not wanting the moment to come but knowing that it must.

The sea beyond the balcony is still — I look closer and see tiny ripples glistening in the morning light. I worry that Katerina won't wake up, what I would do if this were to happen. I try to avoid the dawning realisation that this is probably our last trip together. The reality of it is suddenly too close. I know, intellectually, what it means that the cancer is now in Katerina's liver, that she has diabetes, that her appetite is waning. But a part of me refuses to accept it.

A few weeks later, I visit Katerina at her parents' home and watch as she takes a few sips of a chicken broth her mother has made for her before pushing the bowl away. The look of pain on her mother's face – *she won't eat; she has to eat to get better* – but Katerina is no longer hungry at all.

Soon after, we have a picnic on the grounds of Heide, an artists' colony turned gallery in Melbourne's east. Katerina doesn't touch the gourmet takeaway goodies. Dolores has brought a tape recorder and 'interviews' Katerina, who tells us how much we mean to her and what her favourite colour is.

We go for a walk through the picturesque gardens; walking down a grassy slope, George and I support Katerina's weight.

'Could this be it, Spiri?' she asks.

'You won't even let me feed you,' I say with a wry smile. 'That can't be good.'

She gives me a long, pained look. We don't have to speak.

One week later, we sit around Katerina's bed in hospital. Alex, her brother, brings a pomegranate from his garden, and we share it in the common room where we keep vigil. We rub ice on Katerina's dry lips, hold her head up to open her airways, helping her gently along on her way. I make phone calls in the lobby – a few of Katerina's friends, her counsellor, her music therapist – letting them know that if they want to come and see her, they should do it very soon.

Today, many people important to Katerina are here – her parents, siblings, aunts and uncles, cousins and dear friends. We know one another more intimately after our vigil of the past few days. We share stories about Katerina: how she inspired us, her pithy mottos. Everyone is here but Katerina. Her absence is like an ache, jagged, too painful to touch.

I concentrate instead on the large snapper on the stainless steel platter in the middle of the table. Steaming bowls of fish soup are lined up beside it like an expectant orchestra facing their conductor. It's almost a shame to ruin the symmetry of it, but the soup's maker, Theia Evangelia, presses us to *faye, faye,* eat, eat.

There is nowhere to sit in the room filled with black-clad bodies. I hold the bowl in my hand and eat standing up. The broth is rich, the flavours simple and clean. The soup warms me, sating a deeper need for consolation. I suddenly realise how tired I am. The soup brings me back to myself, grounds me. I concentrate on the taste, on the sensation as it trickles down my throat. I scoop up the vegetables and rice, plump with fish stock, from the bottom. There is other food on the table, but this is all I need.

I expect Katerina to come in any minute and say wickedly, 'Just tricking.' But she doesn't.

Theia Evangelia's psarosoupa (fish soup)

Serves 6 to 8

Evangelia is Katerina's maternal aunty. A short time after Katerina passed away, Evangelia invited me to her home to show me how to make this *psarosoupa*. We cooked and ate together. Some hours later I left, laden with homemade bread, an oversized tub of soup, a bag of garden greens and a few homegrown peaches, my stomach and my spirit sated.

Ingredients
3 litres vegetable stock
2 large potatoes, peeled and quartered
3 medium carrots, peeled and quartered lengthwise
2 onions, peeled and quartered
2 celery sticks, trimmed and cut into 8 pieces
1 tomato, quartered
1 lemon, peeled and quartered
½ small bunch continental parsley, chopped
¼ cup olive oil
1 teaspoon salt
Pepper to taste

1 kilogram bony fish such as gurnard, salmon, trout, snapper,
flathead, whiting, Murray cod or Australian herring. A mixture of
bones, head and flesh is best, although you can also use a whole
fish. Wash the fish, sprinkle it with salt and place it in the fridge.
¾ cup medium-grain rice
1 extra lemon, to serve

Method

In a large pot, combine the stock and all the ingredients except
for the fish, the rice and the second lemon. Simmer on moderate
heat until the vegetables are soft, then remove them with a
slotted spoon and set them aside. Place the fish (including any
bones, heads, et cetera) into the stock. When the fish starts to
come off the bone (in approximately 20 minutes, depending
on the size of the pieces), it is cooked. Remove it with a slotted
spoon and set it aside.

Strain the stock through a fine sieve, then return it to the pot
and put it back on the heat. Add the rice and cook until it is soft
(approximately 15 minutes).

If you are using a whole fish, place it on a serving platter. If
you're using fish pieces, flake the meat off the bones and place it
in a serving dish. Arrange the vegetables around the fish. Serve
the stock and rice in soup bowls, with wedges of lemon on the
side. Each person can add vegetables, fish and lemon juice to
their bowl as per their preference.

The festival of the queue

Even if you are a priest, get in line

Greek proverb

The queue for souvlaki is twenty people deep. The people at the back look to those in front of them for information.

'Can I pay for the souvlaki here?'

'You need to buy a ticket first. Then you line up.'

'What's the wait? Haven't they got any left?'

'They've run out of cooked meat. It'll be another twenty minutes.'

The queue for *loukoumades,* plump fried honey doughnuts, is nearly as long. Dozens of us wait outside a window that looks into a kitchen. We can see the soft dough being fried up, tantalisingly close. The *loukoumades* are taken out of the fryer, drained in a colander, tossed in honey syrup, sprinkled with cinnamon and put into paper bags. These arrive to us one bag at a time. We hold out our hands, our tickets, our money.

We remind me of photos I have seen of the starving masses, queuing for bread during the depression years. But we aren't starving. All around the grounds are picnic tables laden with food and drink: Greek salads and bread; feta cheese and olives; wine and cordial; dips and desserts. But the elusive souvlaki and *loukoumades* are worth waiting for. Everything is *tis oras*, of the moment, made to order. The meat was carved off the spit a second ago, the salads freshly cut, the pitas cooked and kept warm in deep basins.

Those who already have their souvlakis are sitting around under the olive trees. Most groups are made up of three generations. A grandparent near us runs around, trying to feed morsels of souvlaki to a two-year-old who has better things to do than eat. I'm here with Mum, and it is just the two of us. We are at the Festival of the Grape at the Holy Monastery of Panagia Kamariani in Red Hill. I've brought her away for a weekend of pampering. It's the first time we've ever been away, just me and her. It is novel to have her all to myself, with no neighbours or friends or phone calls vying for her attention. Mum keeps trying to pay for things, and keeps wondering how George and the kids are faring back in Melbourne. Now that I see bigger family groups together, I wish they were here too.

The grounds of the monastery are packed and the priest, Reverend Elefterios, looks proud to have gathered us all to his metaphorical table. He has cultivated the land here for three decades, tending the olive trees and beehives and a thriving chook yard. We could well be in Greece except for the swaying gumtrees. In his sermon earlier this morning, he told us that the Festival of the Grape was observed by his own father, also a priest, back in Greece, always during August, at the height of the grape season. Mum and I stood up the back as he spoke; Mum and some other women took it in turns to sit on the few available seats. Most sat down slowly, painfully.

The Greeks left their country poor and worked hard, Reverend Elefterios said, and should be proud of what they have achieved. He too arrived poor, with just the shirt on his back. Murmurs of recognition rippled through the church. People nodded. *Yes, me too, me too.*

After the service, the priest leads the congregation outside and we gather in front of a tent piled high with boxes of grapes. He chants, blessing the grapes. He invites us each to come and get a small bag of grapes to eat or take home. An usher tries to get everyone to line up in single file, but the queue is three deep and chaotic.

'Please line up. In a row,' the usher implores to no avail.

I have to laugh. Some cultural habits are so ingrained, they'll never change.

Now, when I finally make it to the head of the doughnut queue and get back to Mum with my hard-earnt *loukoumades*, she looks concerned.

'I was getting worried. You took so long.'

'The queues were huge.'

'They're starting the grape pressing.'

A crowd has gathered. The priest stands beside what looks like a sandpit and calls all the children to come forward.

'Who's going to be the first to start pressing the grapes?' the priest calls out, voice booming.

A little boy volunteers.

'You were the first last year. Now give someone else a turn,' the priest teases. 'Come on, boys and girls, come on, don't be shy.'

Dozens of children step up, as do their parents and grandparents, cameras at the ready. The kids take off their shoes and the priest throws the first batch of grapes into the pit. The children squeal with delight and step onto the juicy lobes. Box after box of grapes goes in. The kids slip and slide and the priest is delighted. This is the new generation, and he does his best to make sure they are having fun.

Finally the crowd disperses and the ushers take the grapes away. Mum has enjoyed the spectacle, but is a little perturbed that the grapes and the juice are likely to be discarded.

'They should use it to make wine. Why are they throwing it away?'

'No one has washed their feet, Mum. And I guess it would have been too dangerous to put the grapes into a sack and have the kids climb on top of it.' I don't know the words for 'public liability' in Greek.

Mum isn't convinced. 'In our village, we didn't worry too much about washing our feet.'

I shrug. Things have changed.

Mum gets up painfully from her chair – her knees are giving her grief. 'Let's go home. George and the kids will be waiting.'

'I'm sure they're having a good time without us.'

'Still, you need to go back to your family.'

We pack up our things, grab the bag of leftover *loukoumades* to take home and slowly make our way to the car to join the long line that snakes its way out of the grounds.

Chrysoula's loukoumades
(Greek doughnuts in honey syrup)

Makes 20 to 30 small doughnuts

Ingredients

Doughnut mixture
2 tablespoons white vinegar
1 tablespoon sugar
½ teaspoon salt
2 teaspoons dried yeast
4 cups lukewarm water
4½ cups self-raising flour
5 cups vegetable oil for frying

Syrup
1½ cups honey
½ cup water
Peel from half a lemon

Garnish
Cinnamon
1 cup crushed walnuts (optional)

Method

To make the doughnut mixture, combine the vinegar, sugar, salt, yeast and water in a bowl and mix well. Add the flour and mix well. Cover with cling wrap and a folded blanket and place the bowl in a warm spot for about 1 hour, or until the dough has doubled in size.

To make the syrup, place the honey, water and lemon peel in a saucepan. Bring to a slow boil and cook for 10 minutes.

Heat the vegetable oil until it is very hot. Using a wet spoon, drop one ball of dough at a time into the pan until you have 6 or 7 doughnuts. Agitate with a slotted spoon to cook evenly, and take them out once they have turned a golden-brown colour. Set them aside to drain on a tray. Continue this process until the mixture has all been cooked. Dunk each doughnut in the syrup, arrange on a serving dish and sprinkle with cinnamon and/or crushed walnuts if desired.

Laying down bricks and mortar

Everything in its time and mackerel in August

Greek proverb

When I see the cement truck parked out the front of our house, I know my dream of a village oven is dead. The sentiment is village – but the construction is most definitely city.

George has been mumbling about formwork and besser bricks and rebars in his sleep. He is on a first-name basis with the staff at our local hardware store. I was worried the project might be getting out of control, but the cement truck confirms it beyond a doubt.

'They didn't have cement trucks in the village, George. This is going to be the most over-engineered oven in the Southern Hemisphere.'

'Well, the slab has to be solid enough to hold the oven.'

'How big is this oven going to be?'

'Big enough to bake eight loaves at a time, a few pizzas and a roast. But maybe not all at once. When we fire it up, it's got to be worthwhile.'

I have to admit, I am excited. 'Maybe we can have a once-a-month firing at our house, book our family and friends in. We'll let the neighbours know – they can bring food to put in it too.'

'I hope it works.' His brow furrows. He's in deep now.

I hope so too. This is turning out to be a much more expensive project than we envisioned – cement trucks don't come cheap. Not to mention the space the oven is going to take up in the yard. What with the garden beds, the clothesline, the barbecue, four bikes and the trampoline, our suburban yard is looking very congested.

George's friend Joseph knocked on the door at 7.30 this morning, just before the cement truck arrived.

'Sorry I'm late – I slept in. No, we can have coffee later. Let's get to work.'

Joseph's family is from Lebanon. In his mother's village, every house had a wood-fired oven. He too is a cartographer, but has also run his own tiling business in the past. He knows a thing or two about concrete. My husband gets his level and his T-square out. He is worried that the wooden frame has buckled with the recent heat, but his friend shrugs. It should be right.

My husband carts the concrete in his new red wheelbarrow and Joseph spreads it out. By 8.30 they are done. We have a shiny grey concrete slab in the middle of the yard. When it dries a little, George will smooth it over and neaten the edges.

'It looks so beautiful,' I proffer. 'Maybe we should just keep the slab and not build the oven on top of it. Perhaps it could be a dance floor.'

The men laugh. Joseph says he has never heard a concrete slab called 'beautiful' before. But they quickly turn their attention back to besser bricks, the best way to cut them in half, and how to hold up the second cement slab that will go on top of the stand. Clearly it is time for me to go inside.

Later that evening, the kids admire the slab. It's too late to initial it – the concrete has already set – but they are excited about mosaiking the oven once it's ready.

'I think a sun would be good,' Dolores says. 'Perhaps on top of the dome, with rays coming down the sides.'

'I love that idea. But you would need to look at it from the top to get the full effect. What about if the entrance of the oven represents the sun, and the rays come off that? Maybe in mirror tiles – lots of gold and burnt orange ...'

George has other ideas. A map. A Maltese fishing boat. A portrait of our family. All in little bitty tiles. Dolores and I roll our eyes.

'Maybe let us project-manage the mosaiking,' I say. 'We'll need a name for the oven. What about Helios? That's Greek for sun.'

We all agree that this is a fitting name. But we're a long way off from accessorising. George's friend Zeki comes to help pour concrete between the besser bricks to stabilise the base. Zeki, an engineer, is originally from Ankara in Turkey. Afterwards, over a lunch of frittata, olives, tomatoes, feta, bread and some leftover okra stew, Zeki suggests we place a time capsule in one of the hollow bricks in the base of the oven.

'Like the ruins at Petra or Pompeii,' pipes up ten-year-old Emmanuel.

In coming weeks, we schedule blocks of time between work and family commitments to finish building the oven. George scribbles constantly in his notebook. One morning, as I am preparing lunch boxes, his brow furrows.

'I don't think it's going to be ready by Easter, Spiri. Perhaps by the first day of winter?'

That afternoon, I consult Mum. 'How long did the wood-fired ovens in the village take to build?'

'Oh, about a day. There was a man in our village who built them. He made them with branches. He'd bend them into the shape of a dome, then pack rocks and mud around them. I think it was done by the end of the day.' We laugh. They didn't have hardware stores or Gantt charts in Mum's day, but their ovens managed to stay up for generations.

Despite George's worries and the mirth of our friends about how long it's taking, I have no doubt that the oven will work – so much thought and careful engineering has gone into it. I respect that George has done it slowly, thoroughly. My mother-in-law's words come back to me. A successful partnership is based on patience.

GEORGE ON BUILDING
A WOOD-FIRED OVEN

In countries like Italy and Greece, the skills to build wood-fired ovens would have been passed down from person to person. In Australia, it's not part of our heritage, so those of us who want to build one generally have to draw on books, courses and online forums.

I enrolled in a one-day course to build a wood-fired oven run by a Cypriot-Australian baker, Mark Dymiotis. But kids came along and I just kept putting it off. Then my father-in-law got seriously ill and so I postponed doing it. That was nine years ago.

There are many books out there about building wood-fired ovens. It can be a bit overwhelming choosing a design. After doing a lot of reading, I decided that I wanted an oven that heated up quickly, cooled down slowly, and wouldn't collapse. I also wanted my favourite baking dish to fit into the entrance of the oven.

If the oven or its door is too small, dishes won't fit into it. If it's too big, it will take a long time to heat up. Your choice of design will depend on what type, and the amount, of food you want to cook. I wanted to fit eight bread loaves into a single firing, so I decided on a 90-centimetre diameter. When fired, the oven should stay hot for a day or more, and so that you can stagger the cooking process.

One of the books I sourced was *The Bread Builders: Hearth Loaves and Masonry Ovens* by Alan Scott and Daniel

Wing. It is very comprehensive, particularly when it comes to the history of ovens, how to build a barrel-style vault oven, and how to make sourdough bread. Vault ovens are rectangular and ideal for baking bread.

There are many books out there on building clay ovens, too. These are cheaper and quicker to build. You can use materials from the back yard, but these ovens can crack and need to be rebuilt every few years.

In the end, I decided to build a dome-style oven. This is the traditional type of oven you find in Italy. It heats up quickly, is self-standing, burns fuel efficiently, and holds its heat for a long time. It also heats more evenly, as (unlike in vault ovens) there are no pockets of cooler air in the corners. There are thousands of dome-style ovens in Italy. More than thirty such ovens have been uncovered in Pompeii. If it's good enough for the Romans, it's good enough for me.

I found free online instructions on how to build an authentic Italian wood-burning oven from a company called Forno Bravo, based in California. You can download a very comprehensive guide that outlines each step – from building the slab to completing the oven enclosure – as well as a good materials list. They also have great tips on firing and cooking in the oven.

Forno Bravo also has a huge user forum, which is like a global village of oven builders. Here you can share your experiences and frustrations. The forum is good if you have a problem and you want to know how to resolve it. However, sometimes there is a little too much information, and of course different opinions, so it can be a bit daunting. Many people put forward their own designs and their own ideas. For me, it was best to stick to one set of instructions.

I underestimated the time it would take to build the oven. If you're working full time and have kids as we do, you might only be able to do it on the weekends. I would allow six months if this is the case.

You can buy kits with all the materials to build the hearth and dome, or you can buy the materials separately. If I were to do it again, I would buy materials from one place rather than trek across the suburbs to different suppliers, hunting for the cheapest supplies. Our oven will end up costing around A$2500. I know that in villages they would have used found materials, clay and rocks for example, and it would have cost a fraction of that, if anything at all. This oven is a long way from those found in the village.

Through this process, I've learnt that you need some basic skills in carpentry, engineering, concreting, tiling, masonry, bricklaying and insulating in order to build a wood oven. As a qualified cartographer, I have none of these skills. But, I do know about straight lines, angles and measurements. I also know how to wield a level and a T-square. The challenge, but also the joy, has been in developing skills I didn't have. Some of these I learnt by reading, some by asking and most through doing. I took pride in completing many things myself. In order to do things like lay the concrete properly, I got help from mates who knew more than I did. Working with friends isn't just about the skills; it's about bonding, having a bit of fun, sharing the experience.

I walk past the oven-in-process in the mornings. I admire the dew over the freshly laid concrete, the lemon verbena casting a little shadow over it, and it makes me smile. The kids stir me about how much work I've put into the oven, how long it's taking, but that's part of the fun too. People at work have teased and encouraged me in equal measure. Some of my colleagues did an oven-building course years ago but never got around to making one. I think I've motivated them to put it back on their agenda.

Perhaps constructing a wood-fired oven is about a primal urge to go back to basics. There's the attraction of the fire and the appeal of a simpler way of cooking. There is an element of obsession once you get started; I'm already wondering about building a second oven, improving on the first. Spiri shakes her head in dismay.

One of the joys for me has been seeing our daughter get excited about what she wants to cook in the oven, about creating the mosaic, and about inviting her friends to eat with us. And our son made the time capsule with great gusto.

I can't wait to bake bread. I want to see how long the oven stays warm and how many dishes we can cook in one firing. But most of all, I'm looking forward to sharing and eating food with our family and friends. That's really what it's all about.

Epilogue

Mesmerised, I watch as blue-orange flames lick at the pile of twigs collected from our winter garden, framed by the arch of the oven. I take in the first breath of smoke and am catapulted back through time: to my grandmother's village, watching plump orbs of bread come out from the oven's hearth; to a sepia-toned image in my Greek-school reader of twigs atop an old-fashioned cooker; and to a half-barrel filled with burning wood, ready to accommodate a whole lamb on the spit. As the flames get bigger I feel a deep-seated pleasure at creating something so beautiful. I carefully place a log on the flames and turn to George and Dolores.

'You lit it on the first go,' says Dolores, surprised. She and George went through a whole box of matches trying to light the fire earlier.

I'm not surprised. It's as if all these collective memories are guiding my hand – instinctively, I know what to do to get the fire going.

What does surprise me is my fascination with the fire. On this, the first day of firing, George and I tend to it in turns. I stoke it carefully, blowing it when it threatens to die down, exalting as the flames reel up when I add another log. I push the fire around the hearth, curing the virgin bricks. All of this feels strangely *right*. I feel calm, as if I am stepping back into myself. The smell gets into the wool of my jumper, into my hair, so that the fire follows me even when I leave it.

In the afternoon, George and I pull up plastic chairs, facing them at the entrance of the oven. In a show of chivalry, George dramatically takes off his jumper and wipes the grime off my chair. I laugh, reminded of my father-in-law making a similar gesture for his wife the first time I met him fifteen years ago.

Light drops of rain fall into our coffee cups as we sit in front of the dome. Emmanuel comes out intermittently, placing eucalyptus branches into the fire. He stands on the stepladder to see the thermometer and announces the temperature: 120 degrees Celsius, 150, back down to 120. We need to get the balance right – heat the oven too fast at this early stage and it might crack, but if we don't get the heat up, we won't be able to cook pizza tomorrow. Perhaps prematurely, we have invited our families over for lunch to celebrate the almost-finished oven. We have even made a special trip to an Italian supermarket on the other side of town, stocking up on anchovies, artichokes, mozzarella, prosciutto and Sicilian salami. Dolores has helped to make the dough. I stood by, ready to teach her how to knead properly, but she has been making bread with George for years and pummelled the flour and oil and water into a silky dough without my help.

As the rain comes down, we hunker deeper into our coats and watch the fire. I think of my grandparents living off the land in Greece, of my parents sailing across the world to make a home here in Australia, of my family and me, drawn around the strange dome-like structure in the middle of the yard, with its time capsule embedded deep within. Now that George has built the oven, it will be harder for us ever to leave this home we have made for ourselves. I remember the dreams we had for our garden in the early days of our courtship: 'Our garden will flourish and be noisy with boisterous bees and sensual smells as our kitchen will be generous with tall tales and arousing aromas.' I take hold of George's hand and smile.

Wise as you will have become, so full of experience,
you will have understood by then what these Ithakas mean.

The village that grew the book

Just as it takes a whole village to raise a child, so too it takes a whole village to grow a book.

First, there were the midwives who delivered the baby. Thank you to my agent Jacinta DiMase, publisher Helen Littleton, editor extraordinaire Denise O'Dea and the team at ABC Books/HarperCollins for bringing this book into the world.

There were those who oversaw my fledgling creation in its infancy, reading and commenting on early chapters. Thank you Nicolas Brasch, Kerrin O'Sullivan, Fiona Samios, Kathy Petras, Myfanwy Jones, Sam Lawry, Maryrose Cuskelly, Wendy Meddings, Jane Woollard, Shelley Kenigsberg, Jane Scully, Debbie Murray, Lina Scalzo and George Mifsud.

There were those who fed this book with their beautiful recipes and stories. Thank you Kerrin O'Sullivan, Vlasios Tzikas, Chrysoula Tsintziras, Georgia Poulis, John Tsimiklis, Christina and Sevi Skaleris, Lina and Maria Scalzo, Mary Coustas, Irine

Vela, Fiona Pirperis, Miranda Chiappini, Panayioti Stathopoulos, Kanella Karydomati, the New England Cheesemaking Supply Company, Natasha Blemenos, D.O.C Gastronomia Italiana, Katya Goodall, Asimina Tzanoukaki, George Mifsud, Gracie Spiteri, Nikos Vlahos, Mark Dymiotis, Tina Tasiopoulos, Stathis Karydomatis, Magda Softi and Evangelia Skevofylakas.

And finally, to those that gave this book body and soul. To Katerina, whose wisdom and spirit still guide me. To my father, who taught me about the importance of a story well told and embellishments convincingly executed. To my mother, who still gives me daily lessons on how to show love through food. To my husband, whose exquisite photographs grace this book; not only did he complete our wood-fired oven, but he *still* makes me laugh daily (sometimes even more). Finally, to our delicious children Dolores and Emmanuel – how blessed are we that we wished for you, and along you came?

'Ithaka': written by Constantine Cavafy, from *C. P. Cavafy: Selected Poems*, translated by Edmund Keeley and Phillip Sherrard; © 1972 Edmund Keeley and Phillip Sherrard. Reprinted with permission Princeton University Press.

Excerpt from 'Mycenae': written by George Seferis, from *George Seferis: Collected Poems*, translated by Edmund Keeley; © 1967 Princeton University Press, 1995 renewed PUP/ 1995 revised edition. Reprinted with permission Princeton University Press.